Alexander Wiggs

Hal's travels in Europe, Egypt and the Holy Land

A twelve months' tour during which he saw many wonderful things

Alexander Wiggs

Hal's travels in Europe, Egypt and the Holy Land
A twelve months' tour during which he saw many wonderful things

ISBN/EAN: 9783337216658

Printed in Europe, USA, Canada, Australia, Japan

Cover: Foto ©Andreas Hilbeck / pixelio.de

More available books at **www.hansebooks.com**

HAL'S TRAVELS

IN

Europe, Egypt, and the Holy Land;

A TWELVE MONTHS' TOUR

DURING WHICH

HE SAW MANY WONDERFUL THINGS AND A VAST DEAL OF FUN.

BY A. R. WIGGS.

NASHVILLE, TENN.:
PRINTED FOR THE AUTHOR BY J. B. M'FERRIN, AG'T.
1861.

TO

Mrs. Sallie Fleming,

OF

"MYRTLE HALL" HUNTSVILLE, ALABAMA,

This Volume

IS AFFECTIONATELY DEDICATED,

BY

THE AUTHOR.

HUNTSVILLE, ALA., JAN., 1861.

HAL'S TRAVELS.

Now, my friends, if you feel inclined to travel, I would be pleased to have you quit your pleasant homes for a season, and journey with me into foreign lands. I think you will find yourselves amply repaid for all the toils you may undergo, for we shall visit many lands and many peoples, and shall look upon sights both quaint and curious. We will take our staves, bind on our sandals, and provide ourselves with scrip, for our wanderings will be long, and mayhap wearisome. I promise you, however, fair entertainment and genial companions by the way, for we shall refresh ourselves on "praties" with our Irish friends, herrings with the cannie Scotch, roast-beef with bluff, honest John Bull, and rabbits with the hardy Welch; with the polite Frenchman we will partake of wine and frogs, sour-krout with the pursy Dutchman, pipes and lager-beer with the German, goat's-milk and cheese with the Swiss—and then cross the proud Alps, and eat maccaroni with the Italian. We will then visit Egypt, and test the quality of its flesh-pots—sail upon the classic waters of the Nile, view the wonderful ruins of Thebes and Memphis, climb the mighty Pyramids, and—ride donkeys. Thence to the Holy Land, where priests and prophets dwelt; to Jerusalem, where our blessed Saviour lived, and moved, and had his being—preached and taught, and healed the sick—was crucified, buried, and rose again. We will stand upon the mount from which he ascended, and many other of the sacred mountains of Palestine; will quench our thirst at the sacred fountains, and bathe in the waters of the Jordan. Thence to Phœnicia, Syria, Turkey, and the classic land of Greece.

But stop! to make this journey properly, we must begin at the beginning; which we will do on the following page.

HUNTSVILLE TO NEW YORK.

WELL, our trunks are packed—Pittman comes round with his omnibus, and we ride to the dépôt, where the "iron horse" stands panting, impatient to be going. We get aboard. The "steed" neighs—bounds away—and in a few moments we lose sight of dear friends, and the lovely little city of Huntsville. One tear—only one—steals down our cheeks, and then our thoughts are reaching forward to scenes that lie before. We are on the fast line now, and shall only take time to glance hastily at the objects along the way. Reach Chattanooga about night, and "put up" at the Crutchfield House—because we see no other house to "put up" at. In the morning, ride out to Lookout Mountain, and spend the day with the Carey family, who are not only clever people, but know just how to keep a hotel. The scenery from this mountain we shall not find surpassed this side of Switzerland. Return to Chattanooga in the evening, and on the arrival of the eight o'clock train, are joined by Mr. Arthur Robinson, who is to accompany us on our travels. We are heartily glad to see him. At nine o'clock, take the cars, and bid farewell to Chattanooga, not deeply impressed with the excellence of its hotel, but willing to admit that its proprietor is a good man. Run all night, and breakfast at Knoxville—most of our fellow-passengers taking "sugar in ther'n" before attacking the beefsteak and coffee. Leaving Knoxville, we arrive at Bristol, one hundred and thirty miles, in just twelve hours and a half!—nearly eleven miles an hour! Shall remember the clever conductor on that part of the line, because he stopped several times to let us pick blackberries. Remain three hours at Bristol, and listen with delight to native music, by some real old Virginia negroes, who entertain us with the classic songs of "Walk Jawbone" and "Hoopta-doodendo," accompanied with the banjo, and other variations. Leave Bristol at nine o'clock P. M., run all night, and in the morning find ourselves in the midst of the most romantic scenery of Virginia—the blue Peaks of Otter towering up just before us. Breakfast at Liberty, and take supper at Richmond—a first-class meal only in price. Leave Richmond at sunset, and at daylight next morning find ourselves approaching Washington—the nation's capital. We stop at Willard's, a number one hotel—judging by the bills we pay. Find some half-dozen of our Huntsville boys here, who are out on a general "bust"—seeing the sights, and having a good time generally. They will accompany us to New York. Stop a couple of days in Washington, and look round at the lions. View the Capitol and other public buildings with pride, and conclude that every American who has a heart, and not a gizzard, should be proud of them. Sunday is a quiet day in Washington; most that is to be seen is a horde of clerks and under-strappers connected with the different Departments, strutting about in their Sunday clothes, looking fiercely Democratic. Call upon Secretary Cass, and after assuring him in the most positive manner that we are truly American citizens, and not likely to be drafted into foreign service, he grants us passports for our foreign travels.

Leave Washington, three o'clock P. M., pass through Baltimore at telegraphic speed, and arrive at Philadelphia ten o'clock at night. Spend a couple of days here. Walk through Chestnut street, and stare at her wonderful stores. The stream of people on this street, and the crowd about old Independence Hall, suggest the idea to some of the Huntsville boys that it is the "First Monday." Call on Siter, Price & Co., fix up our financial matters, and leave for New York—the rollicking, jostling, bustling, rip-roaring, go-ahead Gotham, where every thing and everybody centres on Broadway. Here the boys are dumfounded with astonishment, for Chestnut street is not a circumstance to Broadway for bustle and confusion. We stop at the St. Nicholas, the finest hotel in the world.

There are three of us together now, bound for the Old World, Mr. John Gamble, of Limestone county, having overtaken us at Philadelphia. We are wonderfully pleased with the accession. The steamer City of Baltimore lies in her dock, almost ready to put to sea. We take passage on her for Liverpool.

Now, having joined ourselves to "those who go down to the sea in ships," we shall commit ourselves to the vasty deep, looking for protection to that God who holdeth the winds in his fists, and the mighty seas in the hollow of his hand. We leave our native shores and our friends with many regrets, but with anticipations of much pleasure beyond the water. Should we get safely over on the other shore, our friends shall hear from us again; but if otherwise ordered, and we should be in old ocean buried, we hope to meet them all in that haven of rest where sorrow is not known, and where love and harmony shall reign for ever.

LETTER I.*

NEW YORK TO LIVERPOOL.

As I rock and roll on the raging billows this morning, being confined within doors by a chilling rain, I will redeem my promise by penning you a few paragraphs.

Ten days ago, myself and two friends (Robinson and Gamble) wended our way from the St. Nicholas Hotel, New York, to the ocean steamer City of Baltimore, arriving just in time to get ourselves snugly stowed away before she set sail. Found great confusion reigning on board, and the continued arrival of passengers and their friends rendered the confusion worse confounded. The starting moment arrived. The bell rang—and then such crying, blubbering, hugging and kissing took place as is seldom seen, except on similar occasions. The last good-bye was finally said, and the noble steamer glided out of her dock, and took her course towards the open sea. Expected to feel awfully sublime and desperately solemn and romantic upon witnessing the gradual disappearance of the shores of my native land—but did n't. Although the heavens wept, I

---

* This and most of the succeeding letters were addressed to and published in the Huntsville Independent.

remained comparatively unmoved, for the chilling rain falling at the time, and the dense fog, were death to romance. A few hundred yards put us out of sight of both city and shore.

Steamed ahead for two hours, and came to a halt, owing to a brisk head-wind and dense fog. Lay to near Sandy Hook till near nightfall, then went ahead. Spent the evening in reconnoitring and studying my fellow-passengers, of whom we had a large number. Came to the conclusion that we had several "characters" aboard — and was not far wrong. Felt deep sympathy for some of the ladies, (blessed tender-hearted creatures!) who were still wiping their red eyes, sorrowing for those they had left behind. Was somewhat amused at the chattering of a couple of damsels, (of uncertain age,) who made it convenient to impress the fact upon all within hearing, that they were setting out on a European tour, to be gone for at least four months. Have since learned that the elder and more strong-minded of the two intends writing a book! She will no doubt "do" Europe in style. Shall cultivate her acquaintance, and get some ideas upon the art of book-making.

Found it interesting to notice the assiduity with which several young gentlemen labored to keep off sea-sickness. They had started out from New York with a bountiful supply of medicine, of which they imbibed freely and frequently from wicker-covered flasks. They soon grew hilarious, and snapped their fingers at sea-sickness.

Had a pair of Catholic bishops and three or four priests on board. Had no difficulty in singling them out, for their portly persons and sleek round Irish faces bespoke their calling at once. Was mistaken as to one, however, for the jolly red-nosed man I had taken for a priest turns out to be a retired New York merchant. He is travelling with his family for pleasure. Has two grown-up daughters—fine-looking and sprightly. They talk like books, sing like birds, and know how to put on airs. They look "killingly" at my two friends, John and Arthur, but the effect is not yet very perceptible. The father of these damsels has informed me, "with a great burst of confidence," that he is very wealthy, and that the man who gets his daughter will get a prize.

Sunday morning found us far out to sea, with clear sky above, and smooth sea beneath. Looked out upon the dreary waste of waters, and came to the conclusion that the "sublime grandeur" of the ocean, so much spouted about by poets and travelling writers, was all humbug. Saw nothing peculiarly "sublime" about it. All congratulated ourselves that we had escaped sea-sickness. In the afternoon a whale—a live whale—intrepidly came alongside the steamer, blowing and spouting most obstreperously. Not so large a fish as I had expected to see; but perhaps my idea of a whale was extravagant. I can still, however, believe the story of Jonah and the whale.

Late in the afternoon, the wind blew hard, and

the sea looked angry, as the white-caps burst and foamed upon its troubled surface. The ship rolled and rocked like a restless monster of the deep. Conversation flagged, and a serious gravity took possession of most of the passengers. Your correspondent felt remarkably serious. Some living monster seemed to have set up a gallop within his stomach, and while the cold perspiration rolled down his face, he made a bold attempt to go below to his berth. It was necessary for the steward to follow with broom and water, for he soiled the clean deck. There was a heaving on all sides, and a demand for bowls, buckets, etc. Finally got below, and found John in his berth, rolling and groaning. Joined him, while Arthur, more fortunate than we, laughed at us most barbarously.

Monday the sea was still very rough. The sun shone gloriously, but the wind blew fierce and cool. Few made their appearance on deck, and fewer at the table. My appetite has not yet come to me. Hope to find it in Liverpool.

On Tuesday morning the wind was blowing great guns. The sea boiled like a pot. Great waves chased each other, and leaped like so many furious mad bulls, and occasionally mounted even upon the upper deck of our noble vessel, as she struggled and panted to surmount them. It was a fearful day. The heavens lowered and scowled. Two sails were snapped and torn away by the gale. Timid lubbers looked pale, and manifested a weakness in the knees. Friend Arthur "caved in" that day, but John and myself felt too serious to laugh at him. I am now willing to admit that all that has been said and written about the grandeur and sublimity of the ocean is true—no humbug about it. Ay, but the Atlantic is a rough old bruiser—a rollicking, bluff old bully—boxing and tossing about the monster steamer and the light jolly-boat with like ease and impunity—and, withal, more anti-bilious and anti-dyspeptic than all the medicines ever compounded or concocted by that "retired physician whose sands of life have nearly run out." If it was only at play on Tuesday—and that is what the sailors called it—I never wish to see it angry.

Wednesday and Thursday the weather was more pleasant, and as nothing occurred worth writing about on those days, you must indulge me in a little eulogy on hogs. I respect hogs. In fact, I may say that I reverence a fine fat porker. Ever since I read the account of the Apostle Peter's vision on the house-top, when he stopped with one Simon, a tanner, at Joppa, I have had a weakness for swine. Yes, with all their hoggish ways, I love them. They are good things in their place. But I do protest against their being admitted into the saloons of ocean steamers. There they are out of place, and should be put out. We have three of them with us, of the biped breed, in the shape of three huge beef-headed English bulls. They may have been well raised, but if so, they have been out from home long enough to forget their raising. They have no conversation for anybody except each other, and seem to look upon Americans as potatoes too small for their digging. They sit opposite us every day at table, and annoy and disgust every one who sits near them, with their loud talk, bigoted self-importance, and gluttony. At breakfast they monopolize every thing within their reach, and keep the steward trotting for 'am and heggs. At dinner they continually call for roast beef, hale, etc. We can scarcely get a steward to bestow any attention upon us, and it is so annoying, that Arthur has more than once been on the point of throttling the most villainous-looking one of the trio. John and your correspondent would delight in pitching into the other two. One of them I take peculiar pleasure in detesting, more perhaps on account of his looks than any thing else. He is a hard-featured creature, with short chin, very large mouth, huge nose, and pop-eyes, long arms, bowed-back, and bow-legs. If he were a good-looking man, his manners might be bearable; but to see such a looking creature putting on airs makes me mad. One of my friends gives it as his unbiased opinion that these fellows belong to the latter of two classes that inhabit the world—to wit, natural fools, and d——d fools. I merely record this as my friend's individual opinion.

Friday we were among the icebergs. Wind blew cold like winter. Passed three during the day, one of which seemed to be a quarter of a mile in diameter at the base, and towered up two or three hundred feet. I was gazing at it through a spyglass, when a Georgia friend came up and wanted to "look through that brass thing" to see if he could see any bears: said he had heard them say down in Georgia that bears could always be seen on icebergs. I gratified him with a look through the "brass thing," but he discovered "nary" bear.

Saturday, Sunday, and Monday were lovely days; sky clear and serene, and the atmosphere bracing. The sea was blue and beautiful, and I passed much time on deck, watching the waves as they sported and chased each other like gleesome children at play. On such days I love to sit for hours together and watch the rolling and swelling of the deep blue waters. There is a charm about the sea which grows upon one in spite of himself, and I wonder not that seamen become so much attached to the briny deep.

Had Divine service on Sunday, in the saloon. Passengers and sailors, except those on duty, were called together by the ringing of the ship's bell. The Captain led the service, which was Episcopal. The Catholic clergy and their followers refused to be present, fearing, perhaps, that coming in contact with Protestantism might defile them—not a Catholic remained in the saloon. In the afternoon, Catholic service was held, led by Bishop Connor, of Pittsburg. The burden of his discourse was on *Charity!* The Protestants were all present to hear him—*practicing* what he only *preached.* At night we had sacred music, and indulged in some good old camp-meeting songs, which made me think of home and the revival scenes I have witnessed there.

Wednesday morning early, was aroused from my slumbers with the joyful shout of "Land! Land!" Rushed up on deck, half dressed, and after straining my eyes for some time to penetrate the thick fog, descried a long, low, black streak in the horizon, said to be the coast of Ireland. The fog soon blew away, and sure enough, there lay, in all its beauty, the Emerald Isle—the "gem of the ocean." Steamed into the Cove of Cork, said to be one of the finest harbors in the world; discharged about one hundred passengers—among them the Catholic clergy, and the Yankee spinsters who are to travel four months, and write a book! Leaving Cork, we steamed ahead for Liverpool, and landed here early this morning.

So here we are in Liverpool—the great commercial emporium of Great Britain—one of the first commercial cities of the world. We have tramped round most of the day, looking at the magnificent edifices and some fine monuments. Boot-blacks and newsboys annoy strangers a good deal, and beggars are also to be met. We shake all off, and keep the even tenor of our way. To-morrow we go to London, and from there I will write you again. Adieu.   HAL.

LETTER II.

LONDON.

So we are in London at last! London, the capital of Great Britain, the seat of royalty, and the metropolis of the world—the great city, the smoke of whose furnaces ascends up for ever and ever, and then comes down again, leaving its dark impress upon all objects below. London, where Shakspeare lived, and wrote, and played, and swilled his 'alf-and-'alf; where rare Ben Jonson lived, and moved, and had his being; where Goldsmith, and many other poets and philosophers, came well-nigh starving to death, and where Spenser actually did die for want of bread. London, where princes and beggars jostle each other; where millionnaires and gaunt, starving wretches stare each other in the face; where the jungles of infamy and the palaces of luxury are within a stone's-throw of each other; where priests and pickpockets are near neighbors, and where the philosopher and the clown swill two-penny beer from the same pot. Ay, but London is a great city, and to tell of but the half I have seen here would fill a book. One sees so much here, he becomes bewildered and sick, and gets things so jumbled up in his mind that it is next to impossible to get them untangled. My two friends and myself make it a business to keep going and seeing, but when we return to our domiciles at night, we have but an indistinct recollection of splendid palaces, magnificent churches, beautiful parks and gardens, monuments, rich paintings, and an innumerable multitude of people. Each place we visit would require days to get it fairly and fully impressed upon the mind. One should stay a full year in London to see the "lions."

I find that we are known here by all classes as Americans, and are consequently "set upon" by beggars, and continually swindled by cab-drivers. Don't know what it is that betrays our nationality. Can't be our dress, for we dress like the English; nor can it be our language, for we speak plain English; and to suppose it any thing like verdancy in our appearance would be absurd, for we even labor to look wise. Yet we are known and "spotted" as "Yankees" in all parts of London. It may possibly be our good looks. Started out the other morning to find the Thames Tunnel. Policeman tendered his services, saying he knew we were Americans and strangers, and he would conduct us to the proper place to take the down-river boat; gave him pleasure to serve Americans, as he had once visited Mobile. The agent who gave us tickets for the boat, remarked that they were worth eight cents apiece, as we probably understood the American better than the English currency. Reached the entrance to the Tunnel, paid our pennies, and as we passed in, the gate-keeper handed us a printed description of the great and curious work, saying we might take it back to America with us. Passing along through the brilliantly lighted Tunnel, were seen by a musician who sat near the opposite end. He recognized us at a distance of fifty yards, and struck up "Yankee Doodle." We stopped to listen, and then approached him slowly, when he commenced "Hail Columbia." We gave him some pennies and passed on. Upon one occasion we were hailed by a newsboy. We refused to buy the Times, when the little scamp turned up his nose and ran off, crying, "I smell Yankee! I smell Yankee!" And this is about the way we are continually made to remember the fact that we are *foreigners!*

Leaving the Tunnel, we wandered through the venerable precincts of Wapping, that we might see something of *low* as well as *high* life. Passed through "Bleeding-heart Yard," and, not far distant, saw the remains of "Tom-all-alone's," and if we didn't see poor "Joe," certainly saw his successor. He is still kept "moving on." The elder Mr. Turveydrop is still to be met on the street, but begins to look seedy, while the "young man of the name of Guppy" seems to be doing a thriving business in Chancery Lane.

Have visited Greenwich, about six miles down the river, to see the great hospital for superannuated seamen, the Naval School, and the Observatory, from which longitude is reckoned. Same day paid a visit to the Great Eastern steamship, the largest craft ever put afloat—Noah's ark not excepted. London is full of wonders, but this monster steamer is the greatest wonder of them all. She is nearly seven hundred feet long, one hundred and twenty feet wide across the paddle-boxes, sixty feet deep; has nineteen water-tight compartments. Has five large saloons, two of which are seventy feet long. Diameter of the side-wheels fifty-six feet. Has an enormous screw-propeller. Engines three thousand horse-power. Has five decks. Whole ship built of wrought iron. Can spread six thousand yards of canvass! When finished, she will visit the United States. Guess Brother Jonathan will go into big ecstasies, and tear his trowsers, when he sees her paddling about in his waters.

Went Sunday to hear the celebrated Spurgeon preach. It was with difficulty we found the place. Met a respectable "Pecksniffian"-looking gentleman, and asked him if he could tell us where Mr. Spurgeon would preach that day. Hung down his head, hemmed a little, seemed in deep thought, looked up, and asked if we were not Americans? Told him we were. Hung his head again, paused, put his finger to the side of his nose, and repeated the word slowly three times, "Spurgeon, Spurgeon, Spurgeon." Shook his head, rolled up his eyes, and said "No!" Asked a cab-driver, and his reply was, "Two shillin's." Met the elder Mr. Turvey-drop, and put the question to him. Put the head of his cane to his nose, and said he was sure he had heard the name of Spurgeon before—quite sure he had—but really could not tell where, when, nor in what connection. Policeman told us to go to Park Lane. Another policeman said "No — not Park Lane." Finally, we were informed by genteel-looking individual—very genteel, but a little seedy—who spoke with all the confidence of a Micawber—that Mr. Spurgeon preached at Surrey Gardens—quite sure of it, for he lived in that neighborhood. We took a cab, and rode three miles to Surrey Gardens, and found the gentleman's statement correct. Found the great hall densely crowded, and the people still coming in streams. With difficulty we got *standing* room. Got our places just as the preacher commenced his first prayer.

Now that I have heard Spurgeon, perhaps you expect me to give my opinion of the preacher and his sermon. It may be presumption—and is presumption—for me to attempt to criticise the sermon of a man whose reputation is so extensive on both sides of the Atlantic. But I speak for myself, and nobody else, when I say I was grievously disappointed. Perhaps I expected too much—no doubt did—but I say what I believe to be true, and what I felt to be true at the time, that I have heard sermons in the United States that pleased me much better, and were better calculated to lead sinners to repentance. Mr. Spurgeon is a good man and a good preacher, but if he is worthy of his great reputation, then I am dull indeed. His style of preaching is so very different from other preachers in this country, that it has given him a great notoriety, and the people run to hear him in great numbers, because they are ever ready to hear some new thing. While the preachers of the Church of England deliver dry, windy, punctilious, big-worded, written sermons, Spurgeon marches up off-hand, and takes the bull by the horns, just as some of our preachers do. He calls things by their right names — uses language plain and easy to be understood—and hence takes hold of the people. His figures are apt, vivid, and to the point—homely enough, some of them. Voice clear, and words distinct; yet, in declamation, I know stump-speakers in Tennessee that can beat him. There are plenty of preachers in our country who could get up as great if not a greater furor in London than Mr. Spurgeon has. His sermon on Sunday was preached from Matthew xi. 29: "For I am meek and lowly in heart."

Do not infer from what I have said that I think Mr. Spurgeon an ordinary man. He is a great preacher; and we, too, have great preachers on our side of the water—greater, perhaps, than Mr. Spurgeon. My two friends are entirely delighted with him, and differ with me as to his ability. Mr. S. looks to be about thirty or thirty-five years of age, has rather a boyish face, full and round, wears a high shirt collar and white cravat, to make him look ministerial.

But enough of Spurgeon. There are a thousand things I might write about, but shall not do it. You may expect me to give you a description of the splendid House of Parliament, of Windsor Castle,

St. Paul's Church, National Art Gallery, Hyde Park, Regent's Park, St. James's Park, and the thousand-and-one things of national and historical interest here; but you will be disappointed, for I shall not attempt any thing of the sort. I didn't intend from the start to write any such letters. For information on these things I refer you to *any* book of travels, for all travellers who write think themselves in duty bound to describe those places, and I shall not follow in their footsteps. I could not do it without copying copiously from the guidebooks; hence, will not try. If I can't be original, I won't be at all.

Went down the other evening and took a look at Buckingham Palace, the town residence of Her Royal Highness, Queen Victoria. Her Majesty not being at home, we didn't call. She, with her little responsibilities, is on a visit to the Isle of Wight. Left a few days before we reached London. Presume she did not know we were coming.

Shall visit the Tower of London to-morrow, where all the State prisoners have been imprisoned and beheaded from time immemorial. Place of terrible interest, that Tower. Must also visit the House of Lords and the Crystal Palace. Sorry we have not more time to spend in London, for one should not run through it in a hurry. But must be in Paris on the 15th, to witness the great Napoleon *fête*, and the *entrée* of the grand army of Italy. It will be one of the greatest pageants ever seen in the world. It will compensate us in some degree for the disappointment in not getting over here in time to see a great battle fought in Italy.

Hold! hist! There's another hand-organ thundering away! The seventh time that an organ has been played under my window since this letter was commenced! I acknowledge my weakness for music, but must confess that my respect for Italy and for Italians generally is daily giving way under the pressure of too much grinding upon the organ. There is no less than a regiment of stout Italians now in London, assiduously devoting themselves to the profession. It would be a good thing if they could be put on a cotton-plantation in Alabama, under a good overseer.

The hotels of London are not to be compared with those of New York. Upon arriving here we stopped at Morley's Hotel, Charing Cross, said to be one of the finest in London; but to those coming from Philadelphia or New York, it will appear as small potatoes. We soon discovered that the charges ranged at least fifty per cent. higher than in New York, and we took ourselves suddenly away, and would advise our friends, if they ever come to London, and feel economically disposed, to take private lodgings, as we have done.

This letter is long enough. Good-bye.

HAL.

LETTER III.

LONDON.

I HAD an idea before coming to London that it was a great city. Am now convinced that it is all my fancy painted it, and fifty per cent. more. Since my last letter I have been going, going, going continually, and the more I try to find the end of it, the more I can't do it. Have seen it from the "deck" of an omnibus for ten miles at a stretch—viewed it from the tallest towers and steeples—walked it until my feet are blistered, and my muscles sore—and still it seems the same endless London—full of interest, full of magnificent architecture, full of classic localities, and full of wickedness. I have seen the "lions" and the "elephant"—have tramped from "Blackfriars" to "Whitefriars"—have threaded my way from Pall-mall to "Temple Bar"—have run the gauntlet from "Pudding Lane" to "Pie Corner"—forced my way through the mass from "Billingsgate" to "Cock Lane"—scrambled from "Newgate" to "Dog's-Misery"—have cabbed it from "Regent's Park" to "Surrey Gardens"—'bussed it from "The Angel" to the "Elephant-and-Castle"—from "Piccadilly" to "The

Eagle"—and from "Charing Cross" to "Vauxhall Gardens"—in short, have been, it seems, almost everywhere, and yet have seen but little of London, comparatively.

Visited to-day St. Bartholomew's church, in Smithfield Market, to see the ground where so many Christian martyrs were burned during the reign of bloody Queen Mary. Also the tower erected to commemorate the great fire of London, in 1666. It is an immense column, two hundred and two feet high, and located two hundred and two feet from the spot in "Pudding Lane" where the fire originated. After its erection, the following inscription was engraved upon the base:

"This pillar was set up in perpetuall remembrance of that most dreadful burning of this Protestant citye, begun and carried on by ye treachery and malice of ye Popish factio, in ye beginning of Septem, in ye yeare of our Lord 1666, in order to ye carrying on their horrid plot of extirpating ye Protestant religion and old English liberty, and ye introducing Popery and slavery."

As many as six persons have committed suicide by throwing themselves from the top of this monument. Also visited Charter House Square, where sixty thousand of the better class of the citizens of London were buried during the Great Plague. Also Bunhill Fields Cemetery, where rest the mortal remains of Rev. Mr. Fox, the founder of the Quaker sect of religionists; Dr. Isaac Watts, whose hymns will be sung till time shall be no more; John Bunyan, whose "Christian" in the Pilgrim's Progress will ever be the admiration of Christian warriors;

and many others are buried there whose names are familiar to Protestant Christians throughout Christendom.

On Sunday, instead of going to hear Spurgeon again, went to the Wesley Chapel, and after service went to the rear of the church and saw the tomb of the great divine and founder of Methodism. Also the ground where Goldsmith is said to have been buried.

Friend Arthur went again last Sunday to hear Spurgeon, and came back rather chapfallen. Don't now think quite so much of him as he did. Says he didn't preach near so well as on the Sunday before—and took occasion to come down upon American slavery with a vim; quoted the sixth verse of Psalm ciii., "The Lord executeth righteousness and judgment for all that are oppressed," and said that was a "fit legacy left by David to the slaveholders of America." Won't some kind-hearted philanthropist have the goodness to send Mr. Spurgeon a copy of Ross's Bible Defence of Slavery? I am persuaded that the overrated individual might read it with profit. It is said that Spurgeon intends shortly to visit America. If so, I trust our good people will endeavor to hold themselves on the ground. It is not customary, I know, for them to be temperate when famous foreigners go among them. All the talent of America might come to London, and there would not be half the sensation manifested as in New York when Charles Dickens went among them. Guess Spurgeon will meet a similar reception. If so, hope he will write a " Martin Chuzzlewit."

I have been through most of the parks, many of the churches, castles, and towers, but among them all found no spot which brought up such thoughts as the Tower of London, the place where has been shed so much royal and so much innocent blood, and where have been imprisoned many hundreds whose names adorn or blacken the pages of history. This tower is an immense fortress, surrounded with a deep moat which can be filled at any moment with water from the Thames, on the banks of which it stands. In the centre stands a tower, from which the fortress takes its name. Tradition says it was built by Julius Cæsar, some say by William the Conqueror. The arms and armor of England, from Edward the First on down through successive reigns, are still preserved here, as well as thousands of other relics of antiquity. I was in the cell where Sir Walter Raleigh was confined for twelve years. It is small, without a particle of light, and the walls are fifteen feet thick. In front of this cell stands the block on which so many have been beheaded, including kings, queens, lords and ladies. The fatal axe lies beside it, blackened with rust—the same axe which severed the heads of Lady Jane Grey, Anne Boleyn, Sir Walter Raleigh, and hundreds of others. I passed through many cells, but lingered longest to gaze upon the one in which the gentle Queen Anne Boleyn was confined previous to her execution. The history of that tragedy passed before me, and I almost cursed the memory of the bloody Henry VIII. I thought of the splendor and pomp with which she was received at the palace (then in the Tower) on her espousal to the brutal Henry. She was on that occasion escorted by the Lord Mayor and his train, arrayed in scarlet, with gold chains about their necks, in gilded barges of great magnificence, and was received amidst the melody of trumpets and musical instruments, and a mighty peal of guns. This was the reception Henry gave her. The next day she proceeded from the Tower to Westminster, with all the pomp and heraldry of pride and power. She is described as tall and slender, face oval, hair black, complexion rather pale, features and figure symmetrical; and it is said that beauty and sprightliness sat on her lips; and in readiness of wit she was unsurpassed.

This was truly a splendid beginning—but what an ending! Three years after, the tongue of jealousy and slander aspersed her fair name. She was committed to the Tower, a prisoner; arraigned and tried for unfaithfulness to her royal but villainous husband, and pronounced guilty. When her sentence was pronounced, she raised her hands and eyes to heaven, and exclaimed: "O Father! O Creator! Thou who art the way, the truth, and the life, thou knowest I have not deserved this death!" She was conducted to the place of execution without being permitted even to see the cruel author of her death. Those who were eye-witnesses of the scene, record that her beauty on that day was mournfully brilliant. After addressing a few words to those who stood around, she laid her head on the fatal block, and it was severed at one stroke. Her body was thrust into an old chest, and hurried away to the vault of the chapel, in front of which the scaffold stood. The place where the scaffold stood is marked with black stones, while the rest of the court is paved with stones of a light color.

I have visited some of the London theatres, and have seen the boards trod by some of the ancient worthies. Went to the Haymarket last night, and saw a play which might be performed to advantage in some parts of our own country—entitled, "The Contested Election; or, the way M. P.'s get their seats." It was a good "take-off" of the manner in which members of Parliament are made. None but rich men can get a seat in the English Parliament, for almost every elector has his price, and votes for the highest bidder. Have learned this from debates in the House of Commons, where about a dozen cases of contested election are now being tried. The proof shows that nearly all were elected by bribery. The constituencies being small, it is easier for a man to buy them up here than in the United States, where every man is a voter. They have a curious way here of managing elections. The candidate is in the background—gives the canvass up into the hands of a club or committee. He furnishes the money, and the committee hire and send out "electioneerers." The "electioneerers" buy votes, paying each voter his price. The candidate justifies himself by saying that he is a poor hand to electioneer, and merely hires these men to do it for him, paying them for their time, and giving them a certain sum of money extra, to be expended for "refreshments." Several members have been ousted within the last few days. The play above alluded to was got up to take off the cases now being tried, and does it admirably.

The city of London proper is but a small part of London. What is called "The City" is independent of the rest, having its own government. It was a walled city in ancient times. Part of the wall still stands. Temple Bar (an ancient gate) remains as a remembrance of the old wall, dividing the city from the new part of London. It is an immense arch, spanning the street just at the meeting of the Strand and Fleet streets. Upon the top of this arch the heads of desperate criminals used to be placed, to be scoffed at by the public.

People here have a singular idea about time and age. I dropped into a barber-shop the other day, under Temple Bar, to get my hair cut. Found the barber a loquacious fellow, as all barbers are. Told him I thought he had a good stand for his business, being located under the ancient and time-honored Temple. "Bless you, sir," said he, "this haint the hold bar. This is the new 'un. The hold 'un was pulled down, it got so rickety, and this new 'un built. This haint 'ardly two 'undred years hold yet." I thought two hundred years a good old age.

Billingsgate, I am persuaded, is hardly maintain-

2

ing its ancient reputation. I spent half an hour there one day, and did not hear more than half a dozen oaths, and but few indecent expressions. The coarse language of this place is notorious throughout the world.

> There stripped, fair rhetoric languished on the ground.
> His blunted arms by sophistry are borne,
> And shameless Billingsgate her robes adorn.—POPE.

Billingsgate is a fish-market, and is about the loudest smelling place I have found about London, even surpassing the river Thames, if possible.

Don't know but I begin to feel a little more important than I used to feel. It is not common for plain republicans to be admitted within less than bow-shot of royalty, but I have been much nearer; in fact, almost in the very presence of the royal family. Through the intercession of the American Legation, I was granted a card of admission to the *Queen's Stables*. The document was crowned with the royal arms, (to wit: a lion and unicorn rampant,) and read as follows:

> MASTER OF THE HORSE'S OFFICE, }
> ROYAL MEWS, PIMLICO.

Admit Mr. Hal and party of two to view the Queen's Stables.

J. R. GROVES,
Crown Equerry.

Did myself the honor to call at the Master of the Horse's office yesterday, and was well paid for the visit. The finest stud of horses I ever saw, of course. There are one hundred and fifty horses. Great ceremony is observed at these stables. An official received me at the gate in rich uniform—cut off part of my ticket of admission, and handed me over to a cockaded gentleman, who conducted me to another office, where I was required to register my name and place of residence, and deliver up the rest of my ticket. A third individual with gold lace and shiny buttons conducted me into a stable where stood a dozen of Prince Albert's saddle-horses. After explaining to me the qualities of each particular horse, (for he understood "'orse-talk" perfectly,) he handed me over to a fourth, and thus I was conducted through all the stables, coach and harness houses, a different "gentleman" accompanying me through each place. And now you know how near an approach I have made to royalty since my sojourn in London.

Guess I have bored you enough, and will desist. Shall go to Paris to-morrow.

Yours, etc.,   HAL.

LETTER IV.

PARIS.

I am in a state of excitement this morning—bewildered—in fact, I might say, dumfounded—and the reliability of what I write on this occasion may well be doubted. I have seen enough within the last few days to turn the head of a sage, or to completely derange a man of ordinary sense. I am in Paris, and have seen something of *Paris life*. You don't know what that means, nor does any one who has never been here. I have heard of Paris and read of Paris all my life, but had not the most faint conception of its grandeur, beauty, gayety, or frivolity until now. It is the place of places—the city of cities—where voluptuousness abides, and where wickedness doth abound: where the people sit down to eat and drink, and rise up to play—a city that seems to be verging upon the condition of the great Babylon before its downfall—because it seems to me she makes "all nations drink of the wine of the wrath of her fornication."

I have seen enough since my arrival in Paris to keep me writing a week, and to fill six newspapers; but don't be alarmed—I'm not going to do it. I must put a rein upon my scribbling inclination.

The great fête of the age—yea. the greatest the world has ever known, has just closed—a fête got up, directed and managed by Emperor Napoleon III., backed by the city of Paris, and aided and assisted by the entire French nation. My pen shrinks back appalled when I think of attempting to give you even a distant glimmering of the brilliancy of the scenes in Paris during the last two days—to-wit, Sunday and Monday. It can't be portrayed on paper. An attempt to do so would be simply ridiculous. I can mention some things that were done, however. The *entrée* of the Grand Army of Italy, headed by Napoleon and his staff, was a scene of grandeur seldom witnessed. It was not the army alone that constituted the beauty of the scene: it was the manner in which it was welcomed—the immense crowd of people—the thousands upon thousands of flags. banners and devices which greeted the war-worn veterans—the shouts, and the immense showers of wreaths and bouquets showered upon them from the windows, the balconies, and housetops, as they passed the streets. Their march was from the Place du Trone along the Boulevards, (the broadest and most **beautiful** street of Paris,) a distance of nearly **five miles, to** what is called the Place Vendôme, (a square in which stands the great column surmounted with the statue of Napoleon Bonaparte, the whole cast from the cannon taken by him in his various battles.) This square, which is four hundred and fifty feet across, was surrounded with seats, capable of **seating** twenty-one thousand persons, all of whom were of the privileged classes, and entered the place by ticket. Every window, and the balconies of the houses surrounding this square, and even the roofs, were filled with people—the *élite* of Paris. On one side was a crimson velvet canopy over a tribune, where the Empress and her royal guests sat during the four hours and ten minutes that it took the army to pass. The Emperor sat on his horse in front of the tribune during the whole time, and greeted each regiment as it passed. The brilliancy of the decorations of this square cannot be described. It seemed as if millions of dollars had been expended for banners, arches and columns; crimson, blue and purple velvet, trimmed and embroidered with gold lace, were suspended from every window around the square. The Empress sat during most of the time with the little Prince Imperial in her arms. The little fellow was dressed in the uniform of the Imperial Guards. But why should I attempt a detailed account? I will sum it up by saying that the whole distance marched by the army, from the place of starting, about ten miles, back to the Bastile, was a scene of flaunting banners, triumphal arches, crowds of people, both on the streets, in the windows, and on the housetops, and the continual yell of "Vive l'Empereur!" "Vive l'Armee!" "Vive les Zouaves!" etc., etc.

The procession consisted of 69,800 men, and 144 pieces of cannon, besides many thousands of other troops not belonging to the Army of Italy. It took four hours and ten minutes for the procession to pass. There were 63,000 infantry, 2800 cavalry, 2400 artillerymen, 800 engineers, and 300 with the wagon-train. I do not know the number of soldiers not of the Army of Italy, though there were many thousands. There were also 6500 horses attached to the cannon and wagon-train. The regiments marched about sixteen abreast, headed by their respective officers. The order was as follows:

1st. The Emperor and his escort, (from the Bastile to the Place Vendôme.)

2d. The banners taken from the Austrians.

3d. The Austrian cannon.

4th. The wounded — some limping, some with bandages around their heads, and others with their arms in slings.

5th. The Zouaves, composed of Turks, Moors, and desperate-looking Frenchmen.

6th. Artillery and baggage-wagons.

7th. Infantry.

8th. Regiment of Lancers.

9th. Cavalry of the Guard, in glittering armor.

10th. The Emperor and his attendants brought up the rear from the Place Vendôme, down Rue de Rivoli, to the Palace of the Tuileries.

After the street had been somewhat cleared, the Empress and her household followed on to the Tuileries in the State carriages, each drawn by only two horses, and entirely unattended except by the footmen.

We had a good opportunity to see the whole of

the procession, having a stand in a balcony in front of our hotel, from which we could see both the army and the masses of people up and down the streets for miles. It is estimated that there were from five to eight hundred thousand people on the streets on Sunday, besides what were in the houses and on the housetops. It seemed to an American like any thing but Sunday. The hundred brass bands, the scores and scores of kettle-drums, the yells of the masses, and the confusion generally, made it seem more like pandemonium than a city professing to be Christian. Hundreds of priests, monks, and friars were pushing and crowding along with the rest, looking any thing but meek and lowly, as would have become their long black robes and shaven pates. The day finally closed with a partial illumination of many of the streets.

But Monday was the big *fête* day. Interesting and brilliant spectacles were got up and carried on during the day in every part of the city. As I could not see all, I chose to go to the Hotel des Invalides, (a church, fortification, and hospital for invalid soldiers, all combined,) in which is the Tomb of Napoleon I., and in which was sung a grand Te Deum, and High Mass was celebrated, which is done twice a year, viz., on Christmas and on the 15th of August. The performance was rather imposing, but did not strike me forcibly. The high dignitaries of the Church were dressed in rich gold-embroidered robes, and looked ferociously pious; but during their wails, lamentations, waving of censers, and beseechings of the Virgin Mary to pray for the repose of the soul of Napoleon I., I could not but think of the impious manner in which they had desecrated the Sabbath but the day before.

After the service concluded, I spent the rest of the day in wandering about from place to place, seeing the various shows and sights got up for the occasion. The large plot of ground in front of the Invalides (from fifty to one hundred acres) was crowded with exhibitions of all kinds. There were five or six circuses going on, four theatres, the whole fronts being entirely open; several platforms on which were performing rope-dancers, dancing-girls, tumblers, etc.; innumerable Punch and Judy shows; monkeys and ponies performing; one or two dozen "flying-jennies" on which twenty or thirty persons could ride at once; several sham-battles; four very tall greased poles, on the tops of which were hung watches and other trinkets, prizes for any one who could reach them. I noticed one chap who had started up with his pockets full of pulverized chalk which he rubbed upon the pole as he ascended. He had almost reached the prize, but my attention being called to something else, I did not see how he came out. Balloons in the shape of mammoth bulls, lions, leopards, and men, were sent up at intervals during the day, and late in the evening a very large balloon was let off with two men in the car attached. They went very high, and soon disappeared in the distance. All these exhibitions were free to the public, being paid for by the government.

Late in the evening I wandered through the large open spaces of the Champs Elysees, Place de la Concorde, the Tuileries Gardens and Grove, the streets de Rivoli, Boulevards, and the Place Vendôme, and found them all crowded alike with a dense mass of men and women. It would be impossible almost to exaggerate the number of people. Were I to say I saw a thousand acres of human beings, I should fall short of the mark, and I saw but a small portion of the city.

But now I come to the illumination at night. What shall I say? What *can* I say about it? Its beauty was a thousand degrees beyond any thing I had dreamed of. If I were to study and write for twelve months, and employ every word in the English language that signifies, either directly or remotely, the beautiful, you would have but a faint glimmering of the scene I would attempt to paint. Every street, every house, every garden, every fountain, every tree, every column, monument, and statue, was brilliant. The number of lights was beyond calculation. Figures and devices of every fantastic shape could be seen — festoons, eagles, chicken-cocks, banners, palaces, pyramids, etc., etc., could be seen on every hand. The whole city was as light as day, and the streets as densely crowded as could be. Our hotel (de Rivoli) fronts the Tuileries Gardens, and the scene from our balcony was as fine as could be had from any point. We could see for miles.

The grand fireworks commenced about 9 o'clock,

and if Vesuvius ever presented a finer appearance, it was certainly astonishing to the natives. The fireworks, like the illuminating lamps, were of the tri-color—red, white, and blue.

To conclude, it is estimated that there were more people in Paris by far yesterday than were ever here before, and that more money was expended in getting up the *fêtes* than was ever expended since the world began.

I have much more to write, but must reserve it for another occasion. I must see more of Paris, and will next time write you a more interesting letter. For the present, Adieu. HAL.

P. S.—I must not omit to tell you that at one time during Sunday I was within a few feet of Empress Eugenia. I got a good look at her, and must call her beautiful. I pulled off my hat, and smiled and bowed to her. She waved her fan gracefully, and bowed and smiled in return. (The Emperor was not near enough to observe us.) Since then I have felt inclined to cut the acquaintance of my American friends. Don't know what I may do on reflection. I dislike to do it, for I have two most excellent companions, John G. and Arthur R., who, by the way, are enjoying Paris extensively.

LETTER V.

PARIS.

Paris, for beauty and magnificence, surpasses any thing I had dreamed of. Its gay inhabitants, its beautiful gardens, its magnificent palaces, its brilliant *cafés*, its lovely promenades, its cooling fountains, its galleries of paintings and statuary, its gorgeous shops, its bustling boulevards, and its flashing quays—all these things I have heard of from my youth up, but the half had not been told me. Nor is it possible for me to give you any thing approaching a correct idea of Paris. To be known as it is, it must be seen.

I have been studying the French people assiduously for the past three weeks, and have arrived at a conclusion! Yes, sir—I have come to a conclusion! You may say this is preposterous—absurd—ridiculous—for a fresh import all the way from Alabama (a region generally regarded by Europeans as heathendom) to form, and actually *express* in writing, an opinion of this highly enlightened and doubly-refined people after a study of only three weeks! Call it what you please. I have formed an opinion, and shall express it boldly, without equivocation or mental reservation. It is this:

That the French are a strange and unaccountable people! The more I see of them, the more I am constrained to quote the brilliant exclamation of Hans Von Vochensberg, upon his first visit to Paris: "Mine Got! vat a peoples!" and again, when he saw a monkey, with eyes rolled up and hands erect he exclaimed, "Donner and blitzen! vat vill de Frenchman make next?" These classic expressions pass through my mind daily because of the strange things I see. If there be any thing that a Frenchman cannot make or imitate, I don't know what it is. And if they are not a happy people, appearances are deceptive, for they always seem so. Few of them have *homes*. They live in hired apartments, and take their meals at restaurants. It is quite common to see whole families walk into a restaurant together, and take dinner. The mass of the people seem to live out-doors—all classes. The public squares, gardens and groves, are thronged from morning till night. You will see family groups sitting in the shade in those pleasant gardens, chatting merrily, and doing their work as if they were at home. Fathers read the papers, mothers and grown-up daughters ply the needle, little girls skip the rope, and little boys play ball or fly kites. Belles promenade, and young "whiskerandoes" do the agreeable. To a stranger it looks like a perpetual *fête*. Babies are never heard to cry here.

The garden of the Tuileries is a place of general resort; is very extensive, and contains many beautiful fountains, and a great number of statues. A band of fifty instruments plays here almost every evening, at government expense, for the edification of the people—also at many other places of resort. This is one of the means adopted by Louis Napoleon to render the people content, and keep them from taking off his head.

I have not confined my observation alone to the French people. There are many strangers here— many Americans, but more English. It pays well to note their manners. They are a peculiar people — the English are. They delight in hating the "frog-heating hasses," as they call the French, and suffer no opportunity to pass to speak disparagingly or contemptuously of them. The French, in turn, take pleasure in turning up their noses at the peculiarities and bigotry of the John Bulls. It is amusing to hear the English speak of the French and their institutions. I dropped in at the Grand Hotel du Louvre the other evening, and spent a delicious half-hour listening to the conversation of a small squad of angry Britons. One of them, it seemed, had been swindled by a coachman out of ever so many sous; was in consequence very wrathy, and considered himself licensed to say just what he pleased about the entire French nation; and all he said was endorsed by his companions. He termed them a "'eathenish, houtlandish people; hutterly hignorant of the courtesies due a stranger." Believed they would, from the Emperor down, "cheat the heyes out of a man if they could." Thought it strange they didn't "learn to speak

Hinglish." Thought the French language "'orrible gibberish." Met another party in Bois de Boulogne, a magnificent woodland park—the finest, perhaps, in the world. They acknowledged its beauty, but said that "for a display of fine hequipages and haristocracy, it was hinferior to 'yde Park in London." Still another party, at the Jardin des Plantes, conceded that it was very extensive and beautiful, but then "the hanimals were hinferior to those in the Zoölogical Gardens in Regent's Park." As to the public buildings of Paris, they were not to be compared with St. Paul's. Pronounced the French cookery "'orrid." From what I have seen and heard, I am constrained to believe that the English hate (not to say fear) the French with the hatred that only the intensely jealous feel. But the French turn up their noses, and laugh in their sleeves (they are too polite to laugh openly) at the growling British.

But with all the bluff bluntness and dogmatical bigotry of the English people, and with all their scorn and jealousy of every thing not English, I shall favor their success (much as I like the French) whenever there is a war between them and their Gallic neighbors—and that there will be a war between them at no distant day I have no doubt. Such a war, if declared to-morrow, would be popular on both sides the Channel. The reasons why I should favor England are obvious. She is our mother. Her language is the same, her religion is the same, and her government nearly the same. This is more than we can say of any other country upon earth; therefore my cry shall be, " *Vive l'Angleterre!*"

Many of the streets of this city are broad and beautiful. The Boulevards, a succession of wide streets, are said to be the finest in the world. One of them—the Boulevard des Italiens—is the chief thoroughfare for fashion and gayety. Here the Mrs. Harrises and the Flora McFlimseys most do congregate; and here people may be met every day, the worldwide fame of whom would render them "lions" anywhere but in Paris. Should *one* of them chance to visit the United States, his advent would be heralded by telegraph, from Maine to Texas, and the toadies of New York would get up a demonstration.

A stranger in Paris, from a Christian country, is almost forced to the conclusion that this is a God-despising, infidel people. The workshops, liquor-shops, stores, and all other kinds of work and play go on here on Sunday as on other days. Theatres, circuses, gambling-hells, and all other places of amusement and infamy, are open. The public works by the Government and city are carried on. In short, Sunday is little regarded by the masses.

But there is some salt in Paris; some people who worship God in the good old way. Found a little Methodist chapel, last Sunday, and heard an old-fashioned Methodist sermon. It seemed like getting back home; for both the singing and preaching were such as I have often heard there. The congregation was English.

Went to the Opera last night, and witnessed the performance of Robert le Diable. I was greatly pleased with the music, which was the finest I ever heard. I never before heard a hundred voices in chorus, accompanied by nearly as many instruments. The Opera, like every thing else in Paris, is on a grand scale. They bore with big augers here, and whatever they undertake to do they do with a vim.

It is raining here to-day; a thing much less common in Paris than in London. People, however, don't seem to mind it. The streets are pretty well thronged. Crinoline is displayed liberally; and ladies' knees are no secret in Paris. Modesty is a jewel here; yet it is to be found.

I have hardly yet become reconciled to the hours of serving meals here: coffee at eight or nine o'clock, breakfast at twelve, and dinner at six. No two articles of food are ever served on the same plate. The stuff the French call bread, is a libel—a slander upon the genuine article; almost tough enough to draw teeth; innocent of butter, lard, or salt; open as honeycomb, but with none of its sweetness, and is never used until it is stale. It is bought by the yard or foot, to suit purchasers. This is no joke, but a stubborn fact. The bakers furnish it in rolls from a yard to a yard and a half in length, about the size of a man's arm. Go into a restaurant, and you may see these rolls stacked in one corner of the room, one end resting upon the floor, and the other against the wall.

Our party will be divided in a few days. John and myself are going into Germany, on the Rhine, to be there during the vintage, or grape harvest. We are anxious to learn all we can about the cultivation of the grape, and the modus operandi of making wine. Arthur and Camp Turner (who, by the way, I had almost forgotten to tell you is of our party now—and a valuable accession too) will remain here and pursue their studies till cool weather, when they contemplate uniting with us in Italy.

If I had time, I would tell you something about our visit to Versailles, and of the *fifteen miles of paintings* we saw there, representing all the important battles fought by the French nation for fourteen hundred years. The palace covers twenty acres of ground, and the forest belonging to it six thousand acres!

The strong-minded maiden lady—the literary female mentioned in a previous letter—is here. She is "doing up" Paris with a rush. She goes out at all hours of the day, and in all sorts of weather. If there be any sights in Paris that she don't find, they'll hardly be worth looking for. Being of the pantaloons order of ladies, she goes it alone. I love, honor—yea, reverence—a modest, retiring woman; but from a *he* woman, good Lord deliver me!

We go from here first to Brussels, where we shall spend a week or two perhaps.

Yours,   HAL.

P. S.—Dr. Ford, Miss Hobson, and Miss Elliott, of Nashville, are spending a season here. They have just returned from a tour through Switzerland and on the Rhine—one of the most interesting tours that can be made in Europe.

LETTER VI.

BRUSSELS.

In the beginning of this letter permit me to make a few suggestions for the benefit of all Americans who ever expect to travel on this continent. I advise them, in making their preparations to leave home, to lay in a good supply of charity, forbearance, brotherly kindness, and as much patience as they can conveniently carry. They will find abundant use for all these graces at every stage of the journey—especially the latter. I thought I started with a pretty good supply, but it is well-nigh exhausted. A few more such attacks as I have suffered since my arrival in the Belgian capital, and I shall be "done for." Since my arrival here the beggars have stuck to me like the locusts to the Egyptians. The "commissionaires," who seek to guide me over the city, I have found harder to shake off than a New York hack-driver, or a hanger-on about a Niagara Falls hotel. Thus far I have kept them at bay. I have to use my stick to keep off the dirty-faced beggar children, many of whom carry disgustingly besmeared babies in their arms to excite compassion. I don't know which predominates here, the beggars or the black-robed, broad-brimmed Catholic clergy. The number of each is alarming. I am told that their number is correspondingly great or small in all Catholic countries. Where you find one, the other is sure to be. A numerous armed police is always necessary, too, in such countries.

This is the greatest city for bells I have yet found. A stranger is apt to think, from the incessant ringing of ponderous bells, that the town is burning up. Even now while I write, between eight and nine o'clock at night, the din is distracting. If I make any egregious blunders in this letter, you may lay the sin to the bells of Brussels, or to the Catholic Church.

Speaking of churches, this city is somewhat famous for its ancient and costly edifices. There are some here many hundreds of years old. I have visited some of them, and found them quite interesting on account of their age, architecture and paintings. The Church of St. Gudule is the finest church in the city, and one of the finest in Europe. It is truly magnificent, and I found it interesting to wander through and around it for hours. The painting of the windows is not surpassed anywhere. The internal adornments are elaborate, and quite enchanting to all who admire sculpture and paintings. In this church are deposited what are called the *miraculous wafers*, said to have been stolen from the altar at the instigation of a sacrilegious Jew, and subjected to the insults of himself and brethren in their synagogues. And this outrageous and diabolical act is said to have been committed on *Good Friday*, which of course added to the heinousness of the sin. It is said that when these Jewish scoffers stuck their knives in the wafers, jets of blood burst forth from the wounds, and that, by a second miracle, they were struck senseless. The sinful Jews who had done this were denounced by one who had been converted to Christianity, and were seized and put to death by the most cruel treatment, having their flesh torn off by hot pincers before they were burned to death at the stake. This is said to have taken place about the end of the fourteenth century. This "triumph of the faith," as it is called here, is celebrated once a year, on the Sunday following the fifteenth of July, by a solemn procession of the clergy, and an exhibition of the identical wafers. This is Catholicism in Belgium. You may know by this to what degree the intelligence of the people rises. That beggars abound here is not to be wondered at.

But with all its superstitions and gullibility, I must say that Brussels is a beautiful city. The modern part of the city (which my friend Gamble and myself have succeeded in exploring without the aid of a commissionaire) is decidedly handsome, and would not suffer much by a comparison with Paris. Indeed, Brussels has been called, and not without reason, Paris on a small scale. The streets are broad and straight, while the buildings are magnificent, being uniformly four stories high, and nearly all of a snowy whiteness—built of stone or brick, stuccoed. The old part of the city is not so handsome. The buildings are all fine and good, and the streets are kept perfectly clean, but they are very narrow most of them, and run in no particular direction. They wind about every way, and I find it the easiest thing in the world to get lost among them. It would be hard for a snake to put itself into a more awkward shape than the streets of lower Brussels.

And, by the way, speaking of these winding streets reminds me of a little incident I met with to-day. I was threading my way along one of them, and met two well-dressed ladies, who seemed to be wandering about at random. They were looking up at signs, and showed plainly by their actions that they were strangers in the city. Being a stranger myself, I sympathetically halted near them, when they approached me, and one of them asked, "Sir, do you speak English?" Throwing myself back as straight as a policeman, (for I was glad to hear my native language spoken in this modern Babel,) I replied, "Madam, I don't speak any thing else!" "Then, sir," said she, "will you be so kind as to tell us where to find a lace manufactory?" "Madam," said I, "I will not tell you, but *show* you a lace manufactory," which I did in short order. I found them to be a couple of English ladies who had wandered out from their hotel—very polite, and as thankful for my assistance as it is in the nature of the English to be.

And now, being at the lace manufactory, I will

tell you something about it. The lace is all made by hand, no machinery whatever being used in the making of the Brussels lace. Some thread was shown me, so fine, that I was told a pound of it was worth *twelve hundred dollars!* and that when manufactured into lace the pound would be worth nearly three times that amount of money! It was almost like a spider's web. The women who make the lace labor very hard, and frequently ruin their eyes while they are yet young. A lace handkerchief worth ten dollars requires sixty-five days labor; other laces in the same proportion. This city, as Americans all know, is celebrated for its fine laces. Not only the figures but the groundwork of Brussels laces are made by hand. The proprietor of the establishment made desperate efforts to sell me a bill of laces, but I resisted the temptation to buy.

Went out to Waterloo yesterday, and spent the day wandering about over the old battle-ground. Had Sergeant Munday (who was in the battle of Waterloo) for a guide. He is an Englishman, and of course points out all the interesting parts of the field with pride. No man who looks at the ground carefully will wonder at the defeat of the French. The English had great advantage in position. The Duke of Wellington had reconnoitred and chosen the ground with a view to draw Napoleon into a battle there twelve months before the battle was fought. In the midst of the field a great mound of earth has been thrown up to mark the spot where the bones of the thousands of friends and foes lie heaped together. The mound is two hundred feet high, and sixteen hundred feet in circumference at the base. It is surmounted by the Belgic lion, a huge bronze cast, which, with the pedestal it stands upon, is forty feet high. This lion is intended as a memorial of the Prince of Orange, and to mark the spot where he was wounded.

The church and churchyards of Waterloo village are crowded with memorials of English officers. They contain about thirty tablets and monuments to those who fell.

Waterloo is twelve miles from Brussels. Went out on a great lumbering stage-coach, crowded inside and out with passengers, all English, except G. and myself. Had the good fortune to sit facing two prim English spinsters on an outside seat. Took them for sisters from the favor. Both had auburn hair—intensely auburn—in fact, some people would call it red; thin lips, and fiery, spiteful-looking eyes. It would have required more than an ordinary amount of courage to have sought information as to the age of either of those damsels. Held their heads very high, and sat straight as Indians. I tried to draw one of them into conversation, but could n't. Thought I had succceded once, when she ventured a reply to a remark I made about the extremely hard features of the Belgian peasantry. Said she thought the "Belgian childring looked rather hinteresting." Our confab ended here. I amused myself with drumming Yankee Doodle on the footboard, while she elevated her head two or three degrees higher, and looked defiantly at her male companions.

Before getting off the stage upon reaching the battle-ground, we were set upon by a horde of relic-venders, who stuck to us as tenaciously as the Brussels beggars. Every ragged urchin in the neighborhood seemed to have a pocket full of bullets, buttons, and other relics, said to have been picked up on the battle-field. Our guide told us that he was sure that enough such relics had been sold there to supply a dozen such battles as that of Waterloo.

The road between Brussels and Waterloo is thronged with beggars. It is as amusing as it is lamentable to see the eagerness with which the children from five to twelve years old run after the coach. The oldest of them will follow it for miles in a brisk trot, occasionally turning summersaults to attract the attention of passengers. Others hump themselves, throw back their heads, and with their shaggy hair streaming in the wind, and their elbows pointing back like the knees of a grasshopper, will run for nearly an hour without seeming to tire, never taking their eyes off the passengers. If they get a copper or two, all right; if not, they don't seem disappointed.

Now all these things—the manners, customs, follies, superstitions, etc., are interesting to me, for my object in travelling is to see and learn. I think I am getting the full value of my time, trouble, and money. I am learning what books cannot teach.

Tourists generally go in one beaten track, and their wake is so broad that it is difficult to steer clear of it, but thus far I have succeeded in doing so. Those who write books of travel, or for the newspaper press, have a peculiarly easy way of getting up their letters and volumes. It is an easy thing to write either letters or books. For instance, one of these learned and prolific authors will go to a city, and as soon as his name is registered at his hotel, he has a "commissionaire" engaged, and is on the wing seeing the lions of the place. He runs from church to church, from gallery to gallery, and to all the places of interest, and thus, in a few hours, he "does" the entire city. At night he sits down, and, with the assistance of his guide-book and "commissionaire," he compiles a huge amount of matter which he imagines will be read with greediness by the untravelled, and consequently ignorant public. By elaborate plagiarisms from his guide-book, and some marvellous legends told him by his guide, he is made to appear exceedingly learned and well-read. This mode of getting up letters and books of travel will account for the great similarity observable in such productions. With a few items gathered from their guides, such writers not unfrequently are enabled to enter into a learned discussion of the politics of the countries through which they pass. They find many things to condemn, but rarely any thing to commend in a government.

Now such is the track followed by most of the book and letter writers. I have seen many of them since my arrival in Europe. I met one in Paris three weeks ago. He is now here, having visited more than a dozen other cities since leaving Paris. He thinks he is collecting material for a first-rate book. Bah!

Now as I am travelling for my own edification, and not to gather materials for a book, I shall make it a point to stop long enough in every important city I visit, to learn something about it.

I have now been in Brussels since Saturday last, (five days,) and the beauty of this city has grown upon me every day. It is a charming place, and if the climate were more temperate, I should be surely tempted to remain here through the winter. It is the cheapest place to live in I have found in Europe. Every thing is cheap except beef and mutton. Hotel bills are very moderate. Dry-goods of almost every description are astonishingly low. Many English families live here on account of the cheapness of living and the advantageous educational facilities, but it is said that their presence is gradually banishing the cheapness they seek.

I must acknowledge my indebtedness to Gen. E. Y. Fair, our Minister to Belgium, for his many kindnesses; and also to the charming and highly accomplished Mrs. Fair, for her amiable hospitality. Alabama may well be proud of the honor of being so well represented at the court of Brussels.

Farewell.

HAL.

LETTER VII.

BRUSSELS TO OSNABRUCK.

My last letter to you was written from the fair city of Brussels, which place we left on the 10th inst., and I will now proceed to give you a rambling account of what I have picked up along the way since that time.

Our first stopping-place was Cologne, a city renowned both in song and story for many things—its antiquity, its churches, its galleries of paintings, its antique curiosities, its massive walls, its bridge of boats, its castles and towers, its quaint old buildings, its Eau de Cologne, and, more than all, for its great Cathedral. Cologne is a city in which every one must be interested, especially the antiquarian and the architect; whilst those who are willing to be humbugged (and most people like it) will find many things to rejoice their hearts, for in barefaced humbuggery and brazen impudence, Cologne bears off the palm, as will be seen before the conclusion of this letter.

The first great object of attraction in Cologne is the Cathedral, a great building, which is visited, of course, by every stranger. It is a massive Gothic structure, commenced hundreds of years ago, and which is yet unfinished; and so immense is the work, that the present generation will hardly see it completed, although the work is being vigorously prosecuted. It will be the finest, but not the largest church in the world. It is 511 feet long, 231 feet wide, and will be 511 feet high. To finish it, will cost $5,000,000. The choir is 160 feet high. Internally, the church seems to be almost completed, and from its size, height, and disposition of pillars, arches, chapels, and beautifully colored windows, resembles a splendid vision. I attended the celebration of high mass here on Sunday last.

This Cathedral, like all other Catholic churches in Europe, possesses many wonderful curiosities, some of which will challenge the credulity of the most credulous. For instance, we are shown the *shrine of the Three Kings of Cologne*, or *Magi*, who came from the East with presents for the infant Saviour. The bones of these wise men are preserved in a massive silver case. Their names, Gaspar, Melchoir, and Balthazer, are inscribed upon their skulls in rubies. The bedel who exhibits these bones asserts roundly that they are truly and positively the bones of the Magi, and that all others who pretend to exhibit them are impostors. There is also exhibited here a bone of St. Matthew! But the "trump card" of the Cologneans is the church of St. Ursula, and the curiosities it contains. Here the wonderful things of the city are exhibited, and no traveller is permitted to pass through Cologne without being importuned to visit it. Here he is shown the bones of St. Ursula, and the skulls of the eleven thousand virgins who were her companions. On entering the church, these hideous relics meet the eye, beneath, above, and around; they are built into the walls, in the ceiling, and displayed in glass cases in various parts. The saint herself reposes in a coffin behind the great altar, while the skulls of a select few of her associates are permitted to remain near her. We are told, with prodigious seriousness, that this St. Ursula was the daughter of an English king, who, with eleven thousand virgin followers, made a pilgrimage to Rome. On their return, the whole party suffered martyrdom at Cologne, at the hands of the barbarian Huns, because they refused to break their vows of chastity! The skulls of the whole 11,000 have been preserved. Some of them are pierced with bullet holes, which causes some skeptical infidels to insinuate that they have been picked up on various battle-fields. The true believers, however, scout such an idea. In this church is also one of the vessels in which the water was turned into wine at the marriage in Cana of Galilee. Now, all these things, including a piece of the *true cross*, and one of the *identical thorns* with which our Saviour was crowned, are exhibited with imperturbable gravity, (not to say impudence,) and the spectator besought to believe that they are truly what they are represented to be. To see them costs money, of course, but what seeker after knowledge would refuse to pay a few francs to see so many wonderful relics! The student of human nature is richly repaid for his time and money, in witnessing the coolness with which these people assert the genuineness of their relics; while the credulous antiquarian views them with an astonishment only equalled by his delight. The Roman Catholics are great judges of human nature. They know that the people love to be humbugged, and knowing this, they delight in humbugging them. They find it a paying business. They have learned that the wise man is as susceptible as the fool, and will pay his money for being humbugged with equal liberality. Barnum, as a Bishop, would be a jewel to the Catholic Church.

But aside from the churches of Cologne and their curiosities, I viewed the city with much interest. I walked about the narrow streets, looked at the moss-covered walls and sharp antique gables, and wondered how many centuries the storms had beat upon them—strolled upon the old Roman walls and gazed at the old towers—sauntered upon the quay and the bridge of boats, and looked with delight up and down the classic Rhine, admiring the curiously shaped little steamers as they scudded by. And then the people look so odd! The great wooden shoes, the flaring caps, and the short skirts of the peasant women, were objects of interest. The clumsy wagons and carriages, the large horses and small donkeys, to say nothing of the dogs in harness, all came in for a share of admiration.

From what I saw while there, I would say that

the ladies of Cologne were fond of being seen. Large numbers were on the streets at all times. Now in some portions of our country, ladies' feet are little more than traditionary *leg-ends*, but not so with the Prussian ladies. Their feet are palpable facts, not sought to be concealed, but displayed with much boldness. Nor are they wanting in size. A visitor at Cologne will be struck with these facts.

I would write a paragraph about the filthiness of the streets and alleys of Cologne, if I could do so without following in the footsteps of other writers; but as everybody who writes at all about this city gives them a benefit, I shall pass them by. Much ink has been shed and many hard things said about these streets, and some have been so uncharitable as to even abuse them in poetry, which is terrible, you know. Now I remember to have read once a verse or two, by some heartless individual, running somewhat thus:

> "In Col'n, that town of monks and bones;
> And pavements fanged with murderous stones,
> And hags and rags and hideous wenches,
> I counted two-and-seventy stenches,
> All well-defined and genuine stinks!
>
> The river Rhine, it is well known,
> Doth wash the city of Cologne;
> But tell me, O ye powers divine!
> What e'er can wash that river Rhine?"

It was confidently predicted by the people of Cologne, that the writer of the above wicked lines would come to no good end, which proved true; for not many years after, he was suffocated by the stench in one of the alleys of that city. Verdict of the jury of inquest, "Served him right."

Eau de Cologne, so renowned all over the world, is pleaded as an offset to the two-and-seventy stenches observable in the city. It is an article of considerable commerce. There are upwards of sixty manufacturers of the article, and, strange to say, more than half of them bear the name of *Farina*, all claiming to be descendants of the original inventor of the perfume, whose name was Farina. He lived in 1670. Jean Maria Farina is said to be the rightful heir. Don't know how many of them bear the name of Jean Maria.

But let us leave the *perfumed* city of Cologne, and say a word about Osnabrück—a city of smaller size, less note, and less odoriferous, but one which has a name and a place in history, and is withal no mean city. Osnabrück contains about 15,000 inhabitants, and is one of the oldest cities I have seen. It is, I believe, the capital of a province of the kingdom of Hanover—is a walled city, situated very prettily in a level plain, surrounded on nearly all sides by highlands, which present a picturesque appearance. Friend G. and myself have been here several days, enjoying ourselves extensively, having been kindly and hospitably entertained in the families of Mr. L. and Mrs. H. We shall remember Osnabrück and some of its good citizens for many days. Mr. L. and young Mr. H. have kindly showed us all the notable buildings, and other things of interest, including the churches, City Hall, and some very fine Coffee Houses and Gardens in the suburbs. The Cathedral and St. Maria's (Lutheran) are the finest churches in the city. The City Hall is a castellated building, in which the negotiations for the peace of Westphalia were conducted. It contains a curious collection of very old plate. In the open space opposite this Hall stands a bronze statue of Justus Moser. An evening or two ago, in company with the intelligent Mrs. H. and her accomplished daughters, we drove out to the ancient village of Iburg, and viewed the venerable castle and palace from which the village takes its name. The scenery about Iburg cannot be sketched by any thing short of a master's pencil; it would therefore be bad taste in me to attempt it. I would, however, say to all travellers who pass through Hanover, to visit Iburg, and view the surrounding panorama from the heights of the Great Timpen. I would also recommend a visit to Schwitzenhoff, a beautiful place of general resort and recreation for all the good people of Osnabrück. Also "Little Switzerland."

Taking the people of Osnabrück for a sample, I must say that I am much pleased with the Germans. I find them, so far as my acquaintance extends, intelligent, educated, and refined, and also very hospitable. Their great number of places of public resort and amusement, shows them to be a very lively, fun-loving people; philosophers who believe in enjoying time as it passes. This is all right. I should like them more, however, if it were not for their national and individual disregard of the Sabbath. They do not seem to have learned all the Commandments.

We shall start to-morrow for Coblenz on the Rhine, and shall probably make a little trip from there up the Moselle river, on which is said to be some of the finest scenery in Europe, and where the grape is grown to great perfection. Moselle wines are celebrated and quite popular. From there we will wander on up the Rhine at leisure. We wish to see the country as it is, and shall therefore take our time. It is the object of travellers generally to travel over as much territory as they can in as short a space as possible. But we are content to see less and learn more. Adieu.

Hal.

LETTER VIII.

ON THE RHINE.

When Beavers was a candidate for Congress, in 1857, he opened the canvass with a history of the Democratic party, which he continued from day to day, at his different appointments, until he finished it, beginning each day at the place he left off the day before; thus giving to each audience its portion, not, however, in due season. I shall adopt Beaver's plan in this letter, and begin where I left off in my last. That was dated Osnabrück, and it is but proper that you should know my wanderings since leaving that city. Well, I left there about a week ago, and have since that time been lingering among and drinking in the beauties of the Rhine, gliding upon its peaceful bosom, climbing the lofty peaks along its margin, exploring the feudal castles and ruined towers which crown their craggy heights; in short, I have been bathing and basking amid those classic scenes that have been intermingled with my day-dreams from early boyhood. The first grand scenery of the Rhine begins with the "Seven Mountains," not far above the city of Bonn. At Cologne we bought tickets and embarked on a steamer for Coblenz;

but finding that it would be downright stupidity to rush by so much beautiful scenery at steamboat speed, we debarked at Konigswinter, a town just opposite the tallest of the "Seven Mountains," and have since that time been wandering from place to place on foot, which is the only way the Rhine and its neighborhood can be properly seen. He who travels up or down this glorious river by steamer, never stopping, and then boasts of having seen its beauties, is a deceived individual.

At Konigswinter we were met by a swarm of commissioners or guides, each of whom professed to know every inch of ground and every stone upon the Seven Mountains. We succeeded, after a struggle, in fighting our way through them just in time to be set upon by a horde of muleteers, who wanted us to ride up the mountain upon diminutive donkeys, no larger than billygoats. We resisted the temptation to ride, notwithstanding the red saddles, and, with our staves in our hands, started up on foot. It looked like a perilous undertaking to reach the pinnacle of the Drachenfels, (Dragon Rock,) on the top of which stands, or rather seems to hang, a noble old ruin. We reached it, however, and the view amply repaid the toil. This rock and ruin has been rendered more interesting by the verses of Byron:

> "The castled crag of Drachenfels
>   Frowns o'er the wide and winding Rhine;
> Whose breast of waters broadly swells
>   Between the banks which bear the vine;

And hills all rich with blossomed trees,
　　And fields which promise corn and wine;
And scattered cities crowning these,
　　Whose far white walls along them shine,
Have strewed a scene which I should see
With double joy, wert *thou* with me.

"And peasant girls, with deep blue eyes,
　　And hands which offer early flowers,
Walk smiling o'er this Paradise.
　　Above, the frequent feudal towers
Through green leaves lift their walls of gray;
　　And many a rock which steeply towers,
And noble arch, in proud decay,
　　Look o'er this vale of vintage bowers.
But one thing want these banks of Rhine—
Thy gentle hand to clasp in mine!

"The river nobly foams and flows;
　　The charms of this enchanted ground,
And all its thousand turns, disclose
　　Some fresher beauty varying round.
The haughtiest breast its wish might bound
　　Through life to dwell delighted here:
Nor could on earth a spot be found
　　To nature and to me so dear,
Could thy dear eyes, in following mine,
Still sweeten more these banks of Rhine."

From the heights of Drachenfels I counted twelve cities and towns in plain view, besides a number of ruined castles on other points along the river.

We descended about sundown, and slept at our inn at Konigswinter. In the morning we shouldered our carpet-bags, crossed the river, and took our way along the high road towards the village of Rolandseck, above which, on the heights, stands the ruin of the ancient baronial fortress and tower of Rolandseck. There is a little romantic story connected with this ruin. It receives its name from a tradition that the famous Roland, nephew of Charlemagne, chose this spot because it commanded a view of the convent of Nonnenworth, (which convent still stands on an island in the river, just opposite,) within whose walls his betrothed bride had taken the vail, upon hearing a false report of his having fallen in battle. He lived here a lonely hermit for many years, which has furnished the subject of one of Schiller's most beautiful ballads, "The Knight of Toggenburg." The scene, however, has been transferred by Schiller from the Rhine to Switzerland. So says Murray.

After climbing to this height, and viewing the grand scenery from many points, we again descended, and took the highway for the town of Ramagen, in the course of which we met with an adventure not to be forgotten. (I had forgotten to mention that there are now three in our party, instead of but two, young Mr. Hollenberg having accompanied us from Osnabrück. He speaks both German and English, and is quite an agreeable travelling companion.) The road runs immediately through vineyards nearly the whole way. The vines bend beneath the weight of a heavy crop, and, as there are no fences in this country, the luscious clusters hang temptingly over the road. We hailed this sight with a gladness similar to that of the spies who entered the promised land. Seeing so many hundreds of acres of the blushing fruit, and deeming it nothing amiss, we, with that innocence peculiar to ignorance, began to pluck and eat. A long, gangling, blue-shirted fellow, standing in the road some hundred yards ahead of us, raised his long bony arm ominously, and uttered a horrible sentence, in which our friend H. detected the word "police." He then called some half dozen laborers, near by, and with them started for the village of Oberwinter, (I shall always remember the name,) lying just ahead of us. We followed on very slowly, feeling assured that something was going to happen. When we entered the village we saw heads projected from every window, and knowing winks and nods were passed from neighbor to neighbor as we threaded the narrow streets. Young women laughed at us, and the old women looked at us with a sort of pitying expression, while the crowd of boys trudging at our heels momentarily swelled and grew larger. It was evident that everybody in Oberwinter knew that we were in a scrape. Even the dogs barked at us. At the far end of the village we saw a crowd collected, in the midst of which stood the blue-shirted individual, with his arms going like winding-blades. His gestures indicated that we were the subject of his discourse. We trudged on, and, upon reaching the crowd, were surrounded by the rabble, and informed that we must go before the burgomaster of the town, to answer to the charge of stealing grapes. The tongue of the informant was going like a bell-clapper, and the witnesses who had accompanied him were scarcely less noisy. The burgomaster was present, and, in a very loud tone, gave us to understand that we had committed a very grave offence; that he was a man of great authority, and that we should feel the weight of his power. We followed him into his filthy office—a small room redolent of lager-beer and tobacco smoke. He opened a ponderous book, and proceeded to read the law, which was all "Dutch" to us. Then, with his rusty spectacles thrown back, he proceeded to deliver a loud harangue, while his arms swayed to and fro like the sails of a wind-mill. Told us we must go to prison; to which we dissented most emphatically; and my friend John was about beginning to give the old skunk a lesson in civility with the butt end of his cane, and I felt inclined to give the leading witness a similar lesson, when friend Hollenberg quieted the clamor by producing his purse, and asking how much money it would take to get us off. The eyes of the belligerent magistrate brightened, and smiles took the place of frowns. But for all his smiles, John thought a cudgelling due him, which he would have proceeded to administer, had I not persuaded him that discretion was the better part of valor; which to me was evident, when I looked at the crowd of big, greasy, bloused Prussians standing round. The burgomaster told us if we would pay a good round sum of money, (which amount would go for the benefit of the poor,) we should be released. I supposed we should have to pay ten or fifteen dollars apiece, and was prepared to disburse to that extent; but Hollenberg knew his countrymen better than I did, and offered him half a thaler, (about thirty-seven and a half cents;) which he disdainfully refused. He then offered him a thaler, and told him we would give no more. He took it, and we shook the dust from our feet, and departed. As we left the office, a friend said to us, (I know he was a friend, from a remark he made,) "Go, gentlemen, and sin no more." This was the interpretation given to the remark by H. I have made up my mind as to one thing: if ever I catch that burgomaster, or either of the half dozen bloused witnesses, in the streets of Huntsville, I'll—I'll—but there's no use saying what I'll do, for it is dangerous to make threats; but I'll make them sorry they ever saw a bunch of grapes.

Leaving Oberwinter, we soon reached the town of Ramagen, an old town in which are traces of Roman architecture, dating back to the year 375. Remained at Ramagen all night, and the next day made an excursion up the winding valley of Ayr, down which the crystal waters of the little river Ayr flow beautifully. The scenery up this valley is picturesque beyond description. We ascended about fourteen miles to the towns of Ahrweiler and Altenah. Near the latter place is a very high peak of the mountain, on the top of which stands a majestic old ruin, the history of which I could not learn, except that it was built by a robber chief many hundred years ago. While standing upon the tallest pinnacle, a gust of wind took my hat off, and I have not seen it since. Not wishing to return to Ramagen bareheaded, I took a large comforter which resembled two or three yards of fancy carpeting, and wound it around my head, *a la* Turk. I was the admiration of the rustics all along the road to Ramagen, and in the village of Ahrweiler nearly the whole town gathered to see me, and a crowd of little boys followed me for some distance beyond the wall. Some said " Turko," and others said " Zouave." I enjoyed the fun very much.

After returning from the Ayr (or Ahr) valley, which, by the way, is world-renowned for its vineyards, we took boat and proceeded up to Brohl, (one or two hours' run,) from which point we walked to Laacher Sea, where we now are. This is a very singular lake, nearly circular in form, supposed to occupy the crater of an extinct volcano, is about two miles long, and one and a half miles wide, and very deep. The appearance of a deep blue lake hemmed in on all sides by a ridge of hills completely covered with luxuriant wood down to the water's edge is exceedingly beautiful, as well as singular. At one end of this lake, embowered in a forest of large trees, rises a grand old Abbey, with five immense towers, built about seven hundred years ago. The Abbey, with the many buildings attached to it, is enclosed with a massive stone wall. This is not used for church purposes now, but is private property; and many of the halls once occupied by nuns and monks are now used for granaries and cow-stalls. One of the buildings is an inn, in which I now write.

I must now go to bed, for John and Benno have been snoring this hour. Yours, etc.,

HAL.

P. S.—We have passed through many vineyards since our interview with the burgomaster of Ober-winter, but thinking the grapes " sour," we troubled them not.

LETTER IX.

RHINE TO GENEVA.

WHILE "taking mine ease at mine inn," and smoking my fair long pipe, I will scribble you a few items picked up along the way since my last letter.

By glancing at the map, you will see that I am many hundreds of miles away from the place from which I last addressed you. I was then lolling upon the fair shores of the pretty little Laachar Sea, away up in Prussia. Since then I have visited many places. Have wandered upon the "banks of the blue Moselle;" clambered among the ruins of the old "Mouse Castle;" stood upon the heights of the great Neiderwald; have tarried at "Bingen on the Rhine;" have roved through the celebrated vineyards of Johannisberg; groped through the world-renowned wine-cellars of Rudesheim; lingered in the groves and around the hot springs of Ems and Weisbaden; strolled through the streets and gardens of the beautiful city of Frankfort-on-the-Main; have struggled up the high mountains and gazed upon the ruined castles of Heidelberg; have looked and wondered at the great tower of the Strasburg Cathedral; have traversed the romantic hills and valleys of Switzerland; stood upon "the margin of fair Zurich's waters;" walked beneath the dark shadows of the Jura Mountains, and gazed with awe at the snow-crowned, cloud-capped peaks of the terrible Alps; have sailed upon the limpid waters of the lakes of Bienne, Neufchâtel, and Geneva; have been charmed with the beauties of the "arrowy Rhone," and now find myself quietly nestled down in the quiet city of Geneva, long noted for its beauty, the taste of its people, and as the place where they make watches. Geneva is one of the most beautiful cities I have seen, situated at the west end of the lake of the same name—a noble sheet of water which no European traveller fails to see, and which has been rendered classic by the historian, the romance writer, and the poet. It seems that the beauties of this lake well-nigh made a virtuous man of Lord Byron, judging by the following lines penned by that illustrious poet:

> "Clear, placid Leman! thy contrasted lake,
> With the wild world I dwelt in, is a thing
> Which warns me, with its stillness, to forsake
> Earth's troubled waters for a purer spring.
> This quiet sail is as a noiseless wing
> To waft me from distraction; once I loved
> Torn ocean's roar, but thy soft murmuring
> Sounds sweet, as if a sister's voice reproved,
> That I with stern delights should e'er have been so moved."

Thus was the great poet moved to write upon viewing this lake when calm and peaceful. Later he was nigh being lost in a storm, while making an excursion on the lake, when he wrote as follows:

"The sky is changed! and such a change! O night,
And storm, and darkness, ye are wondrous strong,
Yet lovely in your strength as is the light
Of a dark eye in woman! Far along,
From peak to peak, the rattling crags among,
Leaps the live thunder! Not from one lone cloud,
But every mountain now hath found a tongue,
And Jura answers through her misty shroud,
Back to the joyous Alps who call to her aloud!

. . . . .

How the lit lake shines, a phosphoric sea,
And the big rain comes dancing to the earth!
And now again 'tis black—and now the glee
Of the loud hills shakes with its mountain-mirth,
As if they did rejoice o'er a young earthquake's birth."

I have been now two days in Geneva, charmed and delighted with the rugged scenery which presents itself on every hand. The black, steep Jura mountains stretch themselves all along the northern shore of the lake. To the south rise the noble Alps, and away in the distance is seen the gigantic Mont Blanc, with its snow and glaciers glistening in the sun. I shall not be content until I have a nearer view of this giant of mountains.

If I had not begun this with a determination to write a very short letter, I would tell you a great deal about what I have seen within the last week or two, but as I don't wish to bore you or your readers very deep, I will refrain; for it would be as a thrice-told tale, as every nincompoop who travels over the route, if he can write at all, must needs attempt a description. I refer you to various books of travel, where you will find all that I could say.

I have been much interested in the vintage, and have learned what I could about the process of cultivating the grape and making wine. It is interesting to see the Swiss peasantry gathering the grapes. They make a frolic of it, and sing with great glee as they perform their labor. They are hard-looking creatures, both male and female, the latter coarse to an astonishing degree. It is romantic to talk and write about the hardy and frugal Swiss peasantry, and to see them at a distance is very well; but when you come in contact with them, the poetry vanishes. I have not yet seen a handsome or even passable face among the female peasants—though it is said they are virtuous and happy. I doubt not there is rustic virtue among them—a vast deal of it—but they are certainly a most filthy people. They labor in the fields much harder than the negroes of the South, and every woman among them can carry a load upon her head that would make an ordinary mule stagger. They live like hogs—men, women, children, horses, cows and goats, all under the same roof.

But I must close this brief scroll. John, who has just come in, (he has been out to buy us some tobacco,) says it is time to go to bed. We start for Italy to-morrow. Shall cross the Alps by way of the Simplon Pass. Shall have plenty of company. The flat-bosomed lady, who is gathering notes for a book, will probably be in the party—also the bandy-legged gentleman who wears gold spectacles, of whom I intended to tell you, but sha'n't do it now.

Friend Robinson has declined going to Italy, preferring to return home, and will probably go by the steamer that carries this letter, or soon after. He says he is tired of Europe. I regret his determination much, for he is a noble travelling companion, and I had hoped to spend the winter with him beneath the "fair Italian skies." Had also hoped to have friend Turner with us, (who is as clever as boys ever get to be,) but fear we shall not. Don't know what his plans are. He is in Paris.

       Farewell.   HAL.

LETTER X.

GENEVA TO MILAN.

I am at length in Italy—fair, bright, beautiful, sunny Italy!—the land of poetry and popery—of song and sausages—music and maccaroni—of orange-groves and organ-grinders—of roses and rogues—of soldiers and sardines—of minstrels and monkeys—of fat, round-bellied priests, and lean, gaunt, starving beggars—in short, the land where pleasure and misery jostle each other in the streets, and often go hand in hand. Such is Italy, and such are the strange blending of things here. The Italian towns are all strangely marked; houses with colonnades, streets with awnings, shops teeming with sausages, maccaroni and garlic; lazy-looking, loitering lazzaroni, in red nightcaps, and bare mahogany-colored legs, intermixed with mules, burly priests, organ-grinders, and females veiled with the black mantilla: these things fill up the picture of an Italian town, poets and romance-writers to the contrary notwithstanding.

But Milan is a fine city, and, to say nothing of its people and their habits, is a city that any country might be proud of. I have been on the pad all day, seeing its beauties and lions. The first place of interest, and which has been termed, not inappropriately, perhaps, the eighth wonder of the world, is the great Cathedral, the finest building, no doubt, in the world, but not so large as St. Peter's at Rome or St. Paul's, London. It is built of pure white marble, is four hundred and ninety-one feet long, three hundred and thirty-six feet high. There are *ten thousand* spires and pinnacles on this church, and seven thousand of them are surmounted with statues, and the other three thousand will be when the work is finished, which will require at least a century. It was commenced four hundred and seventy-three years ago. The interior is adorned with many fine paintings. The massive windows are of the finest stained glass, representing thousands of Scripture scenes. The scene from the top of the Milan Cathedral can certainly not be surpassed in the world. The spires of perhaps a hundred towns and cities may be seen, while in the far-off distance may be seen the snowy chain of the Alps. Mount Rosa looms up more grandly than any other peak, although Mont Blanc is plainly seen: the former is one hundred and twenty-five miles away, and the latter two hundred and twenty.

Among the other things of interest I have visited in Milan, I may mention the Amphitheatre, (now filled with French artillery,) which is capable of seating thirty-seven thousand people! Here all the *fêtes* of a national character are performed. Also went to see the great original painting of the "Last

Supper," by Leonardo Da Vinci. It is a fresco, in what was formerly the Convent of Le Grazie, but is now used as a barracks for soldiers. The world is flooded with copies of this celebrated painting, which is a proof of its excellence.

I have visited many other places of interest in the city, but it would be a bore to you for me to dwell on them. In fact, I have no disposition to dwell on them now, for I am becoming bored seriously with Milan, not less than six street organs having been furiously grinding near by ever since I commenced this letter. I am fond of music, but too much of a good thing is not pleasant.

But perhaps I ought to tell you something about our trip from Geneva to this city. I will do it for the want of something else to write about, although, like nine out of every ten who attempt to do so, I have no "knack" of describing scenery.

To begin : We left Geneva on the morning of the ninth, just as the god of day rolled proudly and sublimely up above the snowy mountains of the east. The sky was clear, serene and lovely. Not a breath of wind disturbed the placid bosom of the silvery lake which reflected the deep shadows of the black Jura on one side, and the towering Alps on the other. Our feathery craft glided swiftly and gracefully over the still waters like a thing of life, and nothing was there to jar upon the senses save a slight hissing of steam and the flutter of the paddle-wheels, and even that seemed musical. The snowy villages along the shore were as lilies nestling upon the bosom of the waters, while far away in the distance could be seen the beautiful city of Vevay, with its tall spires reflected beautifully in the deep blue lake. Our captain stood leaning lazily upon the quarter-rail, smoking his pipe, while passengers stood in mute wonder at the glorious scenery looming up on every hand. Flocks of happy waterfowl were skimming about in various directions, and anon the nimble trout could be seen to spring high out of the water to seize the unsuspecting butterfly as it dallied above the ripple. All on board that little steamer seemed wrapped in meditation. Your correspondent was in a peculiar mood—bordering on poetry—and had actually got two lines fully composed, when his meditations were cruelly broken in upon by the literary young lady with the scanty breastworks, (mentioned in former letters,) who came up and said, "Why, Mr. Hal, what *is* the matter with you? You are as solemn as if you were going to a funeral. Do rouse yourself and come forward, and see what a thumpin' big fish a sailor has caught. Come, it's in a tub of water in the forward part of the boat." The poetry fled, and up to this time I have not been able to whistle it back. I went and saw the fish, of course.

But to go on with the story. We left the steamer at a town called Bouveret, (pronounced Bouve*ray*, for you know the French take a sort of malicious pleasure in pronouncing things differently from the way they spell them,) at the east end of the lake, took the cars and travelled through the mountain-gorges for about twenty miles, where the railway ceases. Here we took diligence, and continued the journey up the valley of the river Rhone, until about two o'clock at night, halting at the town of Breig, just where the ascent of the Alps begins. All along the route from Geneva to Breig we noticed that the people were idle, and dressed up in their Sunday clothes. We concluded that the ninth of October must be a general Swiss holiday.

At Breig we stopped on the 10th, for we have made it a rule, ever since leaving home, to rest on the Sabbath. Were greatly shocked to see the people of Breig attending to all the ordinary affairs of life, seeming to care no more for the Sabbath than if they had never known such a day. The smith's hammer, the mason's trowel, and the carpenter's saw were heard, while the mowers in the neighborhood were busy gathering in their scanty crops of hay. The stores and shops were all open, and the peasant women were lugging their great burdens about as usual. The churches were there, but no glad bell was heard calling the people to worship. John and I read our Bibles, and deeply commiserated the poor ignorant people, believing that they were ignorant of the holiness of the day. Late in the afternoon John concluded to look over his diary, in doing which he discovered to his amazement that we *were keeping Monday*, and had actually travelled all day Sunday! We could then account for the Swiss holiday.

Tuesday morning we took the diligence, and

started up the mountain, the Simplon Pass. This is the best mountain road ever built. It is a triumph of engineering skill never accomplished before nor since. The world is indebted to Napoleon Bonaparte for it, who, remembering the great difficulty he found in crossing the Alps, determined to make a highway that cannon could be carried over without difficulty. It is a stupendous work, the greatness of which cannot be appreciated without being seen. It winds up the mountain in such a tortuous and zigzag way, that even where it is steepest, it does not rise more than one foot in thirteen. The cost of this road averaged about $25,000 per mile. It took six years to build it, and more than thirty thousand men were employed on it at one time. Houses of refuge—seven in number—are erected at convenient distances, to protect travellers from avalanches, which occur frequently in early summer. For more than two-thirds of the way up, the sides of the mountain are covered with vegetation, and wherever a dozen yards of arable land can be found, there is the hut of the hardy mountaineer. In some places the cabins seem to cling to the sides of the mountain as tenaciously as a bat clings to the wall of a cavern. After gaining two-thirds or more of the ascent, nothing but a picture of desolation surrounds the traveller. The pine has no longer the scanty pittance of soil which it requires for nourishment, the hardy but beautiful Alpine flower ceases to embellish the sterile solitude. The eye wanders over snow and glacier, fractured rock and roaring cataract, relieved only by that stupendous monument of human labor, the *road itself*, winding along the edges of precipices, penetrating the solid granite, striding over the furious torrents, burrowing through dark and dripping grottoes, beneath accumulated masses of ice and snow.

Upon reaching the highest summit or culminating point of the Pass, I made a vigorous effort to work myself up into a poetical mood. Thought of all the romance I had read about crossing the "proud Alps." Jumped up on a large rock, waved my hat above my head, gazed at the country below and the eternal glaciers above; threw my shawl about me, and imagined that it looked very much like Julius Cæsar's mantle; and while it waved in the breeze, and my hair streamed in the wind, I looked away down the acclivity and saw far down in the distance a great lumbering diligence with its long team crawling around a point of the mountain. I thought it looked like a huge ant winding round a potato-hill. The idea was so ridiculous that I involuntarily burst into a laugh, which banished romance. Just then I was enveloped in a passing cloud, and a few spits of snow and sleet together, with the piercing cold wind, warned me that I was exposing myself, when I muffled up, and crawled into the diligence.

We descended the mountain in a sweeping trot, and slept that night in Domo d'Ossolo, Italy. The next day went by diligence to Palanza on Lake

Maggiore, where we took steamer to Arona, and finished the trip to Milan by railroad. Would tell you something about the beauties of Lake Maggiore, but these miserable hand-organs have put my head to aching, so I'll quit and go to bed. Good-night.

HAL.

P. S.—We go to Venice to-morrow. If you find this letter bunglingly got up, just lay it to the organ-grinders, for they have kept up a most horrible squeaking.

LETTER XI.

VENICE.

At last in Venice!—"Beautiful Venice, the bride of the sea"—a city fair to look upon, and as strange as it is fair. Here the houses are palaces, the streets are canals, and the omnibusses, hacks, and pleasure carriages are gondolas. Dwelling in "marble halls" is not a "dream" here, but a reality. The Hotel Vittoria, where we stop, was in olden times a marble palace of great splendor; but now, like many other palaces in Venice, it looks seedy. Indeed, the whole city wears what may be termed a shabby-genteel appearance, though it bears evidences of having once been one of the richest and most magnificent cities of the world. It is beautiful yet, but cities, like belles, must fade before time.

Every thing is so strange, so quiet here. The loudest noise heard is man's voice; no lumbering drays or wagons in the streets—no clattering carriages, nor tramp of horse. There be grown-up men and women too, perhaps, who never saw a horse or wheeled carriage of any description! for such things are not here. Gondolas take their place.

I love dearly to skim about in the graceful gondola. There is poetry about it, especially on a moonlight night. Though I suspect the race of gondoliers is degenerating. When Lord Byron lived here they used to sing as they plied the oar, and we read that he caught the inspiration, and upon one occasion wrote as follows:

> "'Tis sweet to hear
> At midnight, on the blue and moonlit deep,
> The song and oar of Adria's gondolier,
> By distance mellowed, o'er the waters sweep."

These gondoliers don't sing any more. I have listened for one of their songs ever since my arrival here, but have heard "nary" song.

The Grand Canal is to Venice what Broadway is to New York—the great thoroughfare. I have spent much time in gliding up and down this canal, gazing at the great and gorgeous palaces, wonderstricken, with eyes stretched to a size little less than tea-cups. And then the flashing eyes that beam and sparkle from the palace windows, and the graceful forms that lean from the balconies, set my heart all a-flutter. I imagine that Jessica, the fair Jewess, looked as they look, when watching for her Lorenzo; (believe that's the name of the fellow who stole old Shylock's daughter.)

And I have stood upon the Rialto, the splendid arch that spans this Grand Canal. Hard by it is the Exchange, (it is a market now for fishes,) where Antonio and Shylock were wont in former times to talk of trade and commerce, and where Antonio spat upon the Jew's gabardine, and called him

(93)

"dog;" and it was there, or thereabout, the bond was sealed for the pound of flesh. Some of the Shylock family are said to be still found in the neighborhood. The Rialto is a specimen of architecture never surpassed, either in ancient or in modern times. Numerous little shops for the sale of bogus jewelry, cheap goods, and worthless trinkets, are now upon this bridge.

St. Mark's Square is the centre of attraction in Venice. It is an open space of several acres, paved with marble slabs, and surrounded with buildings of great magnificence. These houses are occupied as splendid shops and brilliant cafés, with colonnades. It is a place of general resort, and bands of music often play in it. The *élite* of the city, and strangers innumerable, may always be found in St. Mark's Square. In front of the cafés, people of all nations under the sun may be seen sipping their punch, their wine, or their coffee—playing cards, dominoes, or chess.

On one side of this square stands St. Mark's Cathedral, one of the most quaint as well as most magnificent buildings in the world. It would fill many pages to give any thing approaching a description of this ancient structure, so I shall not attempt it. Nearly the whole of the interior is mosaic of the finest kind, representing many sacred scenes. The four gilded bronze horses, stolen, I believe, by the Venetians from Constantinople, stand above the grand portal of this church. The Doge's palace, of which structure everybody has read something, is connected with this cathedral. In architecture it is a masterpiece, and very large. I have wandered through it, and looked at almost acres of paintings, many of them by Titian, Tintoretto, and other old masters. Titian was a Venetian. Was also conducted through the gloomy prisons of this palace, where many noble, wise, and good men have pined their lives away. Also crossed the Bridge of Sighs, leading from the palace prison to another prison more gloomy still, and from which no prisoner ever returned who entered it by way of this fatal bridge. The prison is separated from the palace by a canal, across which the Bridge of Sighs is suspended, some twenty feet above the water.

A part of the Palazzo San Marco, or St. Mark's Square, opens upon the bay, where two magnificent granite columns stand, one of which is crowned with a winged lion, called St. Mark's lion; (St. Mark is the patron saint of Venice, and every thing important must be called after him.) The story of these columns is this: They were pillaged from some other city, (don't remember what city,) and brought to Venice many centuries ago, but so great was their size that no man could be found who would undertake to elevate them upon their pedestals. After they had lain for a great many years upon the ground, a celebrated gambler of the city proposed to the Doge that he would raise and place them upon their pedestals, upon the condition that he and his friends should ever after have the privilege of gambling between them, without being interfered with by the law. This was granted by the Doge, although gambling was prohibited in all other parts of Venice, and severely punished by the law. The columns were elevated on this condition, but in the course of time the space between them became such a resort for gamblers and desperate characters, that the civil authorities found it absolutely necessary to do something to suppress the scenes there enacted. They could only do it by decreeing that all public executions should take place on the same spot. This broke up the gambling.

We have now been in Venice four days, and have visited a great many churches, palaces, asylums, etc., and have looked at and admired paintings by the acre, and statues innumerable.

It would not take me long to tire of Venice; every thing is so silent and monotonous. I want to be where I can see hills and mountains, and look upon running water. John is already satisfied with Venice.

We came through from Milan by rail, passing through Verona, Padua, etc., the former of which is rendered immortal by Shakspeare, as the scene where figured Romeo and Juliet. The tomb of the fair Juliet is still pointed out to travellers. Verona is also celebrated on account of its great Roman amphitheatre, second only to the Coliseum at Rome. Padua is also very ancient, and is also the place in which some of Shakspeare's characters figured. It is the place of Livy's birth and residence. Giotti, the great painter, also lived there, and his paintings adorn many of the old churches now.

We go from here to Florence, by way of Padua, Rovego, Ferrara, Bologna, etc. Adieu.

HAL.

LETTER XII.

VENICE TO FLORENCE.

AFTER a vast deal of trouble and vexation by the way, I am at length in the classic city of Florence, the centre of art in Europe, and very near the centre of poor bleeding Italy. And being snugly housed in my new quarters, I cannot better spend an hour perhaps than in scribbling you a few lines.

. But what shall I write about? I could write columns of doleful twaddle about the torn and distracted condition of the Italian States. I could get up a most solemn article about the poor down-trodden Italians, who writhe beneath the iron heel of Popery. I might write pages of dreary, nonsense about the black and threatening war-cloud that is now hanging over the whole of Europe, or get up a readable article about the attitude of France and England, who now stand eyeing each other like two furious ram-cats upon the point of a most disastrous clapper-clawing. Or I might scribble long and loud about England and the United States, the San Juan difficulty, and our success in the Celestial Empire, and the discomfiture of the British at the mouth of the Peiho. Again, I might write a stirring appeal to the world in behalf of the Italian patriots who followed the lead of Victor Emanuel and Garibaldi, and loom extensively against the bloody-minded Pope, and tyrannical Austria. I say, I might spread myself on any or all of these subjects, but what would it all amount to? The light that I could throw upon any of them would be so infinitesimally small, that a glass magnifying a thousand times would be required to see it. So I shall pass them all by, and endeavor to pen what you may term an "anti-blue-devil" document; for I hold that he who dispels one vapor from the mental sky of his readers, does more good sometimes than he who convulses nations. Nonsense is a good thing in its place—better on some occasions than volumes of learned lore.

"A little nonsense now and then
Is relished by the wisest men."

So I say. Paradoxical as it may seem, nonsense is sometimes the best of sense—old fogies and long-faced Solons to the contrary notwithstanding.

I am no grumbler. I call upon you to bear me witness that in all that I have written during my travels, I have never written one line in a grumbling spirit. Travellers, you know, are almost universally grumblers. It is their right, and, as they pay for the privilege, they love to enjoy it. Hotel-keepers, waiters, and servants generally come in for their share of censure, while the public conveyances and their conductors are almost universally inveighed against. The English traveller (and his name is legion) never finds any thing on the Continent like it is at " 'ome," hence he is in a grumbling mood all the time. It has been a source of some amusement to me to watch and listen to some of these people. Still, I must say, John Bull is a good fellow at bottom, and I trust the day will never come when we shall be at daggers-points with him; although I go in for our Government holding on to the San Juan Island, even to the bitter end, daggers or no daggers.

But, as I said above, I am no grumbler, but one of the best-natured individuals in the world—a model of patience, a paragon of submissiveness; in fact, a second Mrs. Caudle, who, you know, declared on divers occasions that she was "the patientest thing alive." If it were not so, I should have been in a perfect stew for the last five days. To have undergone what I have in that time would have made Socrates (who was reputed to be a man of great patience) tear his hair and gnash his teeth in very wrath, and Job would possibly have cursed outright, while Samson would have overturned mountains in his anger. Yet I did none of these wicked things. I will give you an outline of the grievances that beset me by the way from Venice to this city.

It was a dull cloudy morning that John and myself took our departure from the beautiful "city of the sea." Upon arriving at the railway-station, our carpet-bags were taken charge of by an Austrian custom-house officer, who, upon our noncompliance with the general custom of slipping a few francs into his hand as a bribe, proceeded to search them most thoroughly, tearing our clothes out, unrolling them, peeping into every hole and corner, leaving them scattered in the most promiscuous manner. In the search he found in each of our carpet-bags a small roll of Turkish tobacco. Upon this discovery his eyes glistened with fiendish delight, and grinning horribly a ghastly smile, he passed it over to a second official, who responded to his chuckle. After weighing the tobacco, and making a great many figures in a business-like way, we were informed that we could take our choice, either to go back to the city under an escort of soldiers, or pay three dollars and fifty cents and go on our way. We chose the latter, shook the dust from our feet, and departed. John bullied them out of a dollar which they wanted him to pay on a cigar-case. This was only our first trouble. Two hours after leaving Venice we arrived at Padua, where we designed taking diligence for this city. The hotel-keeper informed us that the seats in the diligence were all engaged, and that we would have to remain there twenty-four hours, or place ourselves in the tender clutches of a vetturino. He (the hotel-keeper) would be gainer, let us adopt what course we would, for he was the proprietor of the carriages as well as the hotel. We were immediately surrounded by a swarm of vetturinos, who *pretended* to be rivals, but really all the servants of the same proprietor. One of them proposed to carry us to Ferrara in time for the diligence next day, for eighty francs. Another said he would carry us for seventy-five francs. A third very generously proposed to carry us through for sixty. Thinking we would get the passage cheap, we professed to be content to remain in Padua until the next day for the diligence. Finally, one fellow approached us and offered to take us for the low price of fifty francs. We closed the bargain, thinking it dirt-cheap, and found out too late that it was twenty francs more than we ought to have paid. Left Padua in a sweeping gallop, and in the midst of a beating rain.

Arrived at Rovego about eight o'clock at night, where our passports were demanded. Handed them over; and by some sort of hocus-pocus trick they were retained for *twenty-eight hours!* The officer whose duty it was to sign them, was out of place—on a spree, perhaps—and there we had to stay, in a hotel like a dog-kennel, surrounded with beggars and low, greasy Italians. Some people would have got mad under such circumstances. Got our passports at length, and made another start. At Madalena, at the crossing of the river Po, were stopped again, and had to hunt an hour in the rain for another little upstart Austrian officer to sign our passports, and during the whole time were surrounded and set upon by a horde of long, lank, lean, lazy, lounging, loafing, lame, lying, lousy lazzaroni, whose sole business is begging. I amused myself by bouncing the small end of my stick off some of their heads, which is evidence that I am one of the best-natured creatures in the world;

otherwise I should have gone in for breaking necks. John boiled over. Well, in the course of time, we crossed the Po, and reached the city of Ferrara in time to find that we were too late for the diligence, and all the seats even for the next day had been taken. Another struggle with the vetturinos, dozens of whom offered their services to take us to Bologna. Finally struck a bargain with one, and again found out too late that we were swindled worse than before. Got to Bologna and found the diligence again full, and all the seats engaged for two days ahead. Stayed at Bologna twenty-four hours—long enough to see all the sights of the city, and test the quality of the Bologna sausages. Our landlord was a growling, snarling, snappish fellow. John said it was owing to his having eaten so many sausages. The point of the joke "came to me" two days afterwards.

At Bologna we hired another vetturino. He was a real nice fellow, and agreed to put us through to Florence in the most genteel style. Showed us his nice carriage, to which he would hitch *three* splendid horses. We agreed to pay him a round price for the extra fine style in which we were to travel. At the appointed hour we set off in a gallop, really proud of our splendid three-horse turnout. It was two o'clock in the evening. At seven our postilion halted at a miserable inn, which was full of drunken, brigandish-looking fellows, and the landlord of which had a most villainous face. There we had to sleep till morning, or rather *watch;* for it would require a very sanguine man to sleep in a house filled with such ferocious-looking creatures as were there, and that too in a gorge of the Apennines, once famous for robbers. The carousal was kept up nearly all night, and we watched with vigilance, but didn't see "nary banditti." When morning came, we found that our fine vetturino had decamped—taken the back track to Bologna—and had left us to be forwarded in a miserable *one-horse* concern, under the care of a new postilion! We had our choice—either to submit to the outrage, and go on, stay where we were, or walk back to Bologna for the purpose of whipping the proprietor. As travellers never like to turn back, we went ahead. After travelling three or four hours, were again transferred to an old barouche, drawn by two frames of horses, a sight of which would have made a turkey-buzzard smack his lips, and rejoice at the prospect of an early feast. With this turnout we finished the long and tedious ascent of the Apennines, and descended into the beautiful level country on this side. At Pistoja our postilion dumped us down, some twenty miles from Florence, notwithstanding our distinct contract with the proprietor to put us all the way through to this city. The postilion said that his instructions were to bring us no farther; and he would not do it. As Pistoja is a railroad station, we frightened the postilion into buying us tickets, when we took rail and landed here safely, in a little more than five days from Venice.

Now, considering all the troubles and besetments that met us by the way, don't you think we did well to keep our temper? What would Job have done, or what would even Mrs. Caudle have done, under the circumstances? But, as I said before, I don't grumble.

I have not been in Florence long enough to tell you any thing about it. Will do so, perhaps, before long. Can only say that it is a city of great beauty, and is the most beautifully situated of any city I ever saw, being almost surrounded by gently rising mountains, the sides of which are dotted with villas and gardens of much loveliness. The river Arno flows through the midst of the city. I promise myself much pleasure in visiting the many galleries of art here, which are the finest in the world, except, perhaps, those of Rome. Have visited the family of the American Consul, General Mallett, where I was courteously received and entertained. General M. is a high-toned gentleman, and Mrs. M. a most accomplished lady.

Think I shall visit Rome and Naples some time during the winter, provided there is no war in this country. If there be war, I shall be on the right side.

As this letter is long enough, I shall desist for the present, with the cry of, "Three cheers for Victor Emanuel and Garibaldi! Nine cheers for Uncle Sam! Death to Popery and the double-headed Austrian Eagle! Liberty to Italy and the world, mental, moral, and political! So mote it me!

Yours, etc., HAL.

LETTER XIII.

FLORENCE.

The following was written to Dr. Antony, of Huntsville, Alabama:

Dear Doctor:—God bless you! Yes, I repeat it with energy, God bless you! You have made my heart glad. Your letter—the first that I have received from any source since crossing the Atlantic—reached me to-day, and was as a balm, a soothing cordial to my heart. Your kind and pleasant words were like "apples of gold in pictures of silver." Would that I could write a response in equally elegant and pleasant style; but as I cannot, being a plain, blunt man, you must accept such a document as I can pen. But——

Mercy on us! What a noise! what a hubbub! what a rumpus! what a hellabaloo has been kept up in Florence this whole blessed day, and is still, though eight o'clock at night, going on without the least abatement. Bomb—bomb—bang—bang—ding-dong—rattle, rattle! Was the like ever heard! A thousand bells, of all sizes, tones, and descriptions, all ringing at once, and each particular bell, without the least regard to harmony, exerting all its powers to ring louder and more harshly than its neighbor. I am really almost distracted with the noise, and shall make but a poor out writing tonight. To-day is a great Catholic festival—All-Saints' day—but from my heart I pity all saints who have remained in Florence to witness its celebration; for surely they will retire with aching heads. "Old Nick" himself (and he is generally allowed to be a brave one) is made of more plucky stuff than ordinary devils are supposed to be made of, if he has stood his ground to-day. Nay; if he has ears to hear, and wings to fly, I must think he made his escape with the dawn of day. And wise would it have been for every peaceable, quiet, well-disposed person to have followed his example—not that I approve of people following the example of so villainous a vagabond, as a general thing. But any thing to get away from a Catholic festival, where they have as many bells as they have in Florence. If I were not in an ill-humor, I would spend my opinion freely about those tormenting bells, and the people who ring them, but shall refrain from doing so until I am more composed. I might say something harsh, which would no doubt be very lacerating to the feelings of the "holy fathers;" and that would be cruel, you know. Besides, it is not in my nature to wound the feelings of my fellow-men wantonly, more especially those whose mission it is to remit sins, and whose privilege it is to grant indulgences to those who may desire to transgress the holy commandments of God. No; far be it from me to speak harshly or disparagingly of so large and so *very* respectable a body of men, whose rigid, energetic, and persevering piety is no less vividly marked in their sleek, round faces, than in the sacred robes they wear. Nay, let me not offend them; for I would as soon have a legion of devils after me, as an army of pot-bellied priests. The annals of Italy prove that they are a desperate and bloodthirsty people, notwithstanding their fierce sanctity. Then let them ring their bells, eat their wafers, grant indulgences, remit sins, strut the streets, grind the poor, crush liberty, and fill the land with beggars: I shall not say aught against their peace and quiet. But enough about the Catholics and their bells. I must tell you something about Florence.

But hark! There comes "a rapping at my chamber-door."——— "*Entrée.*"

. . . . .

My landlady's daughter has just been in to inform me that an American gentleman in an adjoining house has been found dead in his room. If you will excuse me for a little while, I'll go and make inquiries about it. Hope the bells have not caused his sudden death.

. . . . .

The foregoing was written last night, from which I was called abruptly to the chamber of death. The man was dead—very dead. A Mr. B., of P———, a victim of "cold pison," caused, as he left "a billy-dux a stating," by circumstances similar to those which caused Sickles to murder Key. Yes, he is gone, and is by this time no doubt safely ferried over the river Styx, and landed where all suicides go.

Perhaps you think I speak too lightly of so serious a matter—that I ought to call up a few crocodile tears, and say "poor fellow," and all that sort of stuff. Perhaps I ought, but I cannot. I have a peculiar notion about suicides. They quit the world because they cannot make the world quit them. If they could crush the world, and leave themselves living, they would do it; but as they cannot, they destroy themselves. And besides, they are stimulated to the act by the knowledge that they will be honored with a great funeral procession, and have the sympathies of the world, and that their death and attendant circumstances will be heralded to all parts of the world in the newspapers. If it were law and the custom (and it ought to be) to bury all suicides with their faces down, and stakes driven through their bodies, such occurrences would be few and far between. But you may say that a man is deranged when he takes his own life. Very likely; but would not the reflection upon such a disposition of the body, and the absence of the sympathies of the world, bring about a sober second thought, and prevent that methodical derangement? It seems so to me.

But I must tell you something about Florence, if I can find a starting-point. Would that I could paint you a picture of this lovely city! I know you would be charmed with it, for it is the gem, the crowning jewel of all the beautiful things I have seen in Europe. If it be true that "a thing of beauty is a joy for ever," I could impart to you a lasting joy. But I despair. I feel powerless as an infant. I cannot impart to you even an outline. I have groped about amid magnificence and in beauty until I am sick. You may laugh at me, but it is true! I am sick with seeing. When I wander through the galleries, the palaces, the churches and the gardens, I become faint, and my head throbs with pain, caused by the continued and labored effort of the mind to comprehend the grandeur of the objects presented. I am robbed of more than half the pleasure by the exceeding beauty and greatness of what I see. This is no idle assertion, but a truth. I know not if it be so with others.

But you perhaps expect me to tell you something about the city. And as the galleries of paintings are the first places visited by most travellers, and as it is their custom, almost universally—especially those who write—to tell of what they there see, (and they are generally severe critics,) you may possibly expect a similar tirade from me. You shall not, however, be so bored. I shall not attempt to criticise a single painting. You may wonder that I should so far depart from the general custom— and, indeed, it is to be wondered at—especially when you reflect that I can find so many wise and learned criticisms already prepared to my hands, and nothing to do but to adopt and copy them.

Guide-books are of great advantage to critics, and to descriptive writers generally. But unfortunately for me, I made the sad discovery, when in Paris, that I was no judge of pictures. I made the discovery thus: It was in the Luxembourg Palace, which is filled with the paintings of living artists. I was standing before a picture with some friends, and was pointing out to said friends the peculiar beauties and excellence of said picture. I had selected it as the finest work of art in the room, and was well-nigh going into ecstasies over it, when I heard a voice behind me utter that senseless but very significant word, "Bosh!" Looking round, who should be there but a gentleman in whose taste and judgment I had the most unbounded confidence. Irony and sarcasm were depicted in the contemptuous smiles that sat upon his face. He then went into a critical analysis of the before-mentioned painting, making it as clear as mud to all present that it was one of the most contemptible daubs ever suffered to occupy a public position—a disgrace to the gallery. I wilted, and never since that day have I attempted to criticise a picture.

But this is not telling you about Florence. Just imagine yourself with me, and we will take a stroll over the city, the day being one of the most lovely of the season. Our walk must be a hurried one—just taking time to glance at the things along the way. First we will go to the great Cathedral of St. Maria del Fiore, one of the greatest lions of the city. Does it not loom up grandly? It is built, or rather encased, in polished marble of various colors, and is one of the largest in Italy, being four hundred and twenty-six feet long, and three hundred and fifty-three feet wide; and that dome you see perched up so high is one hundred and forty feet from one angle to the other, said to be the largest dome in the world, except the Pantheon at Rome. By going up to the top of that, you have an excellent view of Florence and the country around. Let us go inside. Here, stop at the door, and look away yonder at the high altar. It is nearly two hundred yards off. Those priests you see officiating there look no larger than grasshoppers. But is not the view a grand one—one vast hall nearly two hundred yards long, and high in proportion? Now let us enter and look at the thousand and one contrivances by which Popery gulls the people. The floor you see is of marble of various colors, worked into many kinds of figures; the walls ditto. The altars are gorgeous, and the stained-glass windows are very pretty. But for fear you may hurt your neck looking up at the frescoes in the great dome, we will retire, and come again when we have more time. As we are a little hurried, we will pass by all the other churches to-day, although there are a hundred worth visiting, representing every style of architecture, and frescoes innumerable.

We will now go to the Pitti palace, if you please. On our way thither we pass by several other palaces, the most imposing of which is that of Ufizzi, which looms up massive and gloomy just on the corner of the Square Gran Duca. We will not enter now, for we would not have time to examine the hundreds of celebrated paintings which it contains. Just by it is the Royal Gallery, the most valuable treasure Florence possesses. Here we might spend a day, and then retire with the determination to come again and again. We will pass this by also, for were you to go in, you would soon be lost in admiration of the famous Venus de Medicis, and other great works of art, and would forget the Pitti palace. Now we will cross the Arno over this magnificent stone-bridge, and in one minute's walk will be at the Palazzo Pitti. Here it is. Is it not enough to make man feel insignificant to look up at those massive walls? See those huge stones of which it is built; rough almost as they came from the quarry, but so large! some ten and some twenty feet long. Is it not astonishing? Don't your head begin to pain you? Mine does. But it will be worse before we get through. We will now pass this sentinel and go in, and as I am anxious to get into the garden in the rear, the famous Boboli Garden, we will hurry rapidly through the various rooms of the palace, where the paintings and statuary you will find rivalling those at the Royal Florentine Gallery. There are fourteen saloons in this palace that deserve our special attention, but they cannot all be seen at one visit, neither will we have time to examine the grandeur of the building itself. First we will enter the *Saloon of Venus.* Here you are enraptured with the frescoes on the ceiling. There are Minerva, Venus,

Hercules, and Cosmo; the Genius of War; Scipio, Antiochus, and his Mistress; Crispus and Fausta; Cyrus and Panthea; Augustus and Cleopatra; Alexander; the Mother and Wife of Darius, etc., etc. Are they not magnificent? Now we enter the *Saloon of Apollo*, in which, as in the previous one, we will only glance at the frescoes. Here we see Apollo and Cosmo; Cæsar studying his books as he walks, that he may lose no time; Augustus listening to the Æneid; Alexander and the Emperor Justinian, etc. Next the *Saloon of Mars*, where we find Mars and Cosmo; Castor and Pollux; Captives loaded with chains, supplicating the Goddess of Victory; Peace and Abundance, scattering blessings. *Saloon of Jupiter :* Jupiter, Cosmo, Olympus, and Hercules; Minerva planting an olive-tree; Mars mounted on Pegasus; Vulcan reposing on his anvil; Diana sleeping; Apollo and Mercury, etc. Now, do not the magnificence of these paintings make you open your eyes with wonder? I doubt if you have seen the beautiful furniture of these saloons as you passed through them, so taken up were you with the paintings. Surely the furniture deserves notice : those splendid vases, ornamented clocks, tables of Florentine Mosaic, etc., etc. But as our time is limited, we will not linger in the palace. We will, however, pass through the Gallery Flora, that you may see the celebrated Venus of Canova, said to rival even the Venus de Medicis.

Now we pass from the palace into the garden, the first view of which makes us halt and gaze and wonder with admiration. The groves, the fountains, the labyrinthine avenues, the cunningly devised arcades of evergreen, the hundreds of statues—wonderful! wonderful! After wandering an hour, and thinking surely we have seen it all, new beauties burst upon us that we knew not of. Were we to tell our friends of but the half we see here, they would give us no credit for veracity. Come let us mount up to the highest point, (for you observe this garden is on a hill,) and take a look down at the city. Is it not lovely as a bride adorned for her husband? And then the villas that dot the hills and vales in all the country around—could man conceive any thing more enchanting? Look out there to the East; there is Fiesole, where ancient Florence stood upon the hill. In the midst of it you see an old tower. That is the tower of Galileo, from which that great philosopher watched the heavens.

Now, contemplating all the beauties you see before and around you, you say, Surely these Florentines are a great people. But you must remember that all these things have been thousands of years accumulating. It is a very ancient city. The Etruscans were here indulging in all the luxuries of life, while the Greeks were still barbarians, and Rome had yet no name. And even then they cultivated sculpture, painting, architecture, and all the arts, with a passion. No wonder, then, that Florence should now be the centre of art.

But let us quit the Boboli Garden now, and take

a stroll to the Casine, that great resort into which Florence empties itself almost every evening. And as we have to pass by my restaurant, we will step in and take a lunch. It is rather an extensive establishment, and you can have any thing you call for; but, as you are my guest, you must submit to the fare that I submit to every day. First, we take soup—any kind you like. Now a dish of meat and vegetables—any kind you are disposed to order— and a small bottle of wine. We end now with a small dessert of fruit, either grapes, figs, pears, or apples. Being through, now, we pay three pauls (about thirty-three cents) each, and retire. This is my dinner, generally. Breakfast costs one paul, (eleven cents,) and supper the same. So you see living is not dear here.

But we will go on to the Casine—an extensive park, or grove, or forest, adjoining the city. You may imagine that it now is Sunday morning, four o'clock; for Sunday is the day, and four o'clock the hour, when we will see most people. We will take our course down the quay along the banks of the Arno, which you see flows through the midst of the city. It is a long walk; but then we will be in such a crowd, and the way is so beautiful, that the distance will be forgotten. Little more than half a mile will put us beyond the city walls, when we will enter immediately into the country. But, mercy on us! what a crowd! what a rush! Everybody is out, and all dressed up in their best, and all, too, looking pleased with themselves and all the world.

And then look at the scores and scores of brilliant and gorgeous equipages! Did you ever see so many and such a variety of turnouts? Look, there is a four-horse coach—four beautiful cream horses. Don't they prance! And, as I live, here comes an eight-horse establishment! and a six-horse, just behind it! Ay; don't the liveried servants flash and shine! And then the ladies! How their eyes sparkle, and how their plumes nod! What an astonishing amount of fine store goods we see! You see at a glance, from the display of fashion, that the season is open in Florence—wide open—and the fashionables are making the best of it. These people are mostly foreigners—only here for the season. Thousands of English, French, Germans, and Americans come to this city to spend the winter. Here we are, at the city gate; and now, amid the jam, we enter the Casine. Is it not lovely? Did you ever see nature and art more happily blended? Those groves, walks, and drives, are perfectly enchanting. Here we are, in a dense crowd. Just yonder we can dive into the bosom of the forest, and in one minute be beyond the noise of the crowd. But we will keep with the company, for they all seem to be making for one place. Here are seats, by the way: we can rest occasionally. We will take the walk on the extreme left, which is on the margin of the Arno. About two miles down we halt, because everybody else does. Here are thousands of people and hundreds of carriages. Now you know why they all stopped. A band of fifty brass instruments strikes up a lively air. What! and on Sunday! Certainly, on Sunday. Now, if we were to tell this to our countrymen, no doubt many of them would roll up their big white eyes to heaven, raise their hands, and thank God that they were not as other men! Music—brass music—on Sunday! Horrible! Well, it may be a very horrible thing, but I am fully persuaded that it is not as horrible as many other things. It gives the people recreation and a place to go to. Were there no such place to resort to, about one-third of these people would sleep away the evening; another third would perhaps spend the time in the drinking-saloons, while the remaining third would wander listlessly about the streets. This is a military band, that plays every day in some part of the city, but only twice a week (Sundays and Thursdays) in the Casine. Don't you think it a good institution, Doctor, and don't you think that every city and town ought to have a band to play, especially on Sunday evenings, even in America? Look on the crowd before us, and give me a candid answer. Did you ever see a more orderly, contented company?

But let us retire from the crowd a few moments, to the river bank; for it is the hour of sunset. You have heard and read of Italian sunsets—of their beauty and exceeding gorgeousness. You shall now see that all you have heard is true. Behold the beautiful tints, the rich, golden streaks that dart up the sky, the gorgeous halo upon the peaks of the Apennines! Is it not enchanting?—

for all the world like a sunset in Alabama!—than which there can be nothing more beautiful, except a sunrise!

The music has now ceased, and the people are wending their way back to the city. Let us join them; but as the walk may seem longer in returning, we will take a carriage—there are plenty here waiting to be hired—and join the mass of aristocratic equipages. Look! look! Do you see that hard-featured lady in that fine carriage? That is old Aunt Harriet Beecher Stowe, who is now spending her time and her ill-got money in Florence. Don't she cut a swell!

Here we are, at my lodgings, No. 1187 Lung Arno. Walk up with me, and we will ring for tea. Walk in. Don't be surprised. My apartments are finely, I may say gorgeously, furnished; which is peculiar to Florence. But, fine as all this furniture is, I only pay eight dollars a month, service included.

Ay; here is Marie, with her tray of tea and toast. Very good; isn't it? It is a good thing to have a good landlady — one who will always send you enough.

Now, tea being over, we will take a smoke, after which, if you feel disposed, we will go out and take a look at the city by moonlight; for the moon is now near the full. Here are some excellent cigars. Take one. I will, if you will excuse me, fall back upon my old friend, the pipe.

Go! O no! Don't think of going yet. It is

quite early. Here—the night being balmy, we will open this door, and take a seat on the balcony, which, you see, overlooks the Arno. And here, while we smoke, I will briefly tell you my plans for the future. For the present I am trying to conquer a language which has thus far proved too hard for me, but which I intend to master, before I am done with it. I have an excellent lady teacher. Well, after I have done that, I shall visit Rome and Naples; after which I shall start for Egypt and the Holy Land. There is a company of Americans here now, who start in January. I have promised to go with them. This is my present design, but laziness, and a love of Florence, may prevent my going.

But, Doctor, with all the beauty of Florence, and all the balminess of the Italian climate, and all the poetical associations of the Arno and the Apennines, I would rather drink from the big spring in Huntsville, and gaze upon Monte Sano, than to enjoy all these things. It would give me more pleasure now to take by the hand an old Alabama or Tennessee friend, than to be perched upon the pinnacle of the tallest pyramid of Egypt.

But you say you *must* go, so I will not detain you. Farewell. God bless you.

Consider me ever yours till further advised.

HAL.

LETTER XIV.

FLORENCE.

We are at length having a taste of winter in Florence. The distant peaks of the Apennines are white with snow, and the tramontane blasts come whirling and dancing and eddying along the streets and around the corners, in the most fantastic, frolicsome, and cutting manner. This being the state of the weather, your correspondent has betaken himself to his domicile, and is now snugly housed before a sparkling wood fire, (a small one, however, for wood is very dear here,) and is just in the humor to bore you with a most unmercifully dull letter, the which you will find to be a hotch-potch of stuff thrown together at random, and in the which, if you do not find any thing *wise*, you will find plenty that is *other*wise.

Perhaps you would like to take a look at this lovely city and its surroundings this morning. If so, you may for the time consider yourself with your correspondent, and he will take much pleasure in conducting you to a point from which you can have a view that will certainly charm you. The view we will take this morning will be a general one, for it would require a month, if not two months, to see the beauties of the city in detail. We will go up to the ancient hill and city of Fiesole, five miles distant, but which indeed looks to be only as many hundred yards. In fact, so bold and striking is it, that it seems to almost jut up against the city walls. From that eminence you will have a view which I venture to say is not surpassed in the world. But in our journey to Fiesole, we will notice a few things along the way. As the wind blows cold, (though the sky is clear, and the sun shines most brilliantly,) we will drop in here at "Café Doney" and take a cup of strong coffee—a very fashionable drink here, and more invigorating than wine or strong drink. This, you observe, is *the* coffee house of Florence. Here you may see people from almost every nation under the sun, at all hours of the day. Those waiters, you see, address every man in his own tongue, whether he be English, French, German, Turk, or Spaniard. It is passing strange that men in such humble positions should be able to speak so many languages—when with us a man who can speak two or three languages fluently is considered quite a scholar.

Now here you see dozens of the Florentine "flower girls," who resort here daily with their baskets of flowers, to furnish strangers with little bouquets. They are very bold, you see, and if you will not buy a bouquet, they thrust it upon you anyhow, pay or no pay, and depend upon your generosity at some future time. You have no doubt heard of these flower girls before—have read of them often—and have perhaps seen pictures of them. They are very pretty creatures—in pictures! You are disappointed when you see them face to face. The average age of them you will set down at not less than thirty-five years. Now here comes one with her great Leghorn hat, the broad brim flaringly thrown back, exposing an enormous expanse of face, about the color of new leather. Another follows in her wake, with pinched features, of a putty color. And there is one whose great fat cheeks forcibly remind you of two prodigious beef-steaks. I know you are amused when you observe the coy glances and assumed modest shyness of these flower girls— or wenches, rather.

But here is another scene of a different kind, and, if I judge you rightly, it will touch you in a tender place. See that little tattered girl with pinched, sharp features, as if age had already come upon her, leading her poor blind father, and modestly holding out her little withered hand, asking alms. Is it not a pitiable sight? "Here, child, here are some sous for you. Go buy the poor old man a loaf of bread, and then lead him to the sunny side of the great palace, where I often see you with him, where he may eat his scanty meal in peace, warmed by the gentle rays of the sun, which shines as benignly upon the poor as upon the rich." And here is a poor old crippled woman. She too must have her breakfast. Two cents will buy her a loaf of bread, and that will appease her gnawing hunger. Who would refuse to give it to her? To give a mite to these poor hungry creatures is a luxury, a balm to the heart of the benevolent. It is better to bleed the pocket than the heart.

Go, old grandmother, and get your breakfast. As to these sturdy wretches who lounge about the streets and beg, I would rather give them kicks than coppers.

Now we will proceed towards Fiesole, but will not have time to stop on the way to see the many beautiful sights. We will stop a moment, however, in the square of the Duomo, and look at the great Cathedral, the Bell tower, and the Baptistry. No man can pass such a place as this without pausing, for the architectural beauty here displayed would charm a Hottentot. Let us approach the Baptistry. It is, you see, a very grand building, of octagonal form, and, like the Cathedral and Campanile, is built of various-colored marble—red, white and black, checked off in chess-board style. We will not enter, but just look at the three enormous doors cast in bronze, the wonder of all who behold them. These doors, or gates, are exquisitely wrought in basso-relievo, representing various Scripture scenes, from the creation on down to the Christian era. The sculpture is as elaborate as beautiful. The great artist Michael Angelo said of them:

> ——"The gates are so miraculously wrought,
> That they might serve to be the gates of heaven."

The interior of this Baptistry, like many of the

palaces and churches of Florence, is enriched with works of art by the great fathers of Italian painting and sculpture—Cimabue, Giotto Memmi, Michael Angelo, and others. But we cannot see them to-day.

We will pass out of the city through the gate of St. Gallo, and proceed on our excursion. Those villas and the richly-cultivated and terraced gardens along the way are perfectly charming, are they not? I know you would like to stop and see all of them, but you must not. Here we are at the beginning of the ascent. See what labor was required to build this road. Like every thing else in Europe, it is built to last for ever—no temporary work in this country. The mountain is steep, but the road is not, so zig-zag and serpentine is its course. It seems but a step from "zig" to "zag," but to follow the road it is hundreds of yards.

And here we are at the summit, the spot from which many a time and oft the great Galileo gazed out upon the heavens, and viewed the caverns, craters, and volcanoes in the moon; the place to which Catiline fled from Rome, and fixed his habitation for a season; where the immortal Dante mused and wrote poetry; and where stood the favorite villa of Lorenzo the Magnificent. Yes, here we are upon classic ground, overlooking scenery that no poet can describe, nor painter delineate. Turn and cast your eye adown the lovely valley of the Arno. See that beautiful stream gliding between richly-embowered banks, and glistening in the sunlight like a thread of silver. See the thousands of white villas that peep from out the gorgeous bowers of orange, palm, and olive on either slope that bounds the valley; and those terraced gardens, flowery walks, stately avenues, and green meadows! Can they be surpassed? And see again, away beyond, towering peaks of Apennine, robed in virgin snow, looking benignly down upon the beauties at her feet, like the hoary patriarch smiling upon his children. And there lies the city at our feet, basking in the noonday sun, as mild and placid as a sleeping infant.

Now turn your raptured gaze away over to the east, toward the lovely Vallambrosa, in whose calm retreats the gods did sport in former times. Sweet Vallambrosa, whose myrtle groves and orange bowers drop milk and honey! where flowers grow, whose lovely tints are painted by the rays of light direct from heaven; where crystal streams and fountains play, and Naiads lave from morn till eve, and shepherds pipe their silvery notes, and maidens dance the livelong day; where fairies meet, and sport, and dance upon the dewy grass where moonbeams play! O lovely valley! How beautiful thy groves, how green thy charming meadows, how enchanting thy nooks and dells, and how sweet and pleasant thy limpid waters! But yet and yet, there's something wanting. With all the gorgeous loveliness and all the charms of Val de l'Arno, methinks one look from *Monte Sano's* brow, or from the rugged heights of brave old *Cumberland*, would be to me more lovely still. And one sweet draught from the great fount that gushes from beneath the cliff that overhangs the Huntsville spring, would be to me more grateful still than waters of Hiperian springs, of which the poets sing. And—and——

Tut! tut! tut! Where in the world am I running to? I did not bring you up on this mount to spout poetically to you, but to show you the scenery. But, my dear sir, you must excuse me. You see my muse has been running at large for some time, feeding and fattening in the rich ambrosial meadows of Parnassus, and, like a colt just taken off the grass, it broke off into a canter before I was aware of it. But now we will jog along soberly back to the city. And now I suppose after what you have seen to-day you are willing to admit that if Paradise was more beautiful, our first parents did sin grievously when they forfeited their title to it for a momentary gratification of the appetite. I think so.

Next Sunday is to be a gala day here. The newly-elected Governor, Prince Carignanie, is expected to arrive here from Turin, and great preparations are being made to receive him. A grand military display will take place in the Casine, where an immense amphitheatre of seats is being erected, and tents or canopies of the most gorgeous description are being put up, in one of which is a great altar, tricked off similar to those in churches. This altar is erected for the Archbishop of Tuscany, who upon that occasion will go through the ceremony of blessing the banners and arms of Tuscany, for we do not know what day they will have to go into battle against his High-Mightiness the Pope. His Holiness is mustering his forces for the purpose of recovering his last temporal power in those States which have deserted him. I presume he has blessed his arms and banners too, which blessing, if there be any virtue in either, is certainly better than that of the Archbishop of Tuscany, as the latter holds or obtained his authority from the former. Guess, though, one is about as good as the other, and equally ridiculous.

On Monday night there is to be a grand ball given to the Prince and to the members of the House of Delegates who chose him to reign over Tuscany. The people are quite enthused, and nothing is talked of but the coming of Prince Carignanie, who is a nephew of Victor Emanuel, King of Sardinia. It is said that the ball will be a most brilliant affair, to come off in the palace prepared for the Prince's reception.

Now to what good fortune, or to whom, your humble correspondant is indebted for an invitation to said ball, he knows not. Certain it is, he has got one. Last night, while quietly seated in my room, heels reared up on the mantel, musing and pondering upon time gone by, and joys departed, alas! never to return, I was roused by a loud rap at my door, when who should enter but a military-looking gentleman with a shining star upon his shoulder, and ever so many golden medals dangling about his bosom. Chapeau in hand, he asked if I were "Signor Hal." Upon being answered in the affirmative, he drew forth a piece of pasteboard about four by six inches, deposited it in my hand, and departed before I had time to ask any questions, or even to find out who he was. I knew it was not a challenge, or he would have waited for an answer; besides, challenges are never printed, except in California. There, I believe, they keep blank challenges on hand ready to be filled up at a moment's notice. After trying for some time to read the document, I gave it up in despair. Summoned my landlady and her daughter, each of whom can speak English a little better than I can speak Italian. By putting our three heads together, we made out that it was an earnest request that "Signor Hal" would make his personal appearance at " Villa del Poggio Imperiale," on the evening of the 21st inst., at a "grande Festa di Ballo."

Upon reading this card I felt considerably lifted up, and my landlady was in ecstasies. She regarded it as an honor to her house, that one of her lodgers should be invited to a ball at the Imperial Palace. She says I *must go;* but, between you and me, I am in the condition of poor Flora McFlimsey—I've got "nothing to wear." Still the old lady earnestly assures me that I *must* go, and that she will see that I am properly rigged out. I shall certainly not buy a suit for the occasion. If I do go, (and I think it likely I shall,) I will write you an account of the proceedings. How I came to get a ticket is a mystery to me, for I know that I have acted quietly and modestly since my sojourn in Florence. But it is hard for a man to hide his candle under a bushel. Genius, like murder, will out.

I guess you think it about time for this document to come to a close—that it is like the old lady's breakfast—"plenty of it, such as it is," but not like her breakfast in another respect, which she said was "good enough, what there was of it." I have kept the promise, however, that I made in the outset.

You must excuse me for neglecting to conduct you into any of the Art Galleries or Studios to-day. I will try to do so at some future time. We will take a peep into the studios of Powers, Hart, and Gault, the American Sculptors, some of these days, when we can see busts and statues of most of the great names of America—Washington, Franklin, Jefferson, Clay, Calhoun, Webster, etc., etc. In either of them you would imagine yourself much less than five thousand miles from home.

Will sail from Naples for Egypt about the 1st of January. It is quite an undertaking, for the great desert that is to be crossed is a more formidable obstacle than the Atlantic. You shall hear from me occasionally along the way.

Think I will spend the Christmas holidays at Rome. Yours, etc.,

HAL.

LETTER XV.

FLORENCE.

This is a cold raw day in Florence. Angry clouds obscure the sun. The winds career and dash along the streets, chilling the blood, and taking unwarrantable liberties with mantillas and petticoats. Pedestrians hurry along, closely muffled in shawls, cloaks, and furs; and beggars are active. Your correspondent is again hovering over his little fire, and but for the consolations of his old and faithful friend, the pipe, would be enjoying a most luxurious spell of the blues. Thinks seriously of migrating to a milder climate—Naples perhaps. Florence is too near the snow-covered mountains for a winter residence.

I mentioned in my last letter that the Tuscan House of Delegates had elected a Governor to reign over them—Prince Carignanie—and that great preparations were making here for his reception. He did not come; but a message came instead, saying that Emperor Napoleon *disapproved* of the proceedings, and preferred that the Tuscans should do without a ruler until a Congress of Nations should decide whether they should choose their own ruler, or the former Austrian Grand Duke (expelled by the late revolution) should be thrust back upon them! This message made the proud Florentines bite their lips with rage and disappointment, and many, no doubt, cursed the French Emperor in their hearts, but gratitude for his past friendship kept them from openly denouncing the usurpation.

But notwithstanding the disappointment, the festivities which were being prepared for the Prince's reception were carried out. The arms and banners of Tuscany were blessed by the Bishops, and an address was delivered, in which it was announced that the Tuscans would submit to no ruler, except one of their own choosing; that the Grand Duke should never again enter Florence, nor should the Pope have temporal dominion over them. This announcement was received with universal applause by the immense gathering of people—especially the troops—the National Guard.

The grand ball did come off at "Villa de Poggio Imperiale," and your correspondent was there! If my pen did not shrink abashed from the attempt, I would try to picture to you the grandeur and beauty—the glare and glitter—displayed on that occasion. The palace is one of the finest in Italy; stands upon a beautiful eminence just one mile from the city gate, and is approached by a broad avenue, richly bordered with trees and flowers. On the night of the ball, this avenue was brilliantly illuminated with thousands of lamps, all the way from the city to the palace. The broad front of the palace was studded with various-colored lights, displaying festoons, and many rich and beautiful devices. I thought nothing could be more enchanting than the fairy-like scene presented on approaching the palace. But upon entering, I was struck dumb with admiration. It was too much for a plain simple republican, all the way from the wilds of America. No expense had been spared in fitting up and decorating the splendid halls for the occasion. Every thing was as fine as fine could be. And then the magnificent costumes of the nobility were dazzling. Nor were the gentry behind the nobility in brilliancy of dress. In short, among the ladies, there was nothing in dress that was not of the finest. There were many English present, and a few Americans. I think the finest-looking lady there was an American—a Miss H——, of N. Y. To my taste she was decidedly *the* belle of the festival. Murmurs of admiration arose wherever she went. She was dressed with more simplicity than any lady there, but simplicity was adornment to her. I am sorry to say that one or two of our American ladies were so *much* dressed, that many lips were curled derisively, and many sly nods and winks were indulged, as they swept haughtily through the saloons.

There were from two to three thousand persons present. The music was enchanting—but nothing seemed more musical or delightful to me than the conversation of the Italian ladies. The language is soft and sweet—every word ending with a vowel—with a stress upon the syllable that gives the word most music. Nothing can be more pleasing to the ear than a conversation between two Italian ladies —refined, elegant Florentine ladies. Their dancing is graceful and beautiful; and although generally slender and delicate, they never seem to tire. I think there were some who danced the entire night, scarcely missing a set. Princess Strozzi was considered the most elegant dancer, and lookers on were enchanted with her graceful movements, as well as her elegant figure. As she moved through the quadrille,

> "Her feet beneath her petticoat,
> Like little mice, stole in and out,
> As if they feared the light."

The dance continued until the gray streaks of the morning were visible in the east, when all retired to their homes and to their virtuous couches to dream of beauty.

I think I mentioned to you in my last letter that there was some doubt about my going to the ball— that, like poor Flora McFlimsey, I had "nothing to wear." My landlady, I think I told you, was determined I should go; that she was ambitious to have her house represented there, and therefore undertook the business of seeing that I was properly fitted out for the occasion. Regarding the honor of her establishment as being at stake, she rested not until she borrowed a dress-coat that fitted me to a T, and an embroidered white satin vest. Next, she rummaged among drawers until she found an elegantly embroidered white cravat, of an antique pattern, which had belonged to her dear, but long since departed husband. A hair-dresser was sent to my room with his instruments, (curling-tongs among them,) with instructions to do my head up *a la mode.* My landlady's daughter, too, sent me ever so many bottles of oils and sweet-smelling essences. The maid was sent back to the kitchen the third time before she gave my boots a sufficient polish to please her mistress. Finally, about thirteen minutes past nine o'clock I was pronounced presentable, and admitted to the parlor, where the boarders were all assembled to see me off. My appearance was pronounced unexceptionable, except that one of the company thought my white kids a little too tight— that they made the hands present rather a "strutting" appearance. At half-past nine I set out, and a little after ten was ushered into the great saloon of the "Villa del Poggio Imperiale," where I trust I did no discredit to my honorable landlady, or her excellent house. The "Americana" has been quite a lion in the house since the ball, and is regarded as no small potatoes.

After all my dreams and fond anticipations, I fear my design to go to Egypt and the Holy Land will be frustrated; and if so, I shall lay the whole blame at the door of that arch politician, Stephen A. Douglas. Yes, if you do not get any letter from your humble servant in those far-off regions, you may blame the "Little Giant." Now, you may think this strange, that Douglas, five thousand miles away, should have any influence upon my travels. But it is so. Not by any thing he is doing now, but by what he did several years ago. If he had not introduced the Kansas Nebraska Bill, the great Republican party would never have had an existence. If the Black Republican party had never come into being, there would never have been any border warfare in Kansas. Had there never been a border war in Kansas, Captain Brown, the notorious "Ossawattomie," would have lived and died unknown. Had he lived and died unknown, the Harper's Ferry rebellion would never have occurred, nor would he have been executed as a traitor and an insurrectionist. And if that rebellion and execution had never occurred, I should have gone on my way rejoicing to Jerusalem. But, strange to say, all these things may prevent my going. And how? you may ask. I'll tell you. You remember I told you in a former letter that I was going with a party of Americans. It happens that this party is composed of live Yankees, the chief of which is one of the "immortal three thousand" New England clergy. This divine and myself have freely and frequently discussed the slavery question. Thought I had him almost converted from the error of his way, until the news of the Harper's Ferry insurrection reached us. Since that we have had two or three stiff quarrels. He argues for Brown, and contends that he was deranged—had gone crazy on account of his troubles in Kansas, and that, instead of being hung, he ought to be confined in an asylum. I contend he ought to be hung a little anyhow—an hour or so—even if he is deranged, that his execution may have a salutary effect upon others who are verging towards the same species of insanity. And upon one or two occasions, when goaded pretty severely, I have insinuated that this same parson would not have far to go to be as crazy as old Brown. He resents the insinuation with dignity, but still I have my opinion. I think the parson has an idea that he will go to old "Aunt Harriet Beecher Stowe" when he dies, and this is another source of rupture between us. So you see it is doubtful about our agreeing well enough to make such a long journey together. If we do not, just lay the blame to Douglas. I must, however, do the parson justice to say that he is a very pleasant and agreeable man in every other respect but upon the slavery question. We meet almost every day in the most friendly manner, but generally part in a huff. The rest of the party are moderate enough. There are four ladies and four gentlemen; three of them are preachers.

I must relate to you a little adventure I had the other day at my restaurant, at dinner. Sitting opposite me at the table was a very prim, nice-looking Englishman, and, what is unusual for an Englishman, he seemed to be of a most social and lively disposition. Entering into conversation, I found him sprightly and agreeable, showing by his manners and conversation that he had evidently had access to good society, and was not altogether unacquainted with books and newspapers; boasted that he was a regular reader of the London Post, the Palmerston mouthpiece. I was pleased with my new acquaintance, so different was he from the great bulk of English travellers, who, as a general thing, are afraid to be social, fearing that they will be regarded as common stock, or, at least, something below the aristocracy and gentry. They go upon the principle that "familiarity breeds contempt," and they are perseveringly resolved not to be contemptible. But here I had found one who feared no contempt on this score. Was extremely agreeable, but, like the rest of his tribe, I found him pugnaciously patriotic. We discussed the San Juan difficulty, and other questions likely to bring about a rupture between our respective countries. He talked fair and reasonable enough for an Englishman, and finally proposed good-naturedly to bet me a bottle of wine—"sparkling Moselle"—that if there ever should be a war between Uncle Sam and John Bull, the former would come out second best; and, to show that he was in earnest, proposed to buy the wine then and there, with the understanding that if the fight should ever occur, and I should lose, I should pay him two bottles, provided we should meet again. I agreed to the proposition, and he bought the wine, over which we cracked several jokes, and parted the best of friends. I came to my room and pondered over the matter, and came to the conclusion that I had not done the English justice in concluding that they were such a cold, selfish people. Since that time I have tried to find my new friend often, for I felt anxious to perpetuate an acquaintance which promised to be so agreeable. I failed to meet with him. I got a glimpse of him yesterday evening, however, in the Casine, dressed in the *gaudy livery of a footman, behind his master's carriage!*

This letter being long enough, and as dry as it is long, I shall close it. Yours, etc.,

HAL.

LETTER XVI.

FLORENCE TO ROME.

After having made up my mind to leave Florence a week or two ago, I took occasion to run round and take a last, long, lingering look at many of its beauties, before doing so. I mounted the great dome of its Cathedral, (the largest Cathedral dome in the world,) and took a last look at the city and its beautiful environs. Went again through the magnificent galleries of the Pitti Palace, and through the Boboli Gardens, the splendid galleries of Ufizzi Palace, the Palazzo Vecchio, and also many of the noble churches. Went again to take a farewell look at the statuary of our American artists, Messrs. Powers, Gault, and Hart, and then with an effort tore myself away from "Florence the Fair."

We started on Thursday morning last—many Americans of us together—about twenty-five. The morning was most lovely, clear, bright, and frosty; the air perfectly calm. The sun rose just as the train glided out of the dépôt, and took its way down the pretty valley of the Arno for Leghorn. The tops of the mountains around us were white with snow, and looked most beautiful in the morning sun. Three hours brought us to the ancient city of Pisa, which is indeed no mean city. Here we stopped a few hours, to see the fine Cathedral, the Leaning Tower, and the Campo Santo, and to make the acquaintance of one hundred and seventeen beggars, more or less. Took the cars at two o'clock, and in an hour more were landed at the Leghorn dépôt. Ran a narrow risk of being torn into several pieces by a horde of hack-drivers, each of whom seemed to take a fancy to me, and desired to take me to the wharf. Finally got to the wharf with whole bones, and, after fighting my way through another army of beggars, enjoying a bit of a "fisticuff" with a hack-driver, quarrelling with a policeman, and bloodying the nose of a gondolier, got safe upon the deck of a miserable little steamer called the "Pompeii." Got aboard just in time to prevent a "fist and skull" frolic between an American friend of mine and the boatman who had rowed him from the wharf to the steamer. The quarrel between them was amusing. The American was doing his level best to curse the boatman in Italian, and the boatman was cursing my friend in most villainous English. These rascally hackmen, boatmen, and porters almost invariably ask double price for what they do, unless you make a distinct bargain with them before they perform the service.

The little steamer was packed full of passengers, and, strange to say, there were more Americans than any others. A strolling band of female musicians came on board and treated us to some very good music, before we set sail; and what was peculiarly cheering to me, they performed "Old Folks at Home," "Old Kentucky Home," and "Yankee Doodle." This brought forth loud applause from the American passengers, and lightened all of our pockets to the amount of many sous.

At four o'clock the steaming apparatus was put to work, and with its coughing, wheezing, spitting, and snorting, we glided out of the harbor of Leghorn, and took our course towards Civita Vecchia, the port nearest Rome. The evening was delightful, the sky perfectly clear, and scarce a breath of wind. The deep blue Mediterranean was almost as calm and quiet as the limpid waters of our own beautiful Tennessee. The sun went down into the bosom of the sea, leaving the sky so beautifully tinged that Claude Lorraine would have jumped up and cracked his heels together with pure delight, could he but have been on earth to witness it.

A little after sundown the bell sounded for dinner, when a terrific rush was made for the cabin, in which scuffle the lady passengers were promiscuously squeezed, and much crinoline was said to be worsted. As you may be somewhat curious to know what good things could induce such a rush, I will append a bill of fare. First course: five spoonsful of hot water, with thirteen specks of grease floating on top, and twenty-three grains of rice at the bottom. This, through courtesy, was called soup. Second course: a boiled Irish potato, about as big as a lump of chalk. Third course: a chicken, cut into forty-two pieces, and some salad, which I thought had a very fishy smell. My right-hand neighbor said he thought it was seasoned with cod-liver oil. Fourth course: a very small dab of spinach. Dessert: one pear and two almonds apiece.

After dinner went out to gaze at the moon. It was nearly full, (much nearer than we were, although just from the dinner-table;) and so beautifully did it shine upon the dancing water, that the scene was enchanting. Many songs were sung; many stories were told; and I am not sure but a little courting was done that night on the deck of that little steamer.

At the proper hour I went down into the cabin, to go to bed, but found all the berths taken. The captain politely informed me that I would have to lie upon the table. I objected to that, emphatically, not wishing to be disposed of in such a summary manner. The captain assured me that if I would suffer myself to be "laid upon the table," it should not be considered a final disposition, but that I should be "called up" at the proper time. He however acknowledged the reasonableness of my objection, and kindly gave me my choice, to either be laid upon the table or "floored." I chose the latter, and with many others spread myself upon the floor, and enjoyed a comfortable night's rest.

I arose the next morning with the sun, went on deck, and got a view of that delectable town known as Civita Vecchia. It is a frightful place; and even now the thought of having to go through it again, terrifies me. If my ink were black enough, I would write you a description of Civita Vecchia and its people, together with my opinion of the Roman laws which govern it. But with ordinary ink I could not do it justice, and will therefore let it pass. Our boat anchored in the harbor at eight o'clock. Our passports were sent on shore, and, after waiting two hours, permission was given us by the police to land. The business of landing was tedious, as only two small boats were employed. Finally we all got ashore, and, as usual, were set upon by the beggars. Our baggage was thrown pell-mell into carts, and trotted off to the custom-house, and we required to follow. The ceremony of examining baggage occupied just five hours; and everybody who touched it had to be paid. After hunting another hour, and walking two miles, we at length found the head of the police department, and got our passports, paying, of course, for the *visé* of the chief. After this, we were suffered to go to a hotel and get our breakfast, now late in the afternoon. About seventy-five porters demanded pay for taking care of the baggage while we ate.

Yet Civita Vecchia, with all its faults, is not without its attractions. After breakfast, leave was kindly given all of us who had any curiosity, to enter the Church of the "Immaculate Conception," and take a look at the celebrated *winking picture*, of which you have no doubt heard. It is a picture of the Holy Virgin which adorns the altar; and a very pretty painting it is. The officiating priest informed us with prodigious gravity, that in 1854 this picture commenced winking its eyes, and continued to do so for three months continuously; that it had winked four times within the last month; that it had been eighteen days since it winked the last time. A statement of this miracle is inscribed in the stone wall of the church, in the form of a bull of Pope Pius IX., ordering the name of the church to be changed on account of it, from Santa Maria to that of the Immaculate Conception—signed, "Pius IX.!" Now, if I had not seen the picture and the inscription, and had not the priest, in his holy robes, informed me of the fact, I doubt much if I could ever have believed fully in the miracle.

After leaving the church of the Immaculate Conception, with its wonderful picture, we started for the dépôt, all taking carriages, of course, as the drivers generously offered to carry us for the small sum of half a paul each. This was cheap enough, but upon reaching the dépôt we had to pay not only the half paul for our own ride, but a paul for each particular article of baggage, however small, besides paying parties for carrying the trunks from the carriages into the dépôt. Finally, near five o'clock, the whistle sounded, and we gladly bade farewell to Civita Vecchia, and bounded off towards Rome. My opinion is, that the man who can get through that seaport, and keep his temper the while, is a philosopher, deserving more praise than was ever awarded to Socrates, or even poor old Job. Even your philosophic correspondent came well-nigh falling into a passion on divers occasions while there.

Two hours' run brought me to the city of the Cæsars—once the mistress of the world, and the seat of art, learning, and eloquence. Yes, by seven o'clock we were in Rome, gazing with awe and wonder at the scenes before us, by moonlight. And here we have been many days, walking amid palaces, clambering among ruins, groping among catacombs, and seeing many things that can be seen nowhere but in Rome. I have viewed the city and its classic environs from the heights of Pincian Hill; from the Palatine and Capitoline Hills; have stood upon the Tarpeian Rock, and upon the towering dome of St. Peter's; have walked upon, around, and beneath the great Coliseum, and have stood beneath the oldest and grandest dome upon earth, the Pantheon. All these things and many more have I seen, and still, for the life of me, I cannot realize that I am in Rome.

Here Catholicism reigns triumphant; stalks abroad at noonday and in the night-time, arrayed in all its pomp and glory. Here ignorance prevails, and superstition reigns over all. The Bible is prohibited, and the people are not allowed to whisper, or even to think that God can be approached in any way except through the priesthood, and by doing penance. Intelligent American people would scarcely believe me were I to tell them but the half of what I hear, see, and learn every day about the humbuggery of the Catholic rulers, and the superstitions of the Roman people. Nothing seems too ridiculous for them to believe. In St. Peter's church there is a bronze statue—a hideous-looking thing—seated upon a pedestal. The image seems to be holding out its right foot, the toe of which all the faithful kiss. I have seen hundreds kiss it, and a cardinal among the number. It is said to have been originally a statue of Jupiter, but it is now called St. Peter. I went to the church of St. John Lateran the other day, and in an adjoining building I saw a staircase up which a company of people were ascending on their knees, kissing devoutly each step as they ascended. I asked the meaning of this, and was told by the priest that the stairs were brought from the Palace of Pilate, in Jerusalem, and were the same that our Saviour passed over when carried before Pilate. He said that all believers who went up these stairs on their knees, were granted ten years indulgence for every step. A notice upon the wall signed by the Pope (Gregory, as well as I remember) confirmed what the priest said. In this same building are preserved a great many valuable relics: the curbing which surrounded the well where Christ talked with the woman of Samaria; a stone table with a hole through it, which we are seriously told was made by a wafer being dropped upon it by a doubting priest, who, while administering the holy sacrament, doubted for a moment that the wafer was really the flesh of the

Saviour! But as I was only in this room for a moment, (it being closing time,) I will wait until I visit it again before I tell you of the hundreds of relics there to be seen. The staircase mentioned above is the same that Martin Luther, the great reformer, was going up when he was converted from the error of his way, and renounced Catholicism for ever.

In the church of Ara Cœli is another wonderful thing. It is a wooden figure of a baby, called the infant Saviour, said to have been carved by a Franciscan pilgrim, out of a tree from the Mount of Olives, and painted by St. Luke. To touch this image is said to be wonderfully efficacious in the curing of diseases, and is a sure preventive of accident, both by sea and land. If it does possess this virtue, I am safe, for I have touched it. It is rigged out in the most gorgeous style, wonderfully rich in jewels, which bespangle it from head to foot—presents from the wealthy whom it has relieved in sickness. No Roman lady of quality ever goes to the "straw" without having this image present, which is said to insure a safe delivery. The priest whose duty it is to take care of this miraculous baby, told us that there was never a day that it was not carried out to attend the sick. It has a coach of its own to ride in. In the church are a great many paintings, representing the accidents which the touching of this figure will prevent, such as horses running away, coaches overturned, shipwrecks, persons falling down stairs, falling scaffolds, assassinations, and hundreds of other accidents to which man is liable. This baby is a great source of revenue to the church, for besides the fees paid for its going out to the sick, all to whom it is exhibited are expected to pay the priest something. All the peasant women in the country have the privilege of bringing their children to touch it once a year gratis, at its festival, the Epiphany. There is a cross in the church, that by kissing, one is allowed seven years' indulgence. Some of the other churches offer still greater inducements to worshippers. These are but a thousandth part of the absurdities here practiced and sanctioned by the Pope.

There is one place here, however, that I visited with feelings of reverence—the house in which St. Paul lived when here. You will remember that he rented a house and lived here two years, and preached the gospel to all who came to him. The floor of the house is now several feet below the surface of the ground, but the old walls remain perfect. The door has been walled up for many centuries, and we now reach it by descending a flight of steps leading from the vestibule of the church of Santa Maria in Via Lata. The identity of this house is one of the Roman traditions that I can believe, because it is reasonable to suppose that the Christians who have lived here ever since the days of St. **Paul** would never have lost sight of the house in which he lived and preached to them. Besides, there are other houses standing here that were built, perhaps, long before it was. The Pantheon, for instance, almost perfect, was built many years before Christ was upon earth.

While standing in that little room, and thinking of the thrilling eloquence of the apostle which its walls had echoed a thousand times—of the humble simplicity of his teachings and manner of his life—and contrasting them with the present pomp of those who here profess to be his followers, I could not but think what wonderful strides the Christian religion had made since his day! If Popery and the manner of Catholic worship be right, the Apostle Paul must have been a stupid old fogy. I take it that he was a sort of Methodist preacher, and instructed all who came to him in a plain simple way, expounding the Scriptures in such a manner that all who desired to do so could understand and believe. Don't think he ever rode in a gilded carriage, or wore a crown with diamonds in it. Nor do I believe that he would have suffered men to kneel to him and to worship him in the street—he or the Apostle Peter either—without rebuking them. But this only shows that they were behind the times. Their successor, the Pope, dresses in purple and fine linen, wears a golden crown, rides in a gilded carriage with a numerous body-guard, and *expects* the people to kneel to him when he passes along the street —and thousands do it. This is the difference between the Pope and his predecessors. His Holiness is evidently aware of the old-fogyism of the Apostle Paul, and hence denies his people the privilege of learning any thing about his precepts. When the apostle left Rome and went over to Ephesus, after having established a good large congregation here, he wrote them a long pastoral letter, full of instruction, and which he no doubt thought would be edifying to them. He wrote it in simple language, that they might the more readily understand it. Now this letter the Pope utterly forbids his people to read, although written directly to them. The book containing this letter is not allowed to remain in the hands of any of them. It is banished from the empire, and no man is allowed to bring it here. (See Paul's Epistle to the Romans.)

A few days ago I visited the Mamertine Prison, where the Apostles Paul and Peter were confined as prisoners before their execution. It is a dismal dungeon at the foot of the Capitoline Hill. It is the same in which Jugurtha was starved to death, and where many of the Catiline conspirators were confined. In the floor of this prison is a well of clear pure water, which is said to have miraculously sprung up to afford water for Paul to baptize the keepers of the prison who were converted under his influence. I drank water from this well. On the side of the wall by the steps of this dungeon is a print of a man's face in the stone. The keeper informed us that it was made by St. Peter's face being knocked against the wall by one of the jailers. The impression is as distinct as if it had been done with a hammer and chisel. It is protected by an iron grating.

In the church of St. John Lateran we were shown

the identical table on which Christ and his disciples ate the Last Supper. It is preserved in a glass case.

There are three hundred churches in Rome, and I believe all of them possess a piece of the true cross, and most of them a thorn from the crown of thorns. I am told, but have not seen it, that one of them possesses a bottle of milk from the breast of the Virgin Mary! This is no joke. I have it from the very best authority.

Perhaps you would like me to tell something about the great St. Peter's church. All that I can say is that it is indescribable. Its interior exceeds any thing I had ever dreamed of. Its size does not exceed its beauty. It would take a much greater mind than I possess even to conceive any thing half so magnificent. It is truly the world's wonder. I have heard it said that it cost *one hundred and thirty-seven millions of dollars!* And, think of it! all this money raised by the sale of indulgences! What a stupendous swindle!

I have visited the galleries of the Vatican, said to be among the richest in the world; and while there saw the modus operandi of manufacturing mosaics, but did not hear the Vatican thunder "nary" time. From the best information I can get, the Vatican contains over six thousand rooms! It is said to cover forty acres!

I shall not attempt to tell you in this letter any thing about the ruins or environs of Rome. I have much to see yet, and may write you again before leaving here. Shall remain here until after Christmas, and then go to Naples. There are many Americans in Rome, several of whom are going to Egypt and Jerusalem.

I am glad to inform you that the bells are not rung here half as much as in Florence.

If this letter is too long, you must blame the elements, not me, for if the rain had not kept me in the house to-day, I should not have written.

When the weather gets better I am going out to Appii Forum, and the Three Taverns, where the brethren went out to meet the Apostle Paul when he was coming to Rome. The meeting was very gratifying to the apostle, and he "thanked God and took courage." It is about three hours travel from here to the Three Taverns.

Peace be with you and all my friends.

       Farewell.   Hal.

LETTER XVII.

ROME.

I HAVE now been in Rome hard upon three weeks, and the time of my departure draws near. My duds are packed, and my passport *viséd* for Naples, and to-morrow morning I shall take my course along the Appian Way for that fair city. I shall remain there long enough to see Naples and its neighboring lions, and then, Ho for the Scripture lands of Egypt and Palestine! I have a longing desire to look upon those holy scenes of which we read in Scripture, before my final departure from this " low ground of sorrow."

My sojourn in Rome has been exceedingly pleasant, and I leave it with regret, for I have not seen one half of the places and things of interest here and hereabouts. To see Rome as it ought to be seen and studied would require months. Sight-seeing is very much like work, and he who follows it well is apt to sleep well of nights. I do. The enjoyment I have had here has been greatly heightened by an elderly gentleman who almost invariably accompanies me in my excursions. He is an original, and I cultivate him to the best of my ability. Will give you a little sketch of him: He is perhaps fifty-five or sixty years of age, but hale and active as a boy; has a great deal more money than classical information, and knows more about "per cent." than the fine arts; has recently married him a young wife, and is in Europe on a bridal tour. His wife being young, and very gay, prefers company of her own age and temper to that of her gray-headed lord. She will drive round the city with the dashing Captain Sucker, or the witty Major Squirt, while her antiquated worser-half contents himself to foot it with me. He good-naturedly lets her have her own way, and lets her have as much pin-money as she wants, which is no trifle, I assure you. She is having two portraits of herself painted by the best masters of Rome, and her bust in marble, made by the greatest sculptor, besides a great number of cameo profiles. She objects to the old gentleman having his portrait painted, saying that none but classical faces should be put upon canvas. He meekly obeys her wishes. Dealers in pearls, diamonds, and other fancy articles, will be sorry when she leaves Rome.

Sometimes Mr. Smith (that is my old friend's name) and myself wander through long galleries of paintings and statuary, and it is not a little refreshing to hear the comments of the old gentleman upon celebrated works of art. The nude appearance of the figures shocks him greatly, and he is not backward in expressing his contempt for the vulgar taste of the Romans. Upon viewing a statue of Venus, a work of great celebrity, he thought the man who made it might have been much better employed. He was much surprised to see what he termed "decent-looking men and women" walking about through the gallery looking at the naked figures together. Said such things would not be allowed where he came from. Upon seeing a bronze figure of Pan, he was indignant. Said that was "running the thing into the ground," to make a statue half man and half beast. We went one day to see the Dying Gladiator, a Grecian work of art much prized by the Romans. Said he thought most any stone-cutter might hew out as good a thing as that. Upon looking at the celebrated painting of the Transfiguration, by Raphael, said he thought it a "tolerable good *photograph*, but not better than Zeph Jones could draw." Told me that Zeph Jones had painted the pictures of his two daughters at home, which were "as like as could be." We went one day to see the ruins of Nero's Palace. He seemed much interested in the exploration, and asked me who Nero was. Told him that Nero, according to the best information I could get, was a *fiddler* who used to play for the Roman Senators to dance. He said Nero must have been a very rich man for a fiddler! When walking through St. Peter's upon one occasion, the old gentleman seemed to be deeply absorbed—dumfounded, in fact—and stood gazing up with his mouth and eyes wide open. I asked, "What do you think of this establishment, Mr. Smith?" After shaking his head, looking wise, and pausing for about two minutes, he replied, "I think the man who got this up must have had considerable gumption!" I thought so too. He don't see what "earthly use" the numerous pillars and columns are that stand in various parts of the city, "with outlandish names on them." In answer to my question as to his opinion of the Coliseum, said he thought it a great waste of money to build such a thing. Two or three days ago the old gentleman expressed a desire to see the holy staircase up which the faithful Catholics crawl upon their knees. We went to it, and, as usual, found many going up—ragged peasants, and ladies in silks and huge crinolines, going up side by side, all alike devoutly kissing the steps as they ascended. A mischievous lady of our party bantered my old friend, saying she would go up if he would, whereupon, to my utter astonishment, both started. But, unlike the devout worshippers, they did not pause upon each step to repeat a prayer, but rushed on as rapidly as they could go. In his anxiety to pass some that were ahead of him, the old man unwittingly placed his knee upon the crinoline of a devout Catholic lady just as she was raising her knee to make another step, which caused a tearing or breaking loose somewhere about her skirts. She looked daggers at him, whereupon he quailed, and turned to descend on his feet. This the attendant priest forbade, (the stairs are considered too holy to be profaned with the feet,) when he turned again and finished the ascent slowly on his knees. He says it was very hard work.

So you see upon the whole I have had a good

time with Mr. Smith, and I hate to leave Rome, on his account, as much as any thing else.

Among the other lions of Rome, I have seen his Holiness the Pope, on various occasions. The first time I saw him was last Sunday week. I'll tell you how it came about. I had understood the old gentleman was to officiate at High Mass, in the Sixtine Chapel, connected with the Vatican Palace. At the proper hour I went over and stood in the long gallery, to watch the assembling of the cardinals, all of whom came in splendid gilded carriages, each with three footmen and a driver. When they had entered, I followed them up the long stairway that leads to the chapel, between files of soldiers, having been first divested of my shawl, by a guard, at the foot of the stairs. On reaching the door at the chapel, I was stopped by two soldiers, and informed that I could not enter without a dress-coat. I thought it hard, but of course had to submit. Going down not in the best humor, I gathered up my shawl to start back to my hotel. The guard, seeing the cause of my discomfiture, proposed to remedy it, and fix me for my appearance before his Holiness, if I would give him a paul, (a dime.) I gave him the paul; whereupon he proceeded to pin up my skirts so as to give me the appearance of having on a dress-coat. Thus fixed, I again ascended the stairs, and marched boldly in, just in time to hear the opening chant, which was as fine, if not the finest music I ever heard. Just after my entrance, his High-mightiness came in by a side door, accompanied by officials, four of whom were required to carry his trail. I was much pleased with the bland smile that rested upon his face. There seemed to be no lurking devil there. He took his seat, and his attendants busied themselves wonderfully in arranging his robes. Two cardinals then lifted the hat from the Pope's head; two others got upon their knees before him, and held up a large book, while another held a lighted candle before the pages for him to read. He read in a clear, loud voice. Then rose to his feet, when all the rest knelt down. He waved his hand, like sowing oats, to indicate that he was scattering blessings upon the kneeling multitude. After that, a velvet cushion, with gold fringe, was brought in by two cardinals, upon which the Pope knelt, being assisted both to get down and to rise, by his attendants. During the service, a file of soldiers stood upon each side of the aisle, from the door nearly back to the high altar, armed with spears and battle-axes.

The exhibition at St. Peter's, on Sunday, (Christmas day,) was splendid. I never before saw any display half so gorgeous. My friend Smith and myself concluded to take a carriage and ride over, (the Madam having engaged to go with Major Squirt.) After starting, we were informed that the hour for the cardinals to proceed to the church had arrived, and that we could not cross the bridge over the Tiber until their carriages had passed. We therefore had to make a circuit of a mile to cross at another bridge. My old friend was wrathy, and

boldly insinuated that if he ever caught one of the
d—d stuck-up cardinals in Boston, he'd make him
shake for his presumption.

We arrived at St. Peter's in time to see most of
the cardinals arrive into the square before the
church. It was a brilliant display. They came in
their holiday coaches, which were gilded all over,
and looked almost like they were made up of solid
gold. A carriage a little less brilliant followed each
of the cardinals, with his chaplain. The three
servants that stood behind each of these carriages
were rigged out in a style that would have made
the most gaudily-dressed monkey envious. Regiments of French soldiers were on duty in front of
the church, and scores of mounted police were galloping about in various directions. Upon entering
the church, we walked between lines of soldiers
extending a hundred yards from the door towards the
interior. There were, perhaps, a thousand of them,
equipped in a far finer style than I ever saw soldiers
before. People poured into the building almost in
one solid mass for nearly an hour, and yet it was
not filled! And with all that great crowd there
was nothing like confusion. I was fortunate enough
to get a good position near the altar, which I kept
throughout the proceedings. At half-past ten
o'clock cannons were fired from Castle Angelo,
and then the Pope made his entrée, seated in a
chair, upon a platform borne upon the shoulders of
twelve cardinals, while eight others supported a
golden-fringed canopy over his head. They marched

slowly from the door to the high altar, the holy father smiling and scattering blessings upon the people as he went. I was within a few feet of him when he passed, and was leaning against the railing of the altar while he performed the ceremonies of consecrating the bread and wine, etc., etc. So you see I had ample opportunity to scan his countenance. I really fell in love with him. To my liking, Pope Pius has the best face I ever saw. He looks really motherly. But he is clay in the hands of the potter: a good man, perhaps; but in the hands of villains, of whom Cardinal Antonelli is chief. The performance was similar to the one I had seen the Sunday before, except there was more display. The robes of the Pope and the cardinals were as rich as it is possible to make such things. The entire furniture of the altar was gold, studded with jewels.

There is certainly no estimating the wealth of the Catholic Church. The man who has rolled in wealth and played with jewels all his life, in our republican country, will be overwhelmed with astonishment upon coming to Rome. At the conclusion of the Christmas service in St. Peter's, the Pope was carried out as he was brought in, and the multitude dispersed to other churches; for scenes of interest were kept up throughout the day at different places of worship.

No good Catholic is supposed to have slept any in Rome on Christmas eve night. The bells were ringing throughout the night, and exhibitions of some sort kept up at the principal churches. There seems to be a sort of puppet-show rivalry between the churches here, to see which can draw the greatest congregations. They publish programmes, and invite the public to come and see their relics, etc., etc. For instance, the Church of St. Marcellus advertised, on Saturday, that they would get up a grand illumination that night, and regale the public with splendid music. Santa Maria Maggiore gave notice that at three o'clock in the morning they would have an illumination, and would exhibit to the public the identical manger in which the infant Saviour was laid in Bethlehem; also a portrait of the Holy Virgin, painted by St. Luke. San Carlo announced a splendid wax-work representation of the Holy Virgin and infant Saviour in the stable with the cattle at Bethlehem. Ara Cœla gave notice that the Bambino, the miraculous wooden baby which heals diseases and prevents accidents, would be on exhibition throughout the night. One of the churches—I do not remember which—was to exhibit the identical swaddling-clothes in which the Saviour was wrapped at his birth. At St. John Lateran the heads of the Apostles Paul and Peter were on exhibition. They are still exposed to the public view. Many other things were to be done at other churches.

The San Marcellus being convenient, I concluded to patronize it. Went and stayed till one o'clock, and was horribly bored. Came home, and went to bed. The Santa Maria Maggiore failing to draw a crowd to witness their exhibition at three o'clock in the morning, consented, "by earnest request," to repeat their performance at three o'clock Sunday evening. I went. The building is only second to St. Peter's in gorgeousness, and perhaps third in size. It is very large. I presume there were from one thousand to fifteen hundred tallow candles burning; but the illumination was dim. They had darkened the windows hardly enough to make the illumination visible. I got a look at the manger, which is preserved in a glass case. The portrait of the Holy Virgin, painted by St. Luke, is so dim that I could make nothing of it. This church is highly estimated in Rome, on account of the miraculous circumstance that caused it to be erected. It is said that a snow-storm once fell on the spot where it stands, and nowhere else in the city. The patch of snow that fell was just in the shape of a church; whereupon its erection was commenced immediately. There is a painting in the church representing the workmen raking away the snow, to lay the foundation.

The Bambino at the Ara Cœla Church is on exhibition again to-day, and people are allowed to touch it gratis.

I went to the church and catacombs of the Capuchins, the other day, and there saw the bones of perhaps a hundred thousand men—thirty or forty wagon-loads of them. They are stacked in arches, and displayed in a thousand fantastic forms. Some skeletons are dressed in the monkish clothes they wore while living, and look hideous. Others are dressed and laid in state, seeming to have been preserved, by some means, from decay. They have dried, like a piece of beef. The walls are covered with festoons and rosettes, and other figures, made with bones; and the dismal abode is lighted by lanterns, curiously made by stringing bones together. Within this charnel-house there is an altar, at which every one who kneels is granted nine years' indulgence; that is, they will be released from purgatory nine years sooner than they would otherwise be. None of our party availed themselves of the liberal offer.

We made an excursion out on the Appian Way, the other day, and, among other things of interest, saw the catacombs of St. Sebastian, an extensive subterranean passage where the Christians formerly worshipped, and where their bodies were deposited during the time of their persecution by the Romans. In the church built over the entrance to these catacombs, we saw, among other relics, one of the arrows with which the martyr St. Sebastian was shot, and the post to which he was tied. Their most highly-prized relic, however, is a stone in which are imprinted the tracks of our Saviour, made when he met St. Peter running away from Rome. The story is, that when the apostle was imprisoned in Rome, he broke his prison, and escaped, one night. He by some means got out of the city gate, and started to make his escape along the Appian Way. At the spot where now stands this church, he was met by the Saviour, and told that he must return to Rome, and be crucified. He did so; and when the Lord departed, he left his tracks deeply imprinted in the stone on which he stood. They are about one inch deep. The priest showed us the stone and told us the story with the candor and simplicity of a child.

If I were to tell you of all the relics I have seen, you would grow tired of reading. It is as strange as it is true, that men who have ideas above the brute, can believe in such absurd things. If I had come to Rome a Catholic, I should leave it something else. The ignorance of the people is certainly the secret of the success of Catholicism. There is a church near my hotel, at the door of which the wind is said to be always blowing. A story is told, that the devil and the wind were once promenading the streets together, when, coming to that church, the devil requested the wind to stop at the door, while he went in to worship. He has never come out, and the wind still waits at the door for him. The ignorant people of the neighborhood cannot be induced to go into the church, except when a priest is present. They firmly believe that the devil is in it. Another superstition is, that the ghost of Nero still walks on Pincian Hill at night, and no one will go up there after nightfall.

A large party of our American friends were presented to the Pope, a few days ago, by Mr. Stockton, United States Minister. Friend Smith and myself, with several others, were on a country excursion at the time, and failed to be presented.

Don't know, however, that we lost a great deal by it. Mr. S. thinks we were fortunate. Those who were presented seemed to be much pleased with the manner in which they were received. Some kissed the hand of his Holiness, and some didn't. He made a pretty little talk to them. Expressed a great admiration for Americans. Said it was a great country, in one sense of the word, but could never become truly great until the true faith was adopted there. He hoped the day would soon come when such should be the case.

Now, if Italy—especially the Roman States—is a fair specimen of the "true greatness" that follows the adoption of the "true faith," I trust it will forever be excluded from our beloved country. It is a most horrid thing. You have but little idea of the poverty, misery, and wretchedness of this country. All the wealth is in the hands of the Church, and, while the thousands of priests and other officials live in luxury, the common people are poor and miserable beyond conception. Were it not for the strangers who visit here, from whom they beg a pittance, many would starve. There is nothing here to give the people employment. I am told that throughout the entire Roman dominions there is not a solitary cotton or woollen manufactory, nor any other kind of manufactory worthy of the name. The streets are full of poor ragged wretches, who would work no doubt if they had any thing to do. They are compelled to beg, to keep soul and body together.

The French soldiers who are stationed here, divide their rations with the miserable creatures.

And this is the "true greatness" his Holiness invites us to! God forbid that America should ever accept the invitation!

Much fear of a revolution is felt here. Comparatively few strangers are here now, on that account. The people of the middle classes are very restive, and the slightest provocation would cause a rising of the masses. If the French troops were withdrawn, it is said the Vatican would be invaded in less than two hours, and certain reforms demanded of his Holiness, the refusal of which would cost him his head. With all his pomp and display, the Pope is sitting upon the brink of a volcano—and he knows it. A few days ago, in one of the coffee-houses here, the portrait of the Pope was taken down, and that of Victor Emanuel put up in its stead. One of the Imperial police ordered the picture taken down immediately, whereupon the coffee-house keeper politely requested the policeman to go to the d—l. For such an act twelve months ago, the perpetrator would have been hurried off to prison and never heard of any more. Now, they dare not arrest him, for fear of a popular outbreak.

I suppose this letter is nearly long enough. I have written rather at random, not having time to take pains, because there is so much to be seen. You see I have omitted the usual "rigmarole" of letter-writers, about the ruins, galleries, etc., etc., because what I could write on those subjects would be but a rehash of what you have read in books and newspapers from your youth up. I can say to you, however, that I have seen those things and enjoyed them extensively. To-day I stood by Pompey's statue, at the foot of which "Great Cæsar fell." A red place is on the leg and foot of the statue, which "they say" is the blood of Cæsar. That is like other Roman traditions.

. . . . . .

I wrote the foregoing last night. Did not get off to Naples this morning. We have understood that the road is infested with banditti, and our little party have determined to go by sea. Will remain here three days longer, and then take ship at that delightful city of Civita Vecchia. I am happy to inform you that my elderly friend Smith is going with us. I shall try to persuade him to go to Egypt. He says he is afraid if he stays in Rome his wife will break him by having "photographs" of herself painted.

Upon reaching Naples, the first place I go to shall be Mt. Vesuvius, for, as Pat said of the oyster, I shall "be afther looking into the *cratur*," after which I will drop you a line. Till then, farewell.

HAL.

LETTER XVIII.

ROME.

I VERILY believe that the most sedate donkey in all Italy (donkeys are the gravest of creatures in this country) would lose his gravity and compromise his dignity, in the presence of my good old friend Smith. I had made up my mind to write you a very grave letter to-night, and had actually commenced one in the most dolorous strain, about the wails and sobs of the dying year—this being about the last hour of the last day of the last week of the last month of the good old year 1859. Yes, I had conjured up some wise sayings for the occasion, and was just on the point of spreading myself on this most fruitful theme for would-be pathetic writers, when lo! who should enter but my venerable friend Smith, looking as much like the ghost of the departing year as it is possible for man to look. His jaw was hanging low, and sadness peered from beneath his shaggy brows. Deep trouble—almost despair—sat upon every lineament of his rubicund face. His usual sprightliness was gone, and I fancied that the crows-feet in the corners of his eyes were more deeply marked than I had ever seen them. Knowing Smith as I have previously known him—always lively and in the best humor in the world—his seriousness only appeared to me in a comic light, and I could not resist the inclination to laugh right out. He was greatly surprised at my rude merriment, and the surprise, added to his woe-begone look, redoubled the comicality of the scene, and I laughed the more. Burton would give all he's worth to be able to put on such a face.

The old gentleman was in trouble, and had come in to unburden himself to me. His handsome young wife was in a pet. He said she was in one of her "tantrums," and had "her back up" furiously; that she had been for four hours engaged, with the assistance of two maids, in packing her trunks for a start to Naples to-morrow morning, and that they were but little nearer packed now than they were four hours ago; he had offered to assist her, but she spurned the offer, and had actually called him an "old fool," which he said was very near correct. Upon his attempting to pacify her, she peremptorily ordered him out of the room. All this he told me "with a burst of confidence," but palliated her offence by saying that she was a "dear good creature" when in a good humor. He thinks that she only lacks a little age and experience, which time will remedy. There was another source of grievance. The old gentleman had gone to a barber-shop to have his hair trimmed, late this evening. Not being able to speak Italian, he measured on his finger, and showed the barber how much he wanted taken off, (about half an inch.) The barber, not fully comprehending his instructions, instead of cutting off half an inch, cut it off to within half an inch of the scalp. He took off his hat to show me how the villainous barber had served him, and I laughed immoderately—could n't help it—at the grotesque spectacle. His hair is of an iron-gray color, and very coarse, and each particular hair bristled straight out. Who could help laughing? But the deep sigh of the old man brought me back to my senses, and I sighed with him—especially when I thought of his domestic troubles.

I spoke of these troubles as little petty annoyances to which every man was liable, and then did what I could to lead the mind of Mr. Smith to other things, which was not hard to do. We talked about what we had seen in Rome, and how we had enjoyed our sojourn and our many pleasant strolls among the ruins, and the great and splendid churches. He soon forgot the "tantrums" of Mrs. S., and actually laughed heartily at some of his own jokes, (he is fond of getting off jokes,) one of which I thought pretty good. We to-day visited the church of the Jesuits, to witness the closing ceremonies of the Christmas holidays. It is a rich church, and I asked him what he thought of it? Said he thought it "the best *organized*" church we had seen in Rome. It contains five organs. That was the best witticism I ever knew Smith to get off. After getting in a thorough good humor, he proceeded to empty his huge overcoat pocket of twenty or thirty pieces of marble and brick upon my table, saying that he wanted to show me some fine specimens he had picked up in his rambles, (for, like everybody else, he gathers relics.) I asked him if he knew where they all came from. Said he knew where some of them came from. Took up a beautiful piece of porphyry and asked where he got it. Did n't know. Asked him where a pretty piece of marble came from. Said he thought he got that from the tomb of the *African* we had visited a day or two ago. (He meant the tomb of Scipio Africanus.) Asked him where he got the piece of brick. Did not exactly remember the name of the place, but knew very well where it was: that great circular concern that stands just beyond the Forum—(the Coliseum.) As to the rest of his specimens, he knew not where they were from. All he cared for, he said, was to know that he had got them in Rome. I thought there was something even in that.

After a chat of nearly two hours over our adventures in Rome, and our anticipated adventures in Naples, speculating upon the weather, and the prospect of a smooth sea to sail over to-morrow, my venerable friend gathered up his rocks and departed for his own room, saying, as a shade of melancholy passed over his face, that he hoped the madam had finished packing. Poor Smith! A kinder-hearted man never trod the earth, but I fear he will never again know any thing of conjugal happiness. He is a good man, and, although he may not know how to keep a hotel, he is worthy of a better wife than the young giddy thing to whom he is yoked. May she grow wiser and better!

I am again packed for Naples, and shall be off to-morrow morning by rail for Civita Vecchia, where I shall again embark upon the deep blue sea. Since my last letter I have been employed in walking about the city, revisiting noted localities that I had seen before, and watching the gayety of the Romans, who have seemed to enjoy the Christmas holidays to the fullest extent. The soldiers, the priests, and the police put on clean shirts the first of the week, and have looked much more decent than usual. Even the monks (the privileged loafers of Rome) seemed to have scraped some of the grease and dirt from their filthy robes and frightful hoods, and have actually tried to look respectable; and the beggars have looked smart and good-humored all the week, and have been more exorbitant in their demands than before. Usually they only ask for "Mezzo biocho," (half a cent,) but this week they have confidently demanded a whole biocho. The principal churches have been all aglow since Sunday last, and most of their relics have been on public exhibition. The wonderful Bambino, the miraculous wooden baby, has been shown every day, gratis, and the peasantry have flocked to see it by thousands. Many have been permitted to touch the sacred thing, and now no doubt feel secure against all accident or misfortune.

I have paid my last visit to the Pantheon, the great structure which has stood whole and perfect throughout so many ages. It was built many years before the birth of our Saviour, and now looks like it might weather a thousand more stormy winters. Its dome is the largest in the world. I have also seen for the last time the great wonder of the world, St. Peter's, the Coliseum, the Roman Forum and its very interesting surroundings, the ruins of the palace of the Cæsars, the Caraculla Baths, and the Arches of Septimus Severus and Titus, both of which have stood much longer than the Pantheon. Have again been in the house of the Apostle Paul, and in his prison. To all these things I have bid farewell, sorry that I cannot remain longer in Rome to see and learn more of its antiquities.

At half-past two o'clock to-day I went to the church of the Jesuits to hear the grand Te Deum, which closes the holidays. The music was heavenly. The proceedings were pretty much the same that I saw in St. Peter's on Christmas day, except that the Pope was not brought in on the platform with the canopy over his head, and the peacock-tails beside him. The old man walked in this time. He was brought to the church from his palace in a coach that looked like it might have been made of beaten gold, drawn by four black horses, followed by the coaches of his cardinals, and guarded by a regiment of soldiers. I thought it strange that the great infallible vicar of God should have to be thus guarded by the puny arm of man, not only in the street, but in the sanctuary! But hark! The clock is now striking twelve. The old year is bringing his last gasp. . . . The clock has ceased! 1859 is no more! Rolled up as a worn garment, and laid away, to be brought forth no more till the great resurrection, when all things, both new and old, shall appear! The new year is before us, and it is meet that we enter upon it with clean hands; and that your correspondent may do his duty in that respect, he will cease scribbling for to-night, and go to bed, with a promise to write from Naples.

Yours, as ever,   Hal.

LETTER XIX.

ROME TO NAPLES.

In company with many others, I left the "Eternal City" the morning of the first instant. Friend Smith and the Madam were along. She was all smiles, and he was in raptures. He told me in the most confident manner that 'he really thought her "the dearest thing in the world;" that she had actually kissed him, the night previous, to heal his wounded feelings. The kiss melted him; and on the spot he promised her a splendid set of corals, as soon as they reached Naples. Said she had promised never to call him an "old fool" again. Smith believes her, and is happy. May his happiness continue!

Two hours' ride on the rail brought us to that delectable sea-port mentioned in a previous letter—Civita Vecchia. The usual number of beggars and porters set upon us; but, being strong-handed, we fought them off. Smith broke his umbrella over the head of a big, greasy, red-capped fellow, and then fell into a cursing fit, which lasted for half an hour. After wandering over the town for an hour, we at length found the proper place—a filthy little den—to get our passports *viséd;* which done, we made a vigorous charge, routed the enemy, and got to the wharf, and from there to the fine steamer Capitol, which lay in the bay. Steamed out of the bay at four o'clock, and took our course towards Naples. The sky was clear, the air was balmy, and the deep blue Mediterranean as calm and placid as a sleeping infant; and to add to the pleasure of a night voyage, the "bright silver moon" was again abroad in the heavens. A little after sunrise on the following morning we entered the world-renowned bay of Naples. As everybody who visits Naples has something to say about the beauty of its bay, the city and its environs, you will excuse me for omitting that part of the ceremony; only I will say that if any one should tell you that the panorama presented is not *perfectly* beautiful, you may take it for granted that that person never saw the sight. A semi-circle of snow-white buildings, extending ten or twelve miles along the margin of a placid bay, backed by an amphitheatre of bold mountains rearing back against the deep blue sky, with the smoky funnel of the terrible old Vesuvius in the midst, could not be any thing else than beautiful—could it?

Naples is a funny place. As soon as our steamer anchored in the bay, it was surrounded by a fleet of the funniest-looking boats, rowed by the most comical-looking men you ever saw, all wearing red caps, a hat being a luxury they never aspire to. And then such a chattering, and such a jabbering, and such pantomimic exertions, offering their boats to take passengers ashore! They were almost as vociferous as a bevy of New York hack-drivers. After remaining on the steamer two hours, the police graciously gave us permission to land; whereupon we bundled ourselves into the funny boats, and were rowed by the comical men to the custom-house, where the officers, in their funny little short-tail coats, and cunning little silver-laced caps, proceeded to dive most savagely into the baggage of every man who failed to slip a couple of pauls into their hands. Any thing can be smuggled into the port of Naples for two pauls, (twenty-two cents.)

And here we are in Naples. What crowds of people, and how filthy they all look! and such chattering and begging—and such poor, hungry-looking wretches! Hard, gaunt poverty is here! And yet, destitute and hungry as they look, they crack jokes and laugh with one another. Many are at work in the open streets, some making shoes, some spinning, some tinkering, and here and there an old woman, seated by a small kettle of coals, broiling fish, which she serves hot from the fire, to all who have the wherewith to pay for them. And merchants in every line are here, hawking their wares—apples, oranges, figs, maccaroni, cakes, pies, bread, nuts, etc., etc.—all yelling at the top of their voices, praising their own merchandise. Babel was a small affair, as far as confusion is concerned, compared to Naples. And here go the donkeys, (the donkey is one of the institutions of this city, and the owner of a donkey is considered a respectable property-holder,) the least imaginable creatures, carrying loads of the most prodigious size. Here goes one with a load of vegetables, enough to load a two-horse wagon, and there goes one under a mound of hay. You see nothing but his ears. Another, with a load of wood. And here comes a little fellow, trotting merrily along, jingling his bells, drawing a two-wheeled carriage with ten burly men and a slouchy woman. As to carrying burdens and drawing loads, the donkey is all in all, here. I say again, Naples is a funny city. It is a large city—second to none in Europe, except London and Paris; well built, with the houses reaching from four to six stories high, and is, withal, as filthy as any four cities I ever saw, leaving out the old part of Rome. I have not yet been able to count the number of odors here; but I think there must be several hundred "well-defined stinks." But let me not be understood as condemning the whole of Naples. There are decent places. One long, broad street (don't remember its name) is filled with rich and brilliant shops, reminding one of Paris; and one or two others are passable, while the King's Garden, which stretches along the bay, is one of the most beautiful promenades I ever saw.

Our first excursion after reaching Naples, was to the resurrected city of Pompeii. It is much more extensive than I expected to find it. It is perfectly wonderful to see a great city brought again to light, after being buried and its site forgotten for more than seventeen hundred years. Two-thirds of the city yet remain buried; but the part discovered shows it to have been a city of much beauty. It must have been very old at the time of its destruction; for the solid stone-paved streets are deeply worn with carriage-wheels. The remains of gorgeous palaces, two large theatres, and an amphitheatre capable of seating twenty-five thousand people, besides hundreds of shops and other houses, have been exhumed. The Villa of Diomedes was a very grand building, and in the large wine-cellar beneath it still remain the wine-jars, just as they were left the day the city was engulfed. The house of Caius Sallust is one of the largest that has been discovered. The floor of every house is of the finest mosaic; finer than any modern mosaics I have seen. Almost every street corner was supplied with a fountain. But it is useless for me to try to tell you about Pompeii in a letter. Its immersion and resurrection are known already to every intelligent reader. Before visiting Pompeii, my friend Smith thought it was a humbug, gotten up by the Neapolitans to get money out of travellers. He is now satisfied that it is no humbug. We spent a day walking about its solitary streets.

But little of Herculaneum has yet been discovered. It lies buried in lava that is harder than limestone, forty feet beneath the surface, and another town now stands above it. We saw all of it in an hour. The theatre is the most important building discovered. It is of immense size. Herculaneum will for ever remain a hidden mystery; for it cannot be exhumed without destroying the city that stands above it; and that wouldn't pay.

We spent one day in the Museum where the things found at Pompeii and Herculaneum are kept. There is much fine statuary, both in marble and bronze; also household utensils of every description. It is intensely interesting to look upon these relics, which are nearly two thousand years old. Loaves of bread, baked so long ago, are exhibited, with the name of the baker stamped upon them.

Yesterday seems to have been the day pitched upon by nearly every American in Naples (twenty-nine in number) to visit Mount Vesuvius. All, with one accord, met at Racina, the town which stands above the submerged Herculaneum. That is the place from which the ascension begins. Our début into the village was hailed with a shout of gladness by the proprietors of donkeys, and all their friends. It was a holiday, and the people were all idle; therefore the crowd which surrounded us was immense. Every man, or at least every man's friend, had a donkey to hire; and each man did his level best to talk louder than his neighbor in praise of his own or his friend's donkey. They quarrelled and cursed each other, and crowded about us in such a manner that we seemed in imminent danger of being trodden under foot. Finally, after an immense amount of hard swearing and scuffling among the donkey men, twenty-nine of the diminutive creatures were saddled and mounted by twenty-nine Americans—nearly an equal number of ladies and gentlemen. Every donkey must needs have a driver, and here a battle ensued among the boys as to who should go as drivers. The stoutest soon fanned out the less muscular, and the conquerors took their places beside the donkeys. At the word of our guide, we started off, single file, in a brisk trot. The ladies not being used to such a mode of locomotion, were frightened; and some of them set up a succession of those interesting little screams peculiar to such of the "dimity institution" as scream at the sight of a lizard or a toad. The donkeys, in response, set up a braying, and this, added to the cries and shouts of the men, women, and children that lined the way on either side, created a noise and confusion hardly surpassed by a mob at a New York municipal election. Friend Smith says he never saw or heard the like before; and Smith is an old man.

A ride of an hour and a half brought us to the foot of the cone, the place where the donkeys must be left, and from which those who would look into the crater must exercise their powers of climbing. It is a serious undertaking, and those who have not good muscles and stout boots had better not undertake it. Of the twenty-nine who started up, only nine reached the summit. Your correspondent was one of the nine. The twenty contented themselves with going to the lower crater, a new one that has not been long in existence. The lava is pouring out of it in a fine large stream. I lighted my pipe, and smoked beside the great stream of liquid fire. Getting to the summit was about as hard an hour's work as I ever did. Two ladies of the party succeeded in getting up. What we saw of the crater was—nothing! We walked along the brink of what seemed a great "jumping-off place," but the smoke was so dense we could not see twenty feet down. The fumes of sulphur were so strong that we could not remain near the brink of the opening more than half a minute at a time.

The funniest part of the business was coming down the mountain, running, jumping, rolling, tumbling, and sliding down the steep cone in the ashes. I enjoyed the fun so much that I was really sorry when the base was reached.

Without being tedious, I will merely say that we returned to our donkeys, and wended our way back to Racina, finishing the descent by moonlight. Got back to our hotel in Naples about 8 o'clock, having been occupied eleven hours in the excursion.

But does it pay? Much as a bargain. It don't more than pay, although it may be about a fair trade. You are *perhaps* compensated for the labor of going up, by the fun of coming down. Certain, you do not *see* enough to make it a paying business. The most interesting part of the day's excursion to me was the row among the donkey men and boys at Racina, and the start from that place. It was rich.

Smith says he never until now believed the story about burning mountains. He's satisfied.

On Tuesday next I leave this funny city of Naples

for Egypt and Palestine. There will be fourteen in the party—all Americans. We sail first to Malta, then to Alexandria, and thence to Grand Cairo. Expect to go up the Nile, and see much of the country once ruled by the Pharaohs. Shall look with deep interest upon the places once inhabited by the Israelites, while in bondage under the tyrannical Egyptians. Will go to the place where they crossed the Red Sea when led out by God under the direction of Moses, and where Pharaoh and his host were drowned. After that we shall go to Jerusalem and many other parts of the Holy Land, about which I will write you after I have seen them.

I am sorry to leave Naples so soon. There are many pleasant excursions in the neighborhood I would like to make. Besides, it is a pleasant place to stop. Living is fine; plenty of macaroni, and an abundance of goats' and asses' milk. The milk-merchants here, instead of carrying their milk round in tin vessels, as in some other cities, go to the houses of their customers with a flock of goats bleating at their heels, and milk them in the houses of those who buy. This insures to the purchaser pure, unadulterated milk. This is sensible.

HAL.

P. S.—Glorious news! Madam Smith has made up her mind to go to Egypt, and so I shall not be so suddenly deprived of the company of my good friend Smith. He does not want to go; but that is nothing. The madam has *made up her mind!* He has just been in to tell me about it. His face is rather elongated this evening.

· We commit ourselves again to the vasty deep on Tuesday, the 10th.

LETTER XX.

NAPLES TO EGYPT.

If you knew the difficulties which surround your correspondent at this time, you would certainly appreciate this effort of his to write you a letter. He is seated in a very narrow little state-room, two by six feet, on board one of the most diminutive steamers that ever attempted the voyage across the Mediterranean, his knees and the back of a book doing the duty of a writing-desk. He is doing his level best to maintain a perpendicular, but evidently fails, as is seen by his head coming in contact, first with the berth on the one side, and the wall on the other, caused by the masterly efforts of the little steamer to mount the ponderous waves so peculiar to the middle of the Great Sea. Still, notwithstanding the waves, and the nausea produced thereby, he persists, determined to get off an epistle of some sort, which, under the circumstances, you cannot expect to be either long or brilliant.

"A life on the ocean wave" will do well enough to talk about, and is a pretty thing when well sung with a good accompaniment, but a life on the ocean wave *in reality* is not the thing it is cracked up to be. The "flashing brine, the spray, and the tempest roar" are sublime things, in the distance, suggestive of any amount of poetry, but, upon a familiar approach, the poetry vanishes like a thing of air. To those who love good dinners and quiet stomachs thereafter, I would say, "Go not down to the sea in ships." I say this from experience, having been for the past four days riding upon the raging billows of the deep blue sea, where sharks do swim, and monsters of the vasty deep do congregate.

Four days ago we glided out of the beautiful Bay of Naples, with as clear a sky and as smooth a sea as heart could wish. Our little party rejoiced with exceeding gladness at the prospect of a pleasant voyage to the land of the Pharaohs. Song and merriment were kept up on board the ship throughout the day, and until a late hour at night. My friend Smith was in ecstasies, and even his handsome young wife condescended to entertain the company with "Annie Laurie" and the "Prairie Flower," which she sang to perfection, accompanied with the guitar. Smith told me he thought her voice angelic.

Early the next morning we found ourselves in the strait, and opposite the city of Messina, on the picturesque island of Sicily. Here our ship stopped four hours, giving us time to "do up" Messina. Without entering into any description of this city, I will only say that it is a second edition of Naples on a small scale, very handsome at a distance.

About the time we sailed from Messina, the

heavens became dark, and in an hour the wind blew great guns, lashing the sea into foaming billows, while the rain came down in torrents. Our little steamer reared and pitched like a little dog in high oats, riding the great waves like a thing of life. The passengers were all huddled together in the saloon, and the most sober stillness prevailed. A more grave and serious company I never saw, except Smith, who boasts that he is never sea-sick. A joke under such circumstances I thought really barbarous—in very bad taste, to say the least—but Smith persisted in getting off two or three of the most shocking kind, which, however, nobody laughed at but himself. The vomiting brought about by the agitation of the waters, he heartlessly called "casting up accounts," and laughed at it as a joke. But the merriment of Mr. Smith was soon brought to an abrupt termination, for the illness of Mrs. S. became very violent. She heaved and groaned in great agony. Said she thought she would die. Smith became earnest, and told her not to think of such a thing. She declared she would die. Smith begged her not to do so. She asserted roundly and positively that she would not live half an hour, when Smith cried—called her his sweet angel, and begged her in the most piteous tones, for his sake, and for the sake of a future generation of Smiths, to live. His earnest persuasions overcame her, and she lived. This affecting scene caused many of us to forget our own sickness for the time, but it returned in time to remind us that the storm was still raging. Towards ten o'clock at night the violence of the storm was spent, but the sea continued rough enough to keep up the sickness most of the night. We thought many times during the night, of the storm that raged on these same waters, some eighteen hundred years ago, when the Apostle Paul was making his voyage across the Mediterranean, an account of which may be found in the 27th and 28th chapters of the Acts of the Apostles. Early the next morning we entered the harbor of Malta, the place where the apostle and his company were shipwrecked. The bay where the wreck occurred is still called St. Paul's Bay. Malta is a large and pretty city—one of the cleanest cities I ever saw—and to show the intense passion of the people for cleanliness, they try to clean everybody who goes there out of their cash. For instance, a party of us went ashore and took breakfast at a hotel—a very small breakfast, consisting of eggs and coffee—for which we paid seventy-five cents each. I desired to lay in supplies there for my Egyptian tour, but found the prices too high for every thing but tobacco. I shall always have *some* respect for Malta for furnishing me a good article of chewing-tobacco cheap—the first I have found this side of New York. The luxury of chewing-tobacco is unknown in other portions of Europe; and I advise all those who are fond of masticating the weed, to bring as much with them when they come over as they can conveniently smuggle in. Otherwise they will fare but middling.

At twelve o'clock yesterday we sailed from Malta.

Sea comparatively smooth. Most of the invalids were sunning themselves on deck. Some got quite lively, and a song could occasionally be heard. We were a mixed company, consisting of Americans, (who predominated, there being fourteen of us,) French, Italians, Greeks, Maltese, Germans, and Turks. We have all languages, and a variety of costumes.

An incident occurred late in the afternoon, worth mentioning, perhaps. Madam Smith had so far recovered as to be able to get upon deck. She looked charmingly pale and interesting, and came up smiling like an aurora. As she walked across the deck, the ship brought a sudden lurch just as her foot came in contact with a coil of rope, which threw the unfortunate lady flat upon her face, and at the same instant a *spanking* breeze came whisking along, and in the rudest manner took unmentionable and unwarrantable liberties with her crinoline, and——— But some scenes are indescribable, and others are not proper to be described. I will only say that the charming and innocent Madam S. retired to her state-room, and has not been seen since the sad catastrophe. Mr. Smith informs me that the occurrence has had a most *shocking* effect upon the Madam's nerves.

This is the fourth day of our voyage. We sailed in sight of the coast of Africa all the forenoon today. An hour or two ago the pilot pointed out to me a dim speck in the distance, which he said was Crete. That is the island where I think the Apostle

Paul wanted to stop and winter, when sailing over this sea. The sea is pretty rough, and with your permission I will stop writing now, and finish at some future time.

. . . . . .

SUNDAY, Jan. 15.—We are sailing this evening over a tolerably quiet sea, though it was rough enough this morning. At breakfast it was announced that we would have preaching in the saloon at 11 o'clock. (We have three New England preachers in our party—all of whom are of the "immortal three thousand.") When the hour arrived, only seven of us, including the preacher, assembled at the place of worship, the rest having suddenly relapsed into sea-sickness. The preacher read the 27th chapter of Acts, and after we had sung some old familiar hymns, he delivered a most excellent discourse from the text, "If God be for us, who can be against us?" Nothing unusual has occurred to-day. We are promised a sight of Alexandria to-morrow morning, and I shall certainly hail the sight with gladness. Yours, etc.,

HAL.

LETTER XXI.

ALEXANDRIA—EGYPT.

AND so I am in Egypt—the land into which Joseph was sold as a slave—the land of the Pharaoh's—the land of the bondage of the children of Israel—the land of Moses and of Aaron, and the land once cursed with ten plagues. I am in the ancient city of Alexandria, built by Alexander the Great more than three hundred years before the birth of our Saviour. It was in a ship of Alexandria that Paul sailed to Rome.

Our débût into this city was funny enough. It was early on Monday morning our ship anchored in the bay. By the time the anchor reached the bottom we were surrounded by a multitude of boats, and no less than a hundred bare-legged, shirt-tailed, turbaned Turks and Egyptians, and about half that number of loose-trowsered brigandish-looking creatures, were mounting up the sides and tumbling into our ship upon every quarter. I thought Naples was *some* for noise and confusion, but it was nothing. Then there was a scramble for the baggage. Every yellow-skinned dog that could lay his hands on an article of baggage seized it, and was for lugging it into his boat, thinking thereby to secure the owner of the article for a passenger to the shore. I held on to my carpet-bag, but had to use my stick freely to keep the creatures from tearing it away from me. Smith cursed and swore like a madman, and vowed he would shoot a score of the scoundrels, but unfortunately his revolver was locked up in his trunk, and his trunk gone he knew not where. The Madam was awfully frightened, and for a time threatened to go into a fit. I assisted in restoring her by procuring from the steward a little brandy and water—a wonderful medicine to promote courage. Smith finally found his trunk in the boat of a big-bearded fellow, who said he had taken it from a thief who was running off with it. Smith gave him a shilling for rescuing his trunk, and took passage with him. The big-bearded fellow was the rogue who had taken the trunk at first, and then invented the lie to ward off the anger of the owner, and to get the shilling for his *honesty*. The hotel-runners were out in force, and pitched into us with as much earnestness as the boatmen. Each one praised his own hotel, and did what he could to disparage his rivals'. As ours is a large party, we had a good deal of fun in receiving bids. Finally we accepted the offer of the proprietor of the Hotel des Indies, where we have fared well (for Egypt) for two days.

This is a strange country. Every thing is so entirely different from what I have seen in America and Europe, that I have gazed and wondered with admiration continually. The flowing trowsers, quaint coats and mantles, picturesque turbans and Fez caps—and then to see all the burdens carried upon camels, instead of wagons—goat-skins of water carried upon asses—all so strange! Unlike our country and Europe, the fashions and manners of the Asiatics never change. They are the same now that they were in the days of Abraham. Few people walk here. Everybody rides the donkey. They stand ready saddled in great herds at nearly every corner. I have been on the back of one of the nimble little creatures almost continually, since my arrival. Nearly all of our party have done the same. Our first jaunt was to Pompey's Pillar, which stands about a mile out, then to Cleopatra's Needles, to the Catacombs, to the ruins of Ancient Alexandria—everywhere. Riding is cheap, and we ride to every place. We go in a gallop nearly all the time, both ladies and gentlemen. It is rare fun, and no mistake. Every donkey has a driver to follow, with a stick. We have a donkey and a driver a whole day for two shillings. We get the worth of our money, and I am sure they earn all they get. The long-legged drivers wear nothing in the world but long shirts, and can run all day. There are twelve of us who usually ride out together; and to see us go dashing at full speed through the streets, with twelve drivers yelling at our heels, makes the quiet old Mussulmans stare with no little surprise. I guess they think the Americans are strange creatures. My friend Smith says he is sorry he did not come to Egypt sooner. Had no idea it was such a funny place. He curses the d—d barbarians for dressing in such outlandish style, and is not a little shocked at the practice of covering up the faces of the women, all but the eyes. He swears he will take an Egyptian donkey home with him. Wants to ride a camel; but we persuade him to wait till we reach Grand Cairo, for which city we leave tomorrow.

Alexandria contains about 80,000 inhabitants. The houses don't seem to be built in any particular form, but seem to be thrown together at random—roofs all flat, and in the Turkish part of the town are seldom more than one story high. The houses are much better, and the streets are of a respectable width in the Frank part of the city. People of all nations, nearly, live here—Turks, Greeks, Assyrians, Maltese, Europeans, Nubians, etc., etc.

We have been beset with a horde of dragomans ever since our arrival, desiring the job of carrying us up the Nile, or anywhere else we may choose to go. We have not got our route fully determined upon yet. We may go from Cairo first to Mount Sinai, or we may go up the Nile. It is too early for our travels in Palestine. We will determine upon a route when we reach Cairo.

Smith says he is glad he came to Egypt, because there are no noted painters or sculptors here. He knows that Mrs. S. would be sitting for more pictures of herself, if she could find a painter. He says he knows she will want to take a camel home with her.

In my rides around here I notice hundreds of Bedouins' tents scattered about over the barren sand hills. They look quite primitive and picturesque. The Bedouins are a filthy, lazy people, and many of them, I observe, wear nothing but a piece of old shirt, and others are in a state of nature. Don't know how they live. A whole family will possess nothing in the world but a tent and the few rags they have on their backs. The poorest people in our country are wealthy, compared to these poor wandering creatures.

BEDOUIN.

I had almost forgotten to tell you that we paid a visit to the Pasha's Palace to-day. It is the neatest and most luxurious establishment I have seen, though not near so large nor imposing as many of the palaces of Europe. We were required to leave our shoes at the door, and were furnished with slippers. The Pasha is not here at present. Has gone up to Cairo. We were not admitted into the Harem, the palace of the Pasha's wives, which stands opposite the one we entered.

I would write a longer letter, but the mosquitoes and fleas are working upon me terribly.

Yours, etc.,   HAL.

LETTER XXII.

ALEXANDRIA TO CAIRO.

A WISE man has said that "much study is a weariness of the flesh." Such being the fact, I shall drop you a few disjointed sentences, gotten up with the very smallest amount of study; for, in this debilitating climate, it takes an industrious man indeed to concoct a studied epistle. You must remember your correspondent is now in Africa, a country in which industry is a rank stranger, and likely to remain so.

Now, for convenience, and as I am too lazy to tell you every thing, suppose you imagine yourself with me in my journeyings since the date of my last letter, which was, I believe, from Alexandria. Leaving the Hotel des Indies on the morning of the 18th inst., we wend our way through the narrow, dirty streets of that city, in the queerest omnibus that civilized man ever saw. An omnibus does not accord with our notions of Eastern locomotion, where camels, dromedaries, and asses have reigned supreme ever since Ham and his progeny peopled the land of Egypt. We are surprised to see an omnibus. But hark! What familiar sound is that? A locomotive whistle, as I live! And is it possible, you ask, that we have to go to Cairo by mere railroad? It is even so, my friend; for a railroad has found its way into Egypt; and as it is the best we can do, we must put up with it. Terrible bore! But here we are, at the dépôt. We buy our tickets, or rather Mr. Smith buys them for us; for, as he is a sharp man to drive a trade, we have elected him treasurer and captain of our party. He is proud of his position, and spares no pains to render satisfaction. We travel as one family, and have all our bills in common, which Mr. Smith invariably disputes and higgles over until they are reduced from ten to twenty-five per cent. He saves us much expense by his shrewdness. You observe that our leader has brought to the aid of his dignity a uniform well becoming a bold captain. At Malta he bought a few yards of gold lace and a military cap. The lace he has had sewed upon his pants, upon his shoulders, and a strip around his cap. Shining gilt buttons also adorn his coat. He is quite an officer in appearance, and acts his part to admiration. He says that a friend of his in Boston told him that if he ever visited Egypt or Spain, he must don the military dress, to inspire awe in the natives. He has followed the advice, not only in dress, but in his noble bearing. Smith we all consider indispensable.

But the bell rings, and we are off for Grand Cairo—Cairo the magnificent—Cairo the Victorious. Here we go, whizzing through the delta, up the valley of the Nile; the richest country, perhaps, in the world. The whole country, you see, is intersected with canals, and at every bound we see machines for raising water, to irrigate the soil. We pass by numerous villages embowered in groves of palm trees. But for the palms, these villages would be the most desolate, forlorn-looking places we ever saw; for they are composed of nothing but mud huts, covered with cornstalks or straw. The inhabitants are miserable-looking creatures, many of them half naked. There is a ghastly sameness about all these villages—and people. Nearly the whole face of the earth is green with crops of luxuriant wheat and clover, with here and there a familiar-looking cotton-field. And now cast your eyes over the beautiful plain upon the left. It is exceeding fair to look upon; "the best of the land of Egypt;" and the numerous flocks and herds you see before you, tell you that you are viewing the land of Goshen. This is the country that Pharaoh gave to the patriarch Jacob, and his sons. It is still good for cattle.

Seven hours' run, and the domes and minarets of the mosques of the capital of Egypt rise before us. That is Grand Cairo, the pride of Egypt, and one of the largest cities of the East. At four o'clock we halt at the dépôt, and here we again find those horrible evidences of European or American encroachment—omnibusses—and, what is still more horrible, we find a multitude of hotel "drummers." We don't like this. It is not the feast we were invited to. We came to the East to find eastern manners and customs, but instead of that we are actually met by men wearing coats and hats, and, what is worse, addressed in plain English; and, even worse than that, importuned to go to *Shepherd's Hotel*, and *Williams's Hotel!* Think of that, will you! "Shepherd" and "Williams" keeping hotel in Grand Cairo! Romance is knocked into the middle of next week!

Our party is now permanently reduced to twelve, just enough to fill an omnibus. Smith drives a bargain with the conductor, and we despairingly get into the lumbering vehicle, with a determination to visit all the hotels, and stop at the one that will take us on the best terms. We go first to Shepherd's, and while Captain Smith (I must give him his title) is chaffering with the landlord about the price, a half-blind, half-naked Arab comes up to the side of the omnibus with matches to sell. I take a box, and give the fellow a rupee to change, (half a dollar.) In five seconds my rupee, in company with the Arab and his basket of matches, is out of sight. I jump out and follow in vain. He is at least a quarter of a mile away. The villainous idlers and shirt-tail donkey-boys about the hotel laugh at my discomfiture.

We leave Shepherd's and drive to four or five other hotels, and finally make a satisfactory bargain with the landlord of the Hotel d'Orient, where we unpack and settle down for a season. Capt. Smith did himself great credit in beating the hotel-keeper down in his price. He contends that as we take lodgings by wholesale, we ought to have them at wholesale prices. Very right.

So here we are in Cairo, surrounded with dragomen, all wanting employment. We are besieged and set upon by swarms of them. We all shake them off, and send them to Capt. Smith. All these dragomen have something less than a peck of certificates each, which they expect us to read, and Smith reads them.

And now another morning has dawned. Having had a night's rest, we will sally forth and see the city. We desire to walk, but the crowd of donkeys waiting at the door is evidence that we are *expected* to ride. We muster our forces, and, with the captain in advance, make a gallant charge towards the open street, but the donkey-boys about the door are too many for us. We retreat ingloriously. Rally and make another charge, but our repulse is more signal than at first. The donkeys have been reinforced. We hold a council, and determine to break through at all hazards. The captain shouts, flourishes his shillaleh, and, with the vigor of Peter McGraw at Donnybrook Fair, makes a bold rush, followed by us all in solid column : knocks down two Arabs, and nearly punches the eye out of a third, but all to no purpose. The column of donkeys and donkey-boys is impenetrable. We hold another council, and capitulate. Twelve donkeys are immediately hired, and a few minutes after, twelve Americans, eight gentlemen and four ladies, are galloping at full speed through the narrow streets of Cairo, followed by twelve Arab boys whose vociferous yells keep the road before us clear. Their yells are incessant, and interpreted would be something like, "O old man! O virgin! get out of the way! on the right! on the left! look to your bare feet! These Americans come, they come, they come! Stand not in the way, O ye children of the true faith!" We make for the citadel—a powerful fortress on a hill overlooking the city. It was into this citadel that Mohammed Ali Pasha inveigled the Mamalukes and had them massacred. Within the citadel is the Pasha's Palace, and the finest mosque in the city. We take off our shoes and enter, and see the faithful prostrating themselves with their faces towards Mecca. We now walk to the edge of the wall of the fortress and look out upon the scene below. Is it not magnificent? The city from here looks beautiful, for the numerous domes and graceful minarets look very picturesque. If Cairo could only be seen from here, we should call it a city of great beauty; but when we enter the narrow, filthy streets, and are continually jostled by loaded donkeys, and camels, and miserable sore-eyed people, we desire to be somewhere else. Few of the streets are wide enough to admit carriages. But from the walls of the citadel we see none of this hideousness. All is fair and comely. Now look away off to the west. Is not that a picture? There is nothing to bound the vision. You see the great river Nile come winding down between its green banks for many, many miles, dotted with hundreds of sailboats. Now look across twelve miles in the southwest. There are the Pyramids of Ghezeh, just as you have seen them in pictures all your life. They look perfectly natural—just exactly as you expected to see them. Don't old Cheops loom up proudly! Does not seem to be more than two or three miles off, but it is twelve. Wonderful pile! We will go and take a nearer view of it some day, so be patient.

But come, let us return to our hotel. We must hold a general council this evening. One portion of our party have got their heads set towards Mount Sinai, and the rest of us desire a trip up the Nile. It is time a decision was come to. Three "highly respectable gentlemen" of most villainous aspect have kindly tendered their services to conduct us across the desert to Sinai. They are true descendants of Ishmael.

But look! Here comes a wedding-procession. Two old fellows lead it, beating something like rude drums; immediately behind them is the bride, closely veiled, supported by two other women, also veiled. The friends of the bride bring up the rear with songs and laughter. She is on her way to the house of her intended, to be delivered over, after which she will no more be seen upon the streets, for a husband never suffers his wife to go abroad in Egypt. The Koran prohibits Mohammedan wives exhibiting themselves in public, and the jealousy of the husbands endorses the prohibition.

Here we are, at the hotel. We take dinner, and

discuss the question as to our future movements. The three "immortal New England clergymen" plead strongly for the Sinai trip, but the rest of us have made up our minds to see Thebes and the crocodiles. The preachers waver a little, and we think our arguments have well-nigh prevailed. We end the discussion and retire to our rooms.

Another day has broken upon us, fair and lovely. This is our third day in Cairo. We take a dragoman and start out on a sight-seeing tour. Remembering our defeat yesterday morning, we quietly yield ourselves into the hands of the donkey-boys, and are soon off in a canter, raising clouds of dust and a terrible clatter. First we will go to the Island of Rhoda, a beautiful isle in the Nile, covered with rich vegetation and some fine gardens. A palace of one of the former rulers of Egypt stands on this island. Here is a picturesque grotto built of stones, shells and coral, said to mark the spot where the infant Moses was found in the bulrushes. Now we will go to the upper end of the island and see the Nilometer, or Nile-measurer. It is a chamber perhaps forty feet square, with a pillar in the centre, marked for ascertaining the rise of the Nile. When the river is rising, the daily rise is proclaimed in the streets of the city each morning, by criers, in the different wards of the town. There is nothing remarkable about this pillar, except its antiquity. It was established many years before Christ.

Now, having seen the grotto, the palace, and the

Nilometer, we will recross this branch of the river, and go to the mosque of the Howling Dervishes, for this is Friday, and their service begins at one o'clock. We go through a shady court into a large square room, the floor of which is covered with matting, and around a circle in the centre are spread some rugs and sheep-skins. The brethren have commenced coming in, and in a few minutes the circle is complete. They take their seats on sheep-skins, and begin a humming noise, which, if we desired to be very courteous, we might call singing. Now contemplate them, as they sit there, swaying their bodies to and fro. There are thirty of them, perhaps; most uncouth-looking creatures; sturdy, undersized, broad-shouldered, bare-legged, splay-footed, horny-fisted, dark-browed, savage-looking, hairy-throated creatures, whose countenances denote the most desperate sanctimoniousness. Now one old fellow of a liver-and-tan color, and a bull-terrier expression, takes his stand in the centre of the circle. A wave of the hand brings the worshippers to their feet. The turbans of all who have long hair are removed. Then, at the word of command, they commence swaying their bodies back and forth, each making a noise, as he bends his body, not unlike the puffing of a high-pressure steamboat. This exercise is continued for one hour, without intermission, the movement gradually growing more rapid, and the coughing noise growing louder, until it resembles a howl. The movement becomes so rapid that the long hair can be heard to crack as the jerk is made. Some of them bend over so far as to almost touch the floor. Their movements are directed by the old priest who stands in the centre. The ceremony is accompanied with a strange kind of music—drums, tambourines, flageolets, etc., which is any thing but harmonious. This jerking movement is carried on until some of the worshippers become so mesmerized that they go into all sorts of strange antics, and some fall down in fits of epilepsy, foaming at the mouth. When this state is attained, the exhibition closes, and visitors are expected to retire. It is wonderful that it does not kill them. No one will desire to see such an exhibition a second time.

The Dervish service being over, we will go to the mosque of Amru, the oldest and most extensive in the city. It is almost in ruins; indeed, much of it has already fallen. There is a superstition among the Moslems, that when this mosque falls, Mohammedanism will cease; that a new prophet will arise, whose prophecies shall supersede the Koran. That time will not be long, judging from the looks of these ancient walls. In this mosque are two upright stone pillars, between which all the faithful must pass. All who pass between them can gain admittance into the kingdom of heaven. Those whose corporeal rotundity renders it impossible for them to get through, can never make the trip to the Moslem heaven; for it is said that they are too fond of the good things of this world. By a very tight squeeze, you see that I can get through, notwithstanding my increased bulk, caused, no doubt, by my sojourn among the savory leeks and onions of Egypt.

Now we will go up into Old Cairo, and visit the old Coptic Church, beneath which is a grotto, in which it is said the Virgin Mary and the infant Saviour dwelt during their stay in Egypt, when they fled from Herod. I know not the authority for the tradition. The house and the grotto bear evidence of great age, and were perhaps here at the time of our Saviour. The Coptic Christians fully credit the tradition.

Having done a pretty good day's work in the way of sight-seeing, we will return to our hotel and—sleep.

Now has arrived our fourth day in Cairo. We have talked over again the respective routes of the Nile and Mount Sinai. The Nile predominates, and Captain Smith and your friend Hal have been deputized to go down to the river, to select boats for the trip. We require two boats: six only can go in one boat. I am decidedly happy this morning; for I have had my heart set upon a trip up the Nile. We jump upon donkeys and gallop down to the river—a mile and a half from our hotel. Here are quite a number of boats, waiting to be hired. How nice and cosy they are! A sight of them makes me doubly anxious to go up the river. Here is a snug little cabin, and six cosy little bunks. Won't we have a nice time! We have selected an experienced and intelligent dragoman, who brought us letters of recommendation from Bayard Taylor, and many other Americans. He goes with us to select the boats, and has promised to faithfully superintend the cleansing of those we select; for, as the Nile boats are nearly all alike, cleanliness is the main point to look to in making a selection. This is very important; for there are still lingering remnants of those terrible plagues once sent upon Egypt by the Almighty. Fleas and bedbugs are not the worst of the vermin met with here. Well, we select two, and go back to the hotel to report, when, O horrible! we find the party again burst up, or nearly so. Mr. Brown has again flown from his agreement, and again declares for Mount Sinai, and is followed by Mr. Jones and two others. And thus we stand—eight in favor of the Nile, and four against it. A split seems inevitable, but we persevere, knowing that men who have already changed twice are likely to change again. We all take donkeys and ride out to the Shubra gardens and country palace of the Pasha, the most beautiful place we have yet seen in Egypt. This closes the day. We will now return to our hotel and discuss the route question again.

Fifth day in Cairo—Sunday. We rest all the forenoon, and in the afternoon go to the American Mission-rooms, and hear a discourse by Mr. C., one of our party, and afterwards a short talk by Mr. W., another one of our party.

Sixth day. Our donkeys are brought out early; for to-day we visit Heliopolis, the ancient city of

On. We mount, and, as usual, leave the city in a lively gallop. We ride some eight or nine miles, part of the way through desert, and part through rich farms. And here we are, at Heliopolis. We see nothing like a city now. There is nothing left to mark the place where the ancient city stood, except one immense granite obelisk, covered with hieroglyphics, which tell the story of its ancient greatness. We see many mounds, where once stood massive buildings, but they have neither shape nor comeliness. Traces of the old walls are plainly discernible, with their gates, but that is all. A little outside the wall is a well of water, held in great esteem by the Coptic Christians, because it is said that Joseph and Mary, with the infant Jesus, drank and rested there, upon their first coming into Egypt. A sycamore tree stands over it, which is said to have been standing at that time. It is the oldest-looking tree I ever saw—nine feet in diameter one way, and three another, being flat.

It was in this city of On that Joseph, the son of Jacob, was married to the daughter of the high-priest. That was a long time ago.

Having seen all that is to be seen here, we will return to the city, and, if we get there in time, will visit some of the Bazaars.

. . . .

You have never been in an Eastern Bazaar before? No wonder you stare with your big eyes. Here you see, in the space of one hundred yards, fifty stores at least; perhaps more. They are stuck in the sides of the houses, like cupboards. The floor is raised perhaps two feet. The merchant sits cross-legged in the middle, smoking his pipe; and if you ask to see an article, he hands it down to you without changing his position; for he can reach any shelf in his little box without moving. He seems perfectly indifferent about selling, seeming to care more about his "chibouk" than for worldly gains. He sits "like Patience on a monument," from morning till night. This one you see puffing smoke, and twirling his fierce moustache, is but a specimen of a thousand. You are surprised at the great number of these turbaned traders. Nothing but a thin partition divides these stores one from another, and the streets on which they are located are so narrow that a merchant can retain his seat and hand his pipe across to his opposite neighbor. When a loaded camel passes through, which we often see, foot passengers have to crouch close to the wall, or they are in danger. But it is getting late, and we will return to the hotel, and again discuss the route question.

Seventh day. Glorious news! The Mount Sinai party has again come round, and announced their *unalterable* determination to go up the Nile. Now for preparations in earnest. Achmet Sciada (this is the name of our dragoman) now has orders to fit out the expedition with the utmost dispatch. We all take donkeys and gallop down to see the boats. The ladies express themselves highly pleased with the appearance of the boats, and the gentlemen are all satisfied. Orders are given to have the fleas, bed-bugs, and other vermin utterly and uncompromisingly destroyed, which Achmet says shall be done. Rats are also to be excommunicated, and cockroaches banished. Capt. Smith and your friend are to superintend these warlike measures. The boats are nice and trim, and look like good sailers. They are perhaps seventy feet long, and are rigged with immense leg-of-mutton sails. Each is to be manned with fourteen men, including the cooks and waiters. We have christened them "Hiawatha" and "Minnehaha." We are indebted to Mrs. Smith, who has a poetical turn of mind, for these names. We will return now to the hotel and finish up the sight-seeing, while the dragoman gets things in readiness for a start. Lunch is ready when we arrive at the hotel. We eat, and now, ho! for the "Petrified Forest."

Again in the saddle, and with our twelve donkey-boys yelling at our heels, we clatter through the streets, and emerge from the eastern gate of the city and enter at once into the desert. Two hours' ride through desolation, where no green thing meets the eye, and we reach what is called the "Petrified Forest." It is an immense field of logs, and stumps, and chips, of all shapes and sizes, looking precisely like wood, but all solid stone. Some have the appearance of oak, and some walnut. There are immense quantities of it. How or when it got here, are questions for wise men to answer if they can.

We gather many specimens, and return to Cairo "with a pocket-full of rocks."

Eighth day. This is a day of sadness. We are told this morning that an American who has been lying here sick for some days, is rapidly sinking. He returned to Cairo a week or two ago from Syria, ill of a fever, which has continued to grow worse daily. He is a Mr. Osborne, of Philadelphia. Our preparations for departure are made without noise or hilarity. . . . .

Mr. Osborne has now breathed his last, and lies in an upper room, cold in death. He died alone, as it were. A few short months ago he left his wife in Geneva, expecting to return about this time. His remains will be interred this evening, and a letter will bear the sad intelligence to the bereaved widow. He died with a Christian's hope. Fortunate man! He has completed his journey but a little sooner than the rest of us. It's all right.

We are busy now, fixing for our departure. There are many little luxuries as well as necessaries that must be bought here, for we are told that nothing can be got above here. We will go up to the European bazaar and get us a couple of American flags, for it will not do to go up the Nile without showing our colors. Mr. Smith is anxious for us to get a young cannon to fire salutes as we meet other boats. We are now ready to start to-morrow. Our dragoman informs us that all the stores are on board, the crew ready, and if we have a fair wind, we shall to-morrow be wending our way towards Thebes, where we shall wander among the greatest ruins in the world. We all calculate on getting us a mummy apiece, and a young crocodile or two. We shall perhaps go to the first cataract, and take a look at the Ethiopians in all their native beauty and *naked* simplicity. We leave the hotel this evening, and shall sleep on the boats to-night. We must not forget to lay in a lot of pipes and a good supply of tobacco, as well as a large supply of powder and shot, for we are told that game is abundant up the Nile. Fishing-tackle must also be remembered. So, farewell for the present.

HAL.

LETTER XXIII.

EGYPT—CAIRO TO THEBES.

ALL aboard! Haul in the plank! Ring the bell! Hoist the sail! Spread the stars and stripes to the breeze, and let us be off!

But hold! There is no breeze. The flag clings to the mast, and the bosom of the majestic Nile is as placid as a lake in summer. We must "wait a little longer."

We moved into our new quarters last evening, and have already settled down into a quietness almost home-like. We found our dear little "Minnehaha" newly painted and varnished, swept and garnished, neat as a pin—in short, all that fancy painted her. We slept in her neat little state-rooms with the sweet assurance that a war of extermination had been successfully waged against the peace-destroying vermin so peculiar to Egypt, and particularly to Nile boats. In other words, we found the "Minnehaha" innocent of bed-bugs. Our friends on board the "Hiawatha" were not so fortunate. They got up this morning with bitter lamentations. We pity, but cannot help them. Achmet (our dragoman) comforts them with the assurance that hostilities shall be immediately recommenced and vigorously prosecuted, until not a living bug or flea is left to tell the tale.

While we are waiting for the breeze, permit me to introduce you to the "Minnehaha," which is to be our home for six or seven weeks to come. See how trim she is, and how gracefully she sits upon the water. Now come aboard. See these cosy little rooms. Here are three of them, eight by ten feet square; two beds in each, which answer the purpose of sofas by day. See how nicely the floors are carpeted, how richly the little windows are curtained, and how beautifully the walls are striped off with red, green, yellow, and white paint. Did you ever see any thing more brilliant? The artist understood the effect of mingling colors—did n't he? A barber's shop was never more striped. Here we have a table, six chairs, two tin candlesticks, a swinging tin lantern, and an abundance of looking-glass—our furniture all told. Now look on deck; here we have cages of turkeys, geese, pigeons, and chickens, besides a quarter of beef and several quarters of mutton. In the hold we have bread, vegetables, flour, and all the etceteras necessary for a two months' voyage—besides a goat to give us milk by the way, and a sheep for future killing. This cat we take along to catch the fleas—a tidy little yellow cat she is. Every thing, you see, is home-like. Here is an awning on the upper deck to protect us from the sun. This will be our general lounging place.

Now take a glance at our crew. There are thirteen in all, including the two cabin-boys. The captain is a noble-looking young Egyptian, tall and brawny, with a flashing black eye. He wears a large turban, which adds not a little to his noble appearance. His dress is one peculiar to the country, being a long blue shirt which reaches several inches below the knees. He disdains to trammel his rich brown legs with trowsers. The sailors, like their captain, are all in their shirt-tails, but none of them, save the helmsman, rejoice in the possession of the turban. Our dragoman dresses in the richest Turkish costume, with a turban of costly Damascus silk. He is a fine-looking fellow, very quiet and gentlemanly in his manners. We like him much.

The scene around us as we lie here at the wharf is quite oriental. You see scores of Egyptian women coming down to the river with the great earthen water-pots on their heads. They wade into the water, wash their feet and legs, fill their pots, and depart. Like the men, they all wear the long blue cotton shirts, with a yard or two of the same material thrown gracefully over their heads, with which they make prodigious efforts to conceal their faces from the gaze of man. Their cotton shirts are so scant and thin that they serve nearly as much to display as to conceal their rather graceful forms. You also see caravans of little donkeys coming down and departing laden with goat-skins full of water. Occasionally a camel is loaded, and waddles off with these water-skins.

But see! our flag begins to float. The wind is rising. The sailors fly to their posts, push out into the stream, spread the sails, we fire salutes, and are off—Hiawatha gallantly leading the way, and Minnehaha gayly tripping after. And now we scud away before the breeze. Farewell to Grand Cairo. We are afloat upon the turbid bosom of the mighty Nile.

And is it really so? Am I on the great river of Egypt, whose waters were once blood? the sands upon whose beach were once lice? Am I in the land of Egypt, and near the very spot where the prophet of God was taken from the bulrushes? And was it here that the locusts came up from the great sea and destroyed every green thing; where the cold, slimy frogs came up and covered the lands, penetrating into the very bedchambers, and infesting the kneading-troughs; where a great darkness came upon the people, and the angel of death was in every house? It is even so! Yonder is Memphis, or Noph, where Pharaoh lived. Moses was brought up there as the son of a princess. Joseph lived there, and Potiphar lived in the neighborhood. It was there that the mighty miracles of God were wrought by the hand of his servant Moses, to convince the heathen monarch of his great power. There still stand the pyramids which Abraham and Moses, and Jacob and Joseph, and all the patriarchs have looked upon as we now see them. And away over yonder is the city of On, which, like its neighbor, Memphis, has fallen before the awful curse of

God, as denounced by the prophets Jeremiah and Ezekiel. It stood in the fruitful land of Goshen, the best of the land of Egypt, which was given to the patriarch Jacob and his sons. Nothing now remains of that once great city but its fallen walls, and one immense obelisk! And this, too, is the land to which our Saviour, when an infant, was brought by Joseph and his espoused Mary to escape the death which the wicked Herod would have administered. Just over there is the subterranean grotto in which he was nourished. The building which stands above it is visible from where we stand, and Christians worship even now in the very place.

But the breeze is blowing briskly, and our little boats stem the current bravely. We pass the Island of Rhoda, and are now opposite Ghezeh, and the great Pyramids, and Memphis. We will not stop to see them now, but wait until our return from Upper Egypt. Mr. Smith is in ecstasies, and Mrs. Smith is on deck, singing,

"O how we fly 'neath the loud-creaking sail!"

The weather is perfectly delicious—neither too hot nor too cold. We are still in sight of the domes and minarets of Cairo. Numerous palm-groves and mud villages are in sight. The scenery is so novel that I shall not be able to confine myself much longer to write. I want to be on deck. So be patient if you can, and I will finish this letter at some future time, should the spirit move me to take up the pen.

. . . . .

It has been many, many days since the foregoing

was written. We are now eighteen days out from Cairo. Expect to see the great ruins of Thebes tomorrow, should we have any wind to help us on—an article we have been wanting for several days. For me to note all the incidents that have occurred along the way up the river would be both tiresome and unprofitable, so I shall not do it. I will say, however, that thus far the voyage has been a delightful one; and I shall always look back upon it as one of the most pleasant seasons I ever enjoyed. Incidents rich and racy, conversations fluent and spicy, and songs solemn and comic, have made time fly on swift wings. We have had head winds and favoring winds, calms and storms, hot suns and chilling breezes—every variety of weather except rain, for it seldom rains in Egypt. We have strolled on the shore, penetrated mud villages, talked to the natives, and rolled in the sand on the margin of the river, and kicked up our heels in the most free-and-easy manner. I never knew what it was before to be perfectly free from care; for, be assured, there is no care on this boat for anybody but the dragoman. He is all in all—the factotum. He is our servant, our master, our guide, interpreter—every thing. He supplies all our wants, and we have nothing in the world to do but to eat, drink, and be merry. We smoke our pipes, drink our coffee, read our books—sometimes—write when we feel like it, sing, talk, and tell yarns with the utmost freedom, dress or not dress just as suits our tastes, and, in fact, do as we list, without regard to the prescribed rules of civilized society. I must confess to a sort of feeling of pity for you poor fellows at home who are compelled to dress up and wear blacked boots and two-story hats every day, starched and ironed shirts, and carefully-tied cravats. In short, you are bound down and hedged about with the most oppressive laws of utter respectability, while we in Egypt kick up our heels with impunity, and snap our fingers at society and its laws. Glorious is life upon the Nile! But the best of our sport consists in shooting game. We roam the fields when we please, and shed streams of blood. Game is so plenty—geese, ducks, pigeons, pelicans, and crocodiles, the latter of which nobody kills, although everybody tries to kill—when they see them. We spend much time on the shore, for when the sailors are dragging the boat, which is more than half the time, we traverse the rich fields, and lounge in the villages, which are as plenty in Egypt as blackberries in North Carolina. Mr. Smith and your correspondent are almost inseparable companions. We talk together, walk together, and shoot together. Smith is not what would be called in Kentucky a good marksman. He will shoot *at* any thing, from a sparrow to a crocodile, but rarely gets any thing. While some of our party think little of bringing down a dozen pigeons at one shot, Smith is well pleased if he can bring down one pigeon in a dozen shots. Pigeons are here by the million. The chief feature in all the villages is the pigeon-houses. They tower much higher than the dwellings, and are invariably built with more taste (if an Egyptian can be said to have any taste) than the huts inhabited by the people—or two-legged creatures who answer the place of people. Smith loves to go into these villages, and to talk or try to talk to these naked and half-naked devils, who are to be found lounging and smoking by the hundred in every town. He invariably takes advantage of them and asks for "backsheesh" before their inordinate laziness will permit them to get the word out. He thus forestalls them, and saves his coppers. A shrewd man is Smith. Perhaps you think I slight the rest of my fellow-passengers by saying nothing about them, and speaking altogether of Smith. The fact is, Smith is the only *original* character we have in the party, and the only man in whom I feel a deep interest. True, Absalom Jones is a "man of parts," but then he is not like Smith. I remember one day our boat arrived at Ossiout, once the capital of Upper Egypt, and one of the largest cities in the country. The town lies back perhaps a mile and a half from the river. As we were to lie there a few hours to give our crew a chance to have a fresh supply of bread baked, Smith and myself mounted donkeys and set off in a gallop for the bazaars. On the way we came up with a crowd of Egyptians in a muss. A fight seemed inevitable. By the time we got into the crowd it had actually commenced. Five stalwart, half-naked, yellow-skinned dogs were pitching into one old man, and giving him particular thunder. Without waiting a moment, Smith plunged into the thickest of the fight, and fell to right and left with his stick in behalf of the weaker party. I was somewhat alarmed, for I thought the villains (either of whom could have demolished their assailant with one blow) seemed disposed to show fight. Smith heeded them not, however, but laid his stick unmercifully on their heads and bare shoulders until the whole five broke and precipitately fled, while the rescued old man ran as fast in an opposite direction. A Frank (a term for Europeans and Americans) can knock an Arab down with impunity, (unless it be a wild Bedouin of the desert,) and fear no evil, especially if he have a gold band on his cap, as Smith had.

I would give you a paragraph or two descriptive of the scenery along the Nile, if there were not already scores of books devoted to this especial thing. Travellers generally think themselves bound to describe scenery—but I don't. One feature, however, strikes me forcibly. It is the total absence of timber, or, at least, any thing like *wild* timber. The palm is almost the only kind of tree to be met with, and it is only cultivated for its fruit—the date. A little accident called my attention more particularly to this. It was the want of a ramrod. Not a stick, or a limb, or a sprig, or a sprout have we been able to find in Egypt long enough or straight enough to make a ramrod even for a short-barrelled fowling-piece. We had not been three days out from Cairo, when my friend Smith shot away his ramrod. He then used mine until two days afterward he dropped it overboard, and we were both left unable to load our guns, and would have continued so but for a small walking-cane which my good friend Tummy Robinson gave me in London. That little walking-cane has enabled us to destroy much game.

Many little incidents have occurred along the way that would be quite amusing if I could do them justice in the telling. One deliciously pleasant evening I remember, not many days ago, when our boat was sailing gently before a quiet breeze, I was lounging on the "sofa," puffing my chibouk, and thinking of dear ones far away; Smith was sitting by, cleaning his gun, and boasting of the execution he meant to do on the morrow; Jones was reading Prime's travels, and Brown was writing up his journal. The ladies, Mrs. Smith and Miss Kissiah Jones, were in their cabin in the arms of Morpheus, for all we knew. Perhaps it will not be out of place for me to say here that Miss Kissiah is as nice a young lady as you would wish to see—neat as a pin, and lovely enough to be just the sort of company one would love to have on the Nile. As for Mrs. Smith, she is *intensely* nice, and as particular in all things as ladies ever get to be. The sight of a cockroach would frighten her, while that horrible insect known in America as a bedbug would, I think, almost drive her into spasms. But as I was saying above, on that delicious evening when we were all lounging and smoking and reading and writing, suddenly we heard in the ladies' cabin something like a faint scream, then a low murmuring of voices, and then a faint and prolonged "O!" like some one giving up in despair. Smith recognized the voice, and rushed in. Mrs. S. had gone off into something like a swoon, while Miss Kissiah stood by, pale and trembling, holding something between her thumb and finger wrapped up in a piece of paper. A tumbler of water brought the madam to her senses, and an explanation followed. Mrs. S. had been prying into the secret recesses and folds of her garments, and had scared up an animal, the precise species of which she did not know, but which she had awful suspicions was the very thing she above all others desired it should not be. Miss Kissiah held the frightful beast tightly in the paper between her fingers. It was brought out for us all to examine. We had no difficulty in deciding that it was indeed the very thing itself that Mrs. S. had feared it was—to wit, a —— shall I write it?—a —— but it is sufficient to say that it was a lineal descendant of the third plague of Egypt. A general examination followed this discovery, which turned up many more of the same sort. Mrs. Smith did not make her appearance at the head of the tea-table that evening. She has lost her buoyancy of spirits, and her color is fast fading. She sighs for a return to civilization. Smith deeply sympathizes with her, and, I regret to say, is not the man he was. Miss Kissiah takes the unfortunate discovery more philosophically, and vows heroically to murder every marauding —— she catches. This species of insect abounds plentifully in Egypt, and he who enjoys the pleasures of Nile travelling must expect to suffer its ills.

If I could do it, I would like to give you some idea of a Mohammedan religious festival—but I can't. We stopped one day at the city of Girgeh, where a fifteen days' festival was going on, and it was a little ahead of any thing I ever saw. As soon as the boat landed we all hastened up into the city, if an immense collection of mud-pens covered with mats and corn-stalks can be called a city. The streets (if little, narrow, filthy, crooked lanes can be called streets) were crowded with an immense herd of creatures very much resembling men and women, cutting up all sorts of monkey-shines, some singing, some beating instruments resembling tambourines, others tapping rude drums, and others snapping their fingers and keeping time by wagging their heads in the most grotesque manner. In an open space near the river-bank stood a tall pole with a rag on it, intended for a banner. In a circle around this pole sat more than a hundred men, mostly old and grayheaded. Within the circle sat many more, all with their shoes off. Some were swaying their bodies, and chanting "Allah-wa, Allah-wa," while others were talking vociferously and making furious gestures. Near this circle was another *standing* circle of Dervishes, going through just such ridiculous contortions and howlings as we had witnessed in Cairo. In the court of a mosque hard by was another just such a crowd. We went into the mosque, followed by about a hundred of the naked and filthy natives, for it is impossible for a "howadji" (a gentleman) to walk in one of these towns without having a bevy of these animals at his heels, and if he does not carry a stick or a cowhide or some other defensive weapon to beat them off, they become oppressively familiar. As we entered the court of the mosque the janizary who guarded the entrance fell upon the crowd at our heels with a huge whip, and beat some of them unmercifully. Such a yelling and scampering I never saw before. The janizary then turned to us and demanded "backsheesh" for the service he had rendered us. Since then we have done our own fighting and saved the backsheesh. This was a fair as well as a religious festival. Tents and temporary huts of corn-stalks occupied every available space, where itinerant merchants were vending the goods, wares, and vegetables peculiar to the country. On our way back to the boats we were set upon by a horde of dancing-girls, dressed in the most gaudy and fantastic style, the fancy articles being principally worn upon the head, neck and arms, while the remaining portion of the person can hardly be said to have been dressed at all. I saw two whose *only* articles of dress were beads and head ornaments. These nymphs occupied a separate group of corn-stalk huts. We almost had to fight our way through them. Some of them had rather good-looking faces; but I have never yet seen a really handsome Egyptian woman. They paint a black streak around their eyes, which they imagine adds greatly to their beauty. We finally fought our way through the "backsheesh"-clamoring "fair ones," got to our boats, and went on our way rejoicing.

My friend Smith is lame to-day. Has been hobbling about two or three days in the most restless and impatient manner, cursing because he has not been able to go ashore shooting. His lameness was brought about in rather an amusing manner. It was thus: A couple of our sailors had a falling out a few nights ago, and finally came to blows. It was dark on deck, and from the noise and confusion which reigned, you would have thought that there were at least fifty in the fight. Not only the two belligerents were yelling and cursing at the top of their voices, but the whole thirteen were making their lungs do service in the most high-pressure style. The ladies became frightened, not knowing but a band of roving Bedouins had attacked the crew. Smith rushed out, and, as is his manner, pitched into the midst of the fight—for Smith is an impetuous man—and the first thing he knew he didn't know much of any thing. On the front part of the deck near the kitchen there is a hatchway, leading of course down into the hold of the boat. We call it the "goat-hole," because in there we keep our mutton and our milk-goat. In the melee Smith disappeared into this "goat-hole," and being somewhat stunned, he lay there until the fight was over, when his head shot up—his iron-gray hair bristling out like spikes—presenting the most ghostlike appearance that I have seen on the Nile. Pale, wounded, bloody, and immeasurably astounded, with his bald head peering up from the dark abyss below, he presented a picture, as revealed by the one dim candle which had been brought to the scene, that would have made the fortune of any comic painter in the world could he have copied it correctly. We lifted the old gentleman out, bore him into the cabin, staunched his bleeding nose, administered a dose of brandy, all of which restored him to himself, when he discovered that a piece of skin about the size of a dollar was missing from the cap of his right knee. Smith has not hunted ducks, geese, or pigeons since. Thinks he will be able to be out to-morrow. I hope so, for we shall probably arrive at Thebes to-morrow.

We have met many boats returning from the up-country during our voyage, two with American colors, and several with French and English. We make it a rule to exchange salutes with all we meet. A day or two ago we met a boat gliding down with an immense English flag and an extensive streamer floating in the breeze. We fired our guns as usual, and waited and listened, but no response came. We were evidently "cut." Smith grew furious—walked the deck, gnashed his teeth, and foamed at the mouth. Wanted to tack about and give chase, and vowed by all that was sacred that he would give them a few guns loaded with something more than powder. Didn't care, he said, as far as he was individually concerned, but the American flag had been insulted, and he was for wiping out the stain then and there. I have no doubt, if he had met a Britisher about that time, something would have happened. Smith isn't afraid. We finally got him cooled down by persuading him that the Englishmen had been up the country for some time, and had in all probability run out of powder.

Yesterday we passed Gheneh, the capital of Upper Egypt, celebrated only as being the place where the governor lives, and for the manufacture of pottery. Before our boat approached within three miles of the town, we were met by a troop of donkey-boys, soliciting the privilege of giving us a ride up to the city. As our boat was going very slowly—the sailors were towing, there being no wind—we accepted the invitation, and once more found ourselves in the saddle scouring away across the sandy plain towards Gheneh, with half-a-dozen black Nubians yelling at our heels, beating the donkeys whenever they could get within striking distance of them. We dashed into the city at furious speed, kicking up a tremendous dust as we went, jostling and discomposing many a pious Mussulman, and knocking the long-stemmed pipes from the mouths of not a few of the leather-headed Arabs as they thronged the narrow lanes. We rushed through the bazaars, and then into the outskirts, and in less than two hours I think we had explored the town thoroughly, threading all the streets and lanes in a lope, to the great astonishment of, and not without serious danger to the frightened natives. We found that about every other house was either a manufactory of, or a place for the sale of pottery. We were assailed again by the fancy girls, who actually blocked up the passage and demanded "backsheesh" in tones of appalling shrillness. A handsome one—that is, a fat one, for "fat" and "beautiful" are synonymous terms in this country—seized the donkey of my good friend Smith by the bridle, and held on so tenaciously that Smith surrendered, and actually gave her a piastre. If it had been a man or a boy, he would have felt the weight of Smith's stick, but Smith is a gallant man. After "doing" the town, and laying in a fresh stock of tobacco, we departed to our boats, to the no small delight of the quiet citizens. It was quite a treat to get on the back of a donkey once more, and we enjoyed it hugely. Riding a good donkey is the very poetry of motion.

A rather laughable incident occurred on board our boat to-day. While we were all taking our after-dinner smoke and siesta, I was aroused by hearing a very loud quarrel begin between Saide Demshiri, our captain, and old Hassan, the helmsman. I went out just in time to see Hassan approach Saide and give him a box upon the cheek. Now Captain Saide is a young man, twenty-two or twenty-three years old perhaps, while Hassan is a venerable old patriarch, who was a helmsman upon the Nile before the captain was born. Saide being young and athletic, I expected to see him demolish old Hassan instanter, which he was just preparing to do when the sailors interfered. When Saide found that he could not get hold of the old fellow, he was, I think, the most enraged and furious individual I ever saw. Captain Smith's rage when the English boat refused to respond to our salute, was as child's-play compared to Captain Saide's demonstrations. His eyes glared like those of a tomcat in a dark cellar. He foamed at the mouth like a hyena. He tore his shirt (the only garment he had on) from the bosom clear out to the tail; snatched off his turban and beat the ground with it, leaving his closely shaven head (all Egyptians shave their heads) bared to the burning sun. Took up handfuls of sand and threw it in the air; covered his head with dirt; snorted, roared, threw himself on the ground, and kicked like a spanked child. Under the command of Hassan, the sailors shoved off the boat, and we left Captain Saide alone in his glory, spread out like a huge bull-frog, with his face in the sand. Our dragoman was on the Hiawatha, a mile or two ahead, at the time of this occurrence. His presence would have prevented it. He will rejoin us to-night. Captain Saide overtook us two hours after we left him, but he is still sullen. I think his chances for a well pair of feet to-morrow are slim. Achmet is not afraid to resort to the bastinado.

This is our twentieth day on the Nile. We are now nearing Thebes and Luxor. Have had no wind for several days to do any good, but we will get to Thebes early to-morrow, wind or no wind.

We have spent no time sight-seeing during our upward trip, but shall devote some five or six days visiting antiquities on our return. It will require five or six days to explore the great ruins here. Have not determined yet whether we will go farther up the river or not. Guess not, as we are anxious to get into Palestine by the middle of March.

Nile-travelling agrees with me well. The flesh-pots of Egypt have had a wonderful effect. I am as fat as a bear, and the pelting African sun has burnt my face as brown as an Arab's. Farewell.

HAL.

LETTER XXIV.

EGYPT—THEBES.

My last letter was closed, I think, on the night of the 14th inst., while the "Hiawatha" and "Minnehaha" were lying tied up to the bank of the river some five or six miles below here. We shoved off bright and early on the following morning, and moved towards Thebes, our hearts beating high with the hope of soon looking upon the remains of what was once, perhaps, the greatest city the world ever saw—and the oldest, for it was doubtless one of the first cities built after the flood. We were all out on deck that morning much earlier than usual, stretching our necks to catch a sight of the great portico of Luxor. Mrs. Smith was up before the sun, and for the first time in many months—perhaps years—saw that glorious luminary make his personal appearance above the eastern horizon. Miss Kissiah was also on the alert. These two ladies were not on deck, but at their little cabin-windows, gazing in a Theban direction for a glimpse of the famed towers of Karnak. While there they saw our favorite and only cat—the yellow cat which had been the faithful companion of our voyage, and general pet of the party—they saw this cat thrown with violence far out into the stream. This horrible *catastrophe* brought forth a scream from Mrs. Smith, and Miss Kissiah followed her example. But screaming did no good: Puss had sunk to rise no more. This occurrence caused, as well it might, no small stir on board the "Minnehaha." The ladies had seen the cat thrown, but had not seen the wicked hand that did the deed. Inquiry was immediately set on foot, but nobody seemed to know who the guilty one was. Suspicion fell upon Mohammed, the black Nubian cook. Mohammed denied the charge with great earnestness, and to make his innocence appear more clear, he swore that there had not been a cat nor the shadow of a cat on the boat for two days; that he had seen the cat with his own eyes jump overboard two days before after a fish, when she was immediately seized and devoured by a ravenous crocodile. We all knew that Mohammed was lying like an Arab, but his cool earnestness was refreshing. Witnesses were then called, when Captain Saide testified that he had seen Mohammed throw Puss over. But this was nothing. It requires two witnesses to establish guilt in this country. Mohammed was on the point of getting off clear, when Abdallah, our favorite oarsman, came forward and substantiated the testimony of the captain. Thus cornered, Mohammed owned up, but justified the act by asserting that the cat had that very morning stolen and eaten a chicken and two pigeons which he was preparing for breakfast. He was dismissed for the time, but with the assurance of the dragoman that a settlement would be entered into at Thebes.

Mrs. Smith was greatly troubled at the loss of this cat, and so was Miss Kissiah; not only on account of their fondness for Puss, but they were superstitious. They fully believed that some evil would befall some if not all of the party. Mrs. S. had never known it to fail, that when a cat was murdered, some misfortune followed soon after, and Miss Kissiah had always "heard" the same thing. They have been in trouble ever since.

Early in the day the great ruins loomed up before us. Our boats were moored under the bank of the river immediately in front of the porch of the grand Temple of Luxor. With impatience, we hurried on shore in the very hottest part of the day, (and hot weather means something in Southern Egypt,) to view the mighty columns and ponderous towers. Our wonder and admiration were great. We looked upon the pile before us, and thought of Rome as a little thing. We looked up at the tall obelisk and the three colossal statues that stand at the entrance to the Temple, and wondered what kind of machinery could have been used to place them there. We walked around and through and upon this vast structure, nor heeded the burning sun, so great was our enthusiasm. Perhaps you have read, but have forgotten when and where, of a temple so large that a populous village now stands in and upon it. It is the Temple of Luxor. We climbed up an immense tower which stands at one of the gateways, by what had once been a flight of granite steps, but which are steps no longer, the foot of man and time having worn them away. Standing up there we had a fine view of the surrounding plains, the frowning walls of Karnak, two miles distant, and the two celebrated colossal statues, Memnon and his nameless companion, standing away across the river. In descending from this tower, your correspondent slipped and fell, and—got up again—but which fall came well-nigh putting a period to his sight-seeing and donkey-riding in Egypt. The accident was not serious, however, a pair of skinned elbows and a few bruises being the extent. A half day's lying up, and all was right, even to the ability to ride a donkey at full speed. A few minutes after this accident, and Mrs. Smith had also to be borne to the boat in a fainting condition, something like a sun-stroke having overpowered her. A little brandy and water restored us both in due time. She was in favor of having poor Mohammed immediately bastinadoed, being more than ever convinced that the drowning of the cat had caused the accidents, and further predicted that misfortumes would continue to follow the party; and then she quoted the "Hiawathian" lines which run somewhat thus:

> "Never jumps a sheep that's frightened
> Over any fence whatever,
> Over wall, or fence, or timber,
> But a second follows after,
> And a third upon the second,

> And a fourth, and fifth, and so on,
> First a sheep, and then a dozen,
> Till they all, in quick succession,
> One by one have got clear over.
> So misfortunes, almost always,
> Follow after one another,
> Seem to watch each other, always,
> When they see the tail uplifted,
> In the air the tail uplifted;
> As the sorrow leapeth over,
> So they follow, thicker, faster,
> Till the air of earth seems darkened,
> With the tails of sad misfortunes."

I was out very early the next morning. I had read and heard of the ancient musical propensities of the great statue of Memnon, (and who has not?) which it is said in ancient times gave forth musical sounds each morning at the rising of the sun. I took a position where I could see the statue and listen, when, as the sun rose and kissed his time-honored and cold, wrinkled brow, judge of my surprise when I heard sounds, not truly musical, but sad and mournful, come floating across the plains and the river, and dying away in the tumult of the mud village that lay behind me. I had thought that Memnon had long since ceased to be musical, and idle curiosity alone had prompted me to listen, not that I expected to hear any sound whatever. My delight was equal to my astonishment when I heard the startling notes. I hurried to the boat with wide-stretched eyes and palpitating heart, to inform my friends and give them a chance to witness the wonderful performance. Smith was the first man out, and heard the sounds distinctly; but a moment after, he pointed out a wheel on the opposite side of the river, slowly revolving to raise water for irrigation, being turned by one solitary ox. It was making a horrible creaking noise. I caved at once. That was the music which had so excited me. Smith had the laugh on me all that day. Old Memnon sat sublimely silent on his cold, stony throne, as he has done for thousands of years.

After breakfast we all gathered together from both boats, crossed the river, and set out for the mountain to see the "Tombs of the Kings." A crowd of donkeys awaited us, (donkeys wait for you everywhere in Egypt,) and I saw at a glance that we should have a scuffle for it. There was just a dozen of us, and about two dozen donkeys, and each donkey-boy would do his level best to out-bully his competitor, and get himself and donkey hired. It is a fearful thing to fall into the hands of donkey-boys, for if you do not beat them off, which is next to an impossibility, they will almost tear you limb from limb. When our boat landed I sprang upon the shore, and fell immediately into the hands of Mohammed Ali and Hassan Asoof. They were stalwart fellows, each large enough to carry his diminutive donkey on his own shoulder. Mohammed Ali swore that he had the best donkey in Thebes, and that Hassan and his donkey were both humbugs; that his own donkey could go like a horse. Hassan retorted the best he could, and said that his donkey could not only go like a horse, but could outrun a jackal. I love a fleet donkey, and was therefore about to mount Hassan's, when Mohammed Ali returned to the charge, and swore by Allah (he was a profane dog) that his donkey could be properly compared to nothing but a steamboat. This decided me, and I mounted the donkey of Mohammed Ali. During the quarrel and scuffle they had each held me by an arm, and had come near pulling them out of their sockets. I did not have time to notice the troubles of my companions, but from the noise kept up, they must have fared worse than I did. We were all at length in the saddle, and fleeing across the broad fields toward the mountain where the kings of Egypt have slept in profound repose for more than thirty centuries; old Achmet, the guide, leading the van, mounted on a donkey which, had it been weighed in the balance with him, would have been found wanting. My own donkey, which Mohammed Ali had said so much resembled a steamboat, was the most miserable thing I ever had backed in Egypt, but little larger and much less nimble than our milk-goat. I complained of the cheat, but Mohammed Ali swore more than a hundred times that it was the best donkey in Thebes, and more like a steamboat than any thing else. But all the beating that Mohammed could bestow could not get him into a gallop. He promised faithfully, however, that on the next day he would furnish me a donkey three times the size, and one that could run like the wind.

It was about two or three hours' ride to the Tombs. In the way, we passed the ruins of the Temple of Kooneh, which, like that of Luxor, was built of enormous stones, every one of which, too, was covered with hieroglyphics, and images of men, women, etc. It was, however, comparatively a small temple. We spent an hour examining it, by which time the heat of the day had fully come upon us. We left the temple, and wound our way up a dreary gorge of the mountain, while the rays of the sun seemed to come down a near way upon our devoted heads. It was, indeed, a pleasant thing to sit down in the shadow of a great rock in such a place and on such a day.

The first tomb we entered is the greatest that has ever been discovered in Egypt. It is called "Belzoni's Tomb," because it was discovered and opened by a man of that name. It is entered by a broad descending passage, which leads into a number of large and elegantly sculptured and painted chambers, all hewn out in the solid stone mountain, and decorated with a great number of elegantly wrought columns which support the roof. The paintings and sculptures represent all the occupations of life, as they were carried on three thousand years ago. There has been but little change since. The dress of the laboring people was the same then as now, being nothing but a simple piece of cloth around the waist, extending about half-way down to the knees; the rest of the body is naked. Boats were rowed and towed upon the Nile then just as they are yet. Water was carried in goat-skins, and the same water-pots were used. In fact, there is no change or improvement in any thing that I can see for all that time. This will sound strange to American ears, where changes are occurring and improvements being made almost daily.

Besides Belzoni's, we went into many other large tombs, all filled with paintings and hieroglyphics like the first. To attempt a description of any of them would be prosy. These are the tombs in which many of the kings of Egypt were laid, but their mummied bodies have been removed, and now grace or disgrace many of the museums of Europe. We sat down in the cool shady entrance of a tomb, took lunch, smoked our pipes, and when the cool of the evening approached, wended our way towards the boats.

In returning, another accident occurred, which again brought up the story of the murdered cat, and confirmed the superstition of Mrs. Smith. My good friend Smith was again the victim. Brown and myself seeing what appeared to be a freshly-opened tomb up the side of the mountain, dismounted and climbed up to it, leaving our donkeys standing in the road. Brown's was a licentious donkey, and was no sooner left to himself than he pitched into the donkey of Mr. Smith, biting, squealing, pawing, and snorting; Smith's donkey resented the attack in such a way as to lay his rider flat on his back on the hard stony road. Poor Smith has been grunting ever since. He refused to pay the donkey-boy the usual "backsheesh," (present,) because his donkey threw him off. Smith is a shrewd man, and never will pay the "backsheesh" unless his donkey suits him—and I have never known him to have a donkey that suited him yet.

The next day we crossed the river again, and went into a great many other tombs. We entered one into which we had to crawl like lizards, so small was the opening. It consisted of six chambers, and contained, I would think, not less than a thousand mummies. I walked upon them, and heard the bones of some crush under my feet. It was strange to see bodies so many thousands of years old wrapped in cloth and undecayed as they were left by their friends. I sat down upon the breast of one big old fellow, and unwound the cloth from the feet of a smaller one, a piece of which I brought away to carry home with me. Also took one of their hands for the inspection of some of my home friends. Smith would not go into this abode of the dead, but stood at the door trembling, while the rest of us left him alone. Smith is not afraid of a living man, but has a mortal dread of entering a tomb tenanted by dead bodies.

Coming out of this tomb, we descended to the Memnonium, or ruins of the Temple of Memnon. This was grand indeed. Its columns were numerous and immense. Every stone inside and outside of this immense structure is covered with hieroglyphies. I do not know how to give you an idea of the magnitude of an Egyptian temple. The stones are so large that you wonder how they were ever hoisted to their places. Every thing you see is on such a scale that you are struck with amazement. In the court of this temple lies a broken colossal statue of Rameses, so large that when you see it, you will give up the effort to comprehend its greatness. To say that it is the largest statue in the world, will give you no idea of it. It is of granite. It is thrown down and broken; thought to have been done by the Persian conquerors of Egypt. What means were used to break it, is a mystery, for gunpowder was unknown in those days. And if the breaking of it be a mystery, how much greater is the mystery as to how it was brought and placed in the court of the temple! for it was certainly brought from a great distance, as there is no red granite in this neighborhood. I suppose it must be the largest block of hewn stone in the world. It weighs, according to Murray, more than *eight hundred and eighty-seven tons!*

Leaving the Memnonium, we went to see two great statues which stand in the plain below—Memnon and his companion. Old Memnon was still silent, and gazed as coldly and steadily towards the east as he did three thousand years ago. He heeds not the rising of the sun, as he did in days of yore; at least, he gives forth no musical sounds now, as then. These statues stand, or rather sit, in a cultivated plain—wheat growing luxuriantly all around them, with scarcely any traces of the great city in the midst of which they once sat. Their height I do not know. They are perhaps as high as any house in Huntsville, although in a sitting posture! After viewing these statues, we returned to our boats, being saluted by the way by all the laborers in the fields, with, "Backsheesh, howadji!" a salutation that I have grown sick of hearing.

The Egyptians are *all* beggars. The first word the children learn is "backsheesh," and they never see a "howadji" that they do not scream it out. If they do you a favor of any kind, they of course expect "backsheesh;" and if you do them a favor, they expect the same thing. So it is "backsheesh" first, last, and all the time. They are all poor devils, seldom possessing more than the cotton shirt or breech-clout which hides their nakedness.

Another day has now dawned. Ho for Karnak, the wonder of the world! Here are our donkeys, waiting for us. We mount, and away. I had forgotten to mention that Mrs. Smith is no longer able to ride a donkey. She has now to be carried in a chair, with a pole strapped to each side, on the shoulders of four Arabs. She enjoys this new mode of locomotion hugely. But here we are, at Karnak. I look up at the great propylon, and feel a dizzy sensation. Enter the court of the temple, and my heart leaps with astonishment. Look up at the enormous columns, and the great stones on top of them, and am sick with wonder. What grandeur! I was not prepared for it, although expecting to see the most ponderous ruins in the world. It is too much for me. Here are in one hall one hundred and twenty-six columns, each thirty-six feet in circumference, with capitals almost double the size, and all so elaborately carved! And this is only one hall! There are many, many others. This temple is said to have covered seventy-five acres of ground! There were four gateways leading into it, each of which was approached by long avenues of Sphynxes. One of these avenues was two miles long, and connected the two temples of Karnak and Luxor. The Sphynxes are nearly all thrown down and broken, and thousands of them buried beneath the soil. Shall I attempt a description of this temple? No. It would fill a book. If I desired to be exceedingly prosy, and to bore you unmercifully, I would copy a few pages from Murray's hand-book, but as I feel kindly towards you, I shall not do it. Every stone in and about the temple (and there are enough to build a city) is completely covered with strange figures and inscriptions. There are so many of them that it is said they have never even been counted! In the midst of this ruin rise two granite obelisks, one ninety-two feet high, and eight feet square at the base, besides the portion that is buried in the ground! They are covered with hieroglyphics, cut about three inches deep, and as well defined as if they had been cut but yesterday. Hundreds of broken statues, of every size and description, are lying in and around this great pile. Some of the paintings on the stones of the temple look bright and fresh, as if recently done. Here are some stones I have measured: they are thirty-six feet long, and five feet square. They formed a gateway, which is now nearly all thrown down.

When we look at these ruins, how small all others seem to us! We think of the many broken columns we saw lying about at Rome as small things indeed. We have never seen a *broken* column in Egypt. They were not made to be broken. We see many lying prostrate, but not broken! They laugh at the tooth of time, and even earthquakes fail to rend them. But for the vandal hand of man, Karnak would have stood whole and entire as long as time. But alas for destructive man! The grace and comeliness of Karnak are gone. But it is only the fulfilment of prophecy. The Prophets Jeremiah, Ezekiel, and Nahum, all prophesied the destruction of Thebes, (or "No," as it was sometimes called.) Like the other great cities of Egypt, it has fallen before the wrath of God! We spend the day among these ruins, and return to the boats.

The next day was Sunday. Some of us went again to Karnak, and some didn't. In the evening we had religious service, as our custom is, on board the "Minnehaha."

Monday we crossed the river again to visit the ruined temple and palace of—of—but the name would be too hard to write, even if I could remember it. I will only say that it was an immense pile of stones and columns, and had once been a building superior to any thing I had seen *out* of Egypt. It dates back as far as the rest of the ruins I had seen. It was partly built by Rameses III. The walls are mostly covered with scenes in the life of that king. After seeing this we returned to the neighborhood of the tombs, where the work of resurrection is still going on. New tombs are often found and opened. The whole side of the mountain which overlooks the plain of Thebes is like a honeycomb, so numerous are the gaping tombs that have been opened and rifled of their contents. We entered one which is now used by Mustapha Agah as a depository for what he finds in his work of resurrection. There were several fine mummy cases, containing bodies which he has recently exhumed. One of them was the body of a princess. There was an open mummy-case standing against the wall, tenanted by a withered body, with its hideous face uncovered. Mrs. Smith mounted upon the top of a prostrate sarcophagus, and delivered the following address to the defunct Egyptian, which she seemed to have memorized for the occasion. The address was written a long time ago by one of the Smith family—Horace Smith, perhaps:

ADDRESS TO A MUMMY.

And thou hast walked about (how strange a story!)
   In Thebes's streets three thousand years ago,
When the Memnonium was in all its glory,
   And time had not begun to overthrow
Those temples, palaces, and piles stupendous,
Of which the very ruins are tremendous.

Speak! for thou long enough hast acted Dummy.
   Thou hast a tongue—come—let us hear its tune;

Thou'rt standing on thy legs, above-ground, Mummy!
　Revisiting the glimpses of the moon,
Not like thin ghosts or disembodied creatures,
　But with thy bones and flesh, and limbs and features.

Tell us—for doubtless thou canst recollect—
　To whom should we assign the Sphynx's fame?
Was Cheops or Cephrenes architect
　Of either pyramid that bears his name?
Is Pompey's Pillar really a misnomer?
Had Thebes a hundred gates, as sung by Homer?

Perhaps thou wert a Mason, and forbidden
　By oath to tell the secrets of thy trade;
Then say what secret melody was hidden
　In Memnon's statue which at sunrise played?
Perhaps thou wert a Priest; if so, my struggles
Are vain, for priestcraft never owns its juggles.

Perchance that very hand, now pinioned flat,
　Has hob-a-nobbed with Pharaoh, glass to glass;
Or dropped a half-penny in Homer's hat,
　Or doffed thine own to let Queen Dido pass;
Or held, by Solomon's own invitation,
A torch at the great Temple's dedication.

I need not ask thee if that hand, when armed,
　Has any Roman soldier mauled and knuckled,
For thou wert dead, and buried, and embalmed,
　Ere Romulus and Remus had been suckled:
Antiquity appears to have begun
Long after thy primeval race was run.

Thou couldst develop, if that withered tongue
　Might tell us what those sightless orbs have seen,
How the world looked when it was fresh and young,
　And the great Deluge still had left it green;
Or was it then so old that History's pages
Contained no record of its early ages?

Still silent! incommunicative elf!
  Art sworn to secrecy? then keep thy vows;
But prythee tell us something of thyself—
  Reveal the secrets of thy prison-house;
Since in the world of spirits thou hast slumbered,
What hast thou seen—what strange adventures numbered?

Since first thy form was in this box extended,
  We have, above-ground, seen some strange mutations:
The Roman empire has begun and ended,
  New worlds have risen—we have lost old nations,
And countless kings have into dust been humbled,
While not a fragment of thy flesh has crumbled.

Didst thou not hear the pother o'er thy head,
  When the great Persian conqueror, Cambyses,
Marched armies o'er thy tomb with thundering tread,
  O'erthrew Osiris, Orus, Apis, Isis,
And shook the Pyramids with fear and wonder,
When the gigantic Memnon fell asunder?

If the tomb's secrets may not be confessed,
  The nature of thy private life unfold:
A heart has throbbed beneath that leathern breast,
  And tears adown that dusty cheek have rolled:
Have children climbed those knees, and kissed that face?
What was thy name and station, age and race?

Statue of flesh—Immortal of the dead!
  Imperishable type of evanescence!
Posthumous man, who quitt'st thy narrow bed,
  And standest undecayed within our presence,
Thou wilt hear nothing till the Judgment morning,
When the great Trump shall thrill thee with its warning.

Why should this worthless tegument endure,
  If its undying guest be lost for ever?
O! let us keep the soul embalmed and pure
  In living virtue, that when both must sever,
Although corruption may our frame consume,
The immortal spirit in the skies may bloom!

Mustapha drives a good business opening tombs and selling the contents. Rich jewels are sometimes found in the sarcophagi with the dead bodies.

Mustapha Agah is a high functionary in Thebes. From the battlements of his house (a mud edifice standing just behind the great columns of the former porch of the Temple of Luxor) float both the flags of Great Britain and America. He is consular agent for both nations. So Mustapha is a great man among the Thebans—higher than the governor himself. I shall long remember Mustapha, and so will every American who visits Thebes—especially if he drinks coffee and smokes the fragrant lataika. Mustapha never fails to furnish his visitors with the chibouk and coffee in true Eastern style. Mustapha is a quiet, pleasant man, perhaps fifty years old, and as black as the ace of spades. He speaks pretty good English, but can neither read nor write. You may think it strange that a United States consul should be unable to read, but then you must remember that Mustapha is in Egypt, and fully competent to attend to all matters likely to come before him, without the aid of letters.

The time has now almost come for our departure. This evening, ere the twilight dews begin to fall, we shall bid farewell to Mustapha, and to the remains of what was once a city of a hundred gates! Mustapha has loaded his little cannon, and will doubtless give us a parting salute, for he pays marked respect to Americans. All the guns and pistols on board the "Hiawatha" and "Minnehaha" are in readiness for one grand discharge. We shall proceed to Grand Cairo, which will occupy from two to three weeks, as we have several stoppages to make along the way. From Cairo we shall make a break for the Holy Land. Will write you again from Cairo.

We have spent six days in Thebes, which is little time enough to see the ruins here. Those who have ample time should stay longer. To those who come here I commend the chibouk and coffee of Mustapha Agah at the British and American Consulate.

But evening approaches, and I must close. The "Minnehaha" has been set in order, and will soon be afloat upon the turbid bosom of the Nile towards the Great Sea. She has many hundred miles to float. If I kill a crocodile on the downward voyage, I shall make a note of it. Farewell.

HAL.

CROCODILE.

LETTER XXV.

THEBES TO THE PYRAMIDS.

Most glorious is life upon the Nile! I have travelled in almost every way that man ever travelled: have footed it upon the broad plains of the far West; have dashed across the same plains on the wild Mustang; have floated upon the bosom of the mighty Mississippi in steamers little less than palaces; have descended the beautiful Tennessee on the primitive "broad-horn;" whizzed from one end of the Union to the other on the "iron steed;" have been towed upon the "raging canal;" steamed across the billowy Atlantic; traversed the wild regions of Switzerland, and crossed the towering Alps, in the great lumbering diligence; rode upon the restless bosom of the blue Mediterranean; rocked through the desert on the back of the fleet dromedary, and galloped over many, many miles on the nimble-footed donkey. In all these ways have I travelled; but for luxurious pleasure, none of them begin to compare with a snug boat upon the Nile. Nile-travelling is "first-class" poetry, compared with which all other modes are commonplace prose, and that of the most prosy kind.

This is now the eighth or ninth week that we have been in blissful ignorance of the world. We have no cares except to eat, drink, and sleep. We are neither cursed with news nor newspapers. Neither pay nor receive visits from gossiping neighbors; nor does the post or carrier-boy leave the daily or weekly paper at our door. Therefore we are happy. We pity our poor deluded friends in America who keep themselves "posted" by reading the papers, and distress themselves sorely when things don't go to please them. Some we know are miserable because they see horrible spectres of the "glorious Union busted up" and clean gone; while other poor devils are utterly miserable because of their inability to bring about said "bust-up." Other some distress themselves grievously in view of the making of the next President, while ghosts and goblins dire haunt the visions of those "illustrious self-sacrificing patriots" who have signified their willingness to yield to the wishes of their countrymen, and to be placed in the Presidential chair. And what painful anxiety must weigh upon those benevolent men who take it upon themselves to arrange and pack committees and delegates for the national farce (by courtesy called "convention") preparatory to making a President! I say, I pity you, my enlightened friends—from my soul I do. Would that you could have a few weeks respite upon the Nile from the painful cares that beset you!

To give you some idea of our ignorance—and

consequent bliss—I will inform you that we do not even know who is Speaker of the House of Representatives, or whether it has a Speaker at all. We heard in Rome (that was a long time ago) that Congress had met, and would proceed to organize, if such a thing were possible, but up to this time we have not heard the result. We have ceased to trouble ourselves with either speaking or thinking of politics, and I almost dread to see the time come when the state of public affairs in Uncle Sam's dominions shall be forced upon me. Two or three weeks ago I ventured to ask my friend Smith what his ideas were about the state of politics at home. I saw a cloud of any thing but pleasure darken his brow; he puffed his chibouk viciously for a few moments, and then, with an emphasis peculiar only to Smith, he replied, "D—n politics!" I said no more, and he continued to puff furiously. I thought strange of this, for Smith was a rampant politician when I first knew him. But such is the effect of travelling in the East—especially upon the Nile.

But this is not telling you of our downward voyage from Upper Egypt. Twelve days ago, just as darkness was settling down upon the ancient city of Thebes—but while it was yet high noon in Huntsville—the Hiawatha and Minnehaha were loosed from their moorings under the towering portico of grand old Luxor, and floated out into the stream, when six guns from the boats announced their departure for the lower country. These guns were responded to by the burning of a pound and a half of Egyptian powder by old Mustapha, whose little cannon thundered forth a report that was echoed by the mountains and cavernous tombs miles away across the river, and we were off, gliding away from the city of forty centuries, which was falling into ruins, perhaps, while the seven hills of Rome were yet a wilderness.

Our progress down the river was slow indeed, owing to adverse winds, and it was not until the afternoon of the following day that we reached the city of Ghena, in the neighborhood of which stands the old Temple of Dendera, one of the lions of Egypt that must needs be seen by all travellers who ascend the Nile. We of course found the omnipresent donkeys waiting for us—they are always waiting, and such donkeys! Wish I could send you a picture of our party as we mounted those donkeys and rode away. You would laugh some. Three of the twelve had bridles, and five had saddles, two of the saddles had stirrups, the rest did n't. The donkeys were of the smallest breed, and almost as woolly as sheep, which they resembled, except the ears. When mounted by their riders, little could be seen but their head and part of their tail. The ears were all the portions visible of those ridden by the ladies—the flowing skirts concealing all else. The donkey on which Miss Kissiah was mounted, though diminutive, was a vicious little scoundrel, and managed early in the excursion to spill his precious burden upon the ground. She bravely remounted, however, and with two Arabs to hold her on, and a

9

third to lead, she managed to stick to him until our return to the boats. Smith's donkey got him off twice—(Smith always gets thrown off)—once by falling, and the second time by lying down. His driver got a sound cursing, but no "backsheesh" that day.

The Temple of Dendera is comparatively of *modern* date, being perhaps something less than two thousand years old! Some portion of it is said to have been built by Cleopatra, and one of the walls is adorned with a sculptured portrait of that queen in bas-relief. Her son, by Julius Cæsar, is standing by her. Like all other Egyptian temples, it is a massive building, every stone of which is carved with images and hieroglyphics. The architecture is magnificent. With the exception of Karnak, it contains some of the largest columns I have seen in Egypt. This temple is almost perfect, but much of it is hid by the ruins of the mud-built city that once surrounded it. The rubbish has all been removed from the interior, and the immense halls stand vacant and desolate, tenanted only by bats and owls.

Finishing up the Temple of Dendera, we returned to our boats through luxurious wheat-fields—cut loose and floated away, with the sincere desire that the next party of travellers may find better donkeys than we found. Three days after, we brought up at the city of Girgeh, the place where we had stopped on the upward trip to see the Dervishes and the dancing-girls. We didn't take donkeys here, but determined to "do" the town on foot. We formed in single column, and marched through the bazaars, stared at and followed by a hundred shirt-tail natives. The ladies of our party were regarded with admiration, and would have been crowded almost to suffocation if we had not kept the crowd back by flourishing our sticks, and occasionally cracking the heads of the more curious. They stand in mortal dread of the cane or "koorbash" of a "howadji." A koorbash is a keen whip, made of the hide of rhinoceros.

The people of Girgeh are not the most noted of Egyptians for cleanliness. Indeed, they may be called, by fastidious people, filthy. It was soon after our visit to this city on the way up that the horrible discovery of the nameless vermin was made among us. Mrs. Smith made the discovery on that occasion, and she contiuues to affirm to this day that they came from Girgeh, which is probable. Returning to our boats after this our second visit, which had been made with the utmost caution, a proposition was made that a general examination be gone into. It was done, and the result was horrifying. The ladies retired to their cabins, and were not long in finding abundant evidence of the presence of the enemy. The gentlemen stripped, and were equally successful. There were voices of lamentation that evening on board the Minnehaha, which were heartily responded to from the portals of the Hiawatha. The ladies almost sobbed, so great was their distress. The gentlemen laughed, and tried to make a joke of it; but the laugh was dry enough, and the ladies refused to be comforted. Smith, as his custom is, tried to be witty on the occasion. Smith is always trying to be witty. He said "there was no use trying to disguise the fact: that we were a lousy set." This remark brought a shower of indignation upon Smith's head from the ladies, each of whom called him a "brute." And it *was* a brutal remark; but Smith is a practical man, and believes in calling things by the right name. There is generally some truth in what Smith says, however homely his language. His wit is not always apparent.

Towards night we loosed from Girgeh, and floated down the river, carrying with us *vivid impressions* of its *inhabitants*. In due course of time—I don't remember how long—we arrived at Ossiout, the largest city in Middle Egypt. Here we of course found donkeys in waiting, and were not long in mounting and setting off for the mountains which lie just back of the city. Our object was to visit the tombs which honeycomb the solid stone cliffs. There are a great many of them, some very large, say forty by fifty feet square, smoothly cut in the solid rock, and adorned with thousands of hieroglyphics and figures in bas-relief on the walls. Seated on some loose stones in the largest one of these tombs we sung several hymns, (it was the Sabbath day,) winding up with some good old camp-meeting songs, after which we departed and went into the city. Passing through the bazaars, we found the crowd so dense that we were obliged to dismount and send our donkeys round another way, while we crowded through on foot. We met a funeral-procession, the largest

I have seen. It was led by banners and drums. The body lay upon an open bier, and immediately following were about fifty mourning-women, whose hideous yells were terrifying. I never heard such weeping. You would have thought the heart of each and every one of them was in the very act of breaking snap in two. They were hired for the occasion, and seemed determined to earn their wages.

In one of the bazaars of this city I saw the first really handsome Egyptian woman that I have met with. If I could wield the pen of a modern novel-writer, I would endeavor to give you some idea of her beauty; for nothing short of that could do her justice. Were I to say that her sparkling black eyes shone like diamonds, and her teeth like pearls, it would not be exaggeration. Nor would it be more than just to say that her swelling bosom and beautifully-rounded arm were such as a Venus might have envied. No Grecian beauty ever possessed features more regular. Showers of coal-black tresses fell in rich profusion upon her graceful neck, and lay nestling upon her voluptuous bosom, just enough of which was exposed to make one anxious to see more. She was dressed in rich Oriental costume, with full flowing silk trowsers, clasped at the ankles with heavy gold bands. Her head, neck, bosom, and wrists were adorned with golden trinkets, elegantly wrought into various devices. I suppose the solid gold ornaments she wore were worth, by weight, at least a thousand dollars. The gracefulness with which she sat, and the mild and modest expression of her beautiful face, belied the calling of this fair creature; for she was a woman of the town, sitting in the market-place, waiting to be hired.

Leaving Ossiout, we next halted at Eekmien, a town containing twenty-five or thirty thousand inhabitants, without counting the dogs, of which latter there seemed to be several regiments. All Egyptian towns swarm with dogs. Eekmien is noted for nothing in particular, so far as I know, except as being the place where General Adem Bey is stationed with the flower of the army of Egypt. Here is the first division of the army, and the favorite soldiers of the Pasha. They are all Nubians, and as black as night; but, black as they are, a finer-looking body of men I never saw, the least one of which is six feet high, and as straight as an Indian. Adem Bey, the commander, is a noble-looking man, standing six feet six in his stockings, and wearing a fierce moustache. He is a brave soldier, and one of the first officials in the Government. Besides being commander of the first division of the army, he is at present acting as Deputy Governor of this portion of Egypt. As to color, General Adem Bey is as black as a stack of black cats in a dark cellar at midnight, but has, withal, a mild and pleasant face. Soon after we landed at Eekmien, my friend Smith proposed that we pay a formal visit to this dignitary. I agreed, of course. So, taking our dragoman, we sallied forth towards the encampment, not, however, until we had put on clean linen, and Smith had donned his regimentals. Smith would carry his gun. He always carries his gun. As we reached the encampment, and were passing up an avenue between rows of white tents and black soldiers, approaching the marque of the General, who had seen us coming from a distance, and dispatched two servants to welcome us to his quarters, it was then and there that Smith compromised the dignity of both of us, and came well-nigh turning our pompous visit into a farce. It was in this wise: Just as the General was advancing to welcome us, in true Eastern style, (for my companion's gaudy gold lace and gilt buttons had inspired him with profound respect, if not awe,) Smith, seeing a flock of pigeons some hundred or two yards away, broke towards them in a brisk run; nor would he stop until he had shot at them. He missed, of course, and then came puffing and blowing back to the tent, evidently pleased that he had had a shot at the birds. The General suppressed a smile, while the servants almost burst with laughter. I confess that my face burnt with mortification, but Smith heeded none of these things. Our dragoman introduced us, giving my friend the title of Colonel. Smith seized the hand of the General, and gave it a genuine Yankee shake. We were invited to seats on the voluptuous divan, by the side of our entertainer, while servants brought us coffee and chibouks. We smoked and chatted with his sable highness for nearly an hour, and found him to be a man of no mean capacity. He had heard of America, and had an impression that it was a great country, but far, O very far away! Said he was glad to see Americans, and hoped we had enjoyed our visit to Egypt. Smith did his best to impress the fact upon our host that Americans were the greatest people in the world, and flatteringly insinuated that the Nubians might rank next. This flattering speech pleased the General wonderfully, and the servants were immediately ordered to refill the pipes and coffee-cups. He showed us his arms and accoutrements; also those of his soldiers. Had all his musical instruments brought in and pompously exhibited. Expressed much regret that our visit had fallen upon the Moslem Sabbath, (Friday;) otherwise he would have given us a chance to review his soldiers on parade. Would also have treated us to a musical entertainment, and a characteristic Nubian dance. But the Koran forbade these performances on Friday, and we had to forego the pleasure. Our visit to Adem Bey was an agreeable one, and but for the approach of evening, would have been prolonged. Smith more than ever believes in the power of gold lace and gilt buttons, being assured that it was his uniform that insured our welcome.

Leaving Eckmien, our next stopping-place was Beni-Hassen, where once stood a considerable town; but a few years ago it was destroyed, and its inhabitants all killed by Ibraham Pasha, except a very few, who escaped by running the gauntlet.

Nothing now remains but the blackened, crumbling walls. The cause of the destruction of this town and people, was their thievish and marauding propensities. It had become dangerous for travellers to stop there to see the many large and curious tombs in the neighborhood, and consequently the Pasha sent his soldiers and wiped it out of existence. The tombs in the mountain back of this town are many and curious; some very large, and nearly all adorned with paintings—better executed than most I have seen elsewhere. One of these tombs is peculiarly interesting, because it is thought by many that it is the same in which the body of Joseph rested until the exodus of the Israelites. One of the walls bears a painting, which it is thought represents the arrival of Jacob and his sons and their families into Egypt, and their presentation to Pharaoh. The number of figures in the painting corresponds with the number of Israelites upon their first arrival. Their flocks and herds and little ones are all represented. It may or may not be Joseph's, but it is at least a very interesting tomb. It is about forty-five feet square, and perhaps fifteen feet to the ceiling, which is supported by several columns.

Below Beni-Hassen we stopped at Minyeh, and visited a very large sugar-manufactory, in which are employed six hundred men. It is managed by French and Russians. We strolled about the town some time, but nothing turned up worthy of note. Nearly half the people of Minyeh seem to be one-eyed, and dogs are numerous. Our next stop was at Benisooef, the first important town above Cairo. We landed about two miles from the town, which being rather an out-of-the-way place, there were no donkeys present (a wonder!) to carry us into the city. We footed it. Went through the bazaars, and laid in a fresh supply of pipes and tobacco. Heard a quarrel there which exceeded any thing in the way of a war of words I ever heard. An old woman was pitching into a shopkeeper in the most approved high-pressure style. The scene was ludicrous beyond description. At first the tongue of the man went like a bell-clapper, but he soon wilted before that old woman. She assumed a thousand grotesque shapes and attitudes, swaying her arms in the air like winding blades, while her long bony fingers contracted and expanded, and clutched, as though she was tearing the very wind-pipe from the neck of her antagonist. Her eyes glared like those of an enraged hyena, while she champed her teeth and foamed at the mouth like a rabid wild boar. She yelled like an Indian, and drew her lean swarthy face into a myriad of frightful contortions. All the time the words flew like bullets, and seemed to take effect, for the man grew perceptibly less at every onslaught. When the old woman was exhausted and nearly ready to fall, a young, athletic woman, about the size of a jackass, and almost as stout, came to her relief, and continued the war in the same strain, until a man in authority approached and put an end to the fun. At the close of this quarrel we hurried to our boats, and floated down the river.

It is now the fourteenth day since we left Thebes. Our progress has been slow, head winds having greatly impeded our course. Our amusements and pastimes coming down have been about the same as when going up—shooting, running, jumping, and kicking up our heels generally. Yesterday being Sunday, our little party of twelve met on board the Hiawatha, and while you were sleeping and perchance dreaming in Huntsville, we worshipped God in the old home fashion, with prayers, and hymns, and spiritual songs—the astonished Arabs standing round and looking on with wonder, as we bowed before the throne of grace.

THE PYRAMIDS.

We are now getting in the neighborhood of the pyramids. Already they begin to loom up in the distance, and the head of the great Sphynx is peering above the sand-hills; but as the wind is strong against us, we shall not reach them before to-morrow, perhaps. After I have seen and climbed some of them, I will write you another letter.

Yours, etc.,   HAL.

LETTER XXVI.

PYRAMIDS TO JERUSALEM.

PREPARE for a long stride—from the Nile to Jerusalem—for this letter must cover all the time and space intervening since my last letter—which, if I remember rightly, was closed late one evening, many days ago, as we floated down the Nile in sight of the pyramids of Sakhara and Dashore. It was the next morning after the close of that letter, I was aroused early by my friend Smith, (who is always up with the lark,) and told that we were near the pyramids. I stuck my head out of the window, and found the nose of the Minnehaha stuck in the mud on the west bank of the river, and the gallant Hiawatha moored alongside—sails all furled. In the distance were the pyramids, just gilded by the rising sun. All our party were soon astir, and Mohammed was ordered to hurry up his cakes, that we might have an early breakfast and be off. Mohammed was unusually spry that morning, and by seven o'clock we were ready to start.

Now, my friend, if you feel inclined to travel, you may imagine yourself one of our party, and make the excursion with us. Here are the donkeys waiting for us. You may mount this little mouse-colored one. No matter about a bridle—a donkey-boy will guide him for you with a stick. Your saddle has no stirrups, but that is all right in Egypt. With Achmet ahead, we will strike out through this large palm-grove. Half an hour's ride, and here we are in the midst of the ruins of old Memphis, or Noph. We look around upon desolation. See nothing here but stupendous piles of broken bricks and fallen walls, with here and there a broken image half buried in the earth. We think immediately of the prophecies concerning this once proud city: "For Noph shall be waste and desolate, without an inhabitant;" and again, "I will destroy the idols, and will cause their images to cease out of Noph." How literally fulfilled! The images and idols are all prostrate and mutilated. We see but one that is worth pausing to look at; it is a colossal statue of Rameses Second, which, when standing, was between forty and fifty feet high. It is fallen now, and its feet broken off—otherwise perfect.

We will hurry on now to the pyramid of Sakhara—some two hours' ride farther. See how it grows upon us as we approach it! Is it not immense? And yet it is a small affair compared with the one we will see to-morrow—Cheops. But even this would be the wonder and admiration of the world if there were none larger. Our dragoman says we cannot ascend this pyramid. We don't believe him—so here we go! He is alarmed, and swears more than a hundred times that we will fall and break our necks. He lies, for here we are on the very pinnacle, waving our hats at the astonished Smith, who broke down when half-way up, and returned to the ground to keep the ladies company.

But let us return to the earth now, and go to the tomb of Apis—the cavern in which were deposited the sacred bulls worshipped by the ancient Egyptians. It is near by. Let us look to our pistols, for we have read Mr. Prime's account of the attack upon himself and party, by a hundred and fifty Arabs, when he visited this tomb. True, he and his bold dragoman put them all to flight, and walked into the cavern without molestation; but they may have picked up some courage since then, and may not be so easily routed as when bearded by the fierce "Braheem Effendi." We are all armed, and Smith, besides his gun, has got the hatchet from the boat, and the carving-knife belonging to our table furniture; while Brown carries his volcanic repeater in one hand and spiked Alpenstock in the other, looking meanwhile as savage as a thunder-storm. The rest of us carry each a copy of Colt's best stuck in our belts. Brave indeed must be the hundred and fifty Bedouins who attack our party! Now, in solid phalanx we move on, Smith nobly leading the van. We approach the cavern, but see not the enemy. Keep a sharp look-out: they may be behind those sand-hills, ready to pounce upon us. We halt, and send Jones ahead to reconnoitre. He returns and reports the coast clear. All right! Let us enter. There is "nary" Bedouin about. No doubt Prime's demonstration, and his threat to throw the old sheik of the tribe "over the river into the Red Sea," frightened them clean away entirely. The brave "Effendi" deserves the thanks of all travellers for frightening away this band of thieves.

But is not this a tremendous hole in the ground? See, it is a finely finished gallery, cut in the living rock, two or three hundred yards in length. Here are twenty-five niches in the sides, each one containing a mammoth sarcophagus, in which the bodies of the sacred bulls were placed after being embalmed. Most of the sarcophagi have been opened, and the bull mummies removed. One of them is in New York, in Dr. Abbott's collection of Egyptian antiquities. Here is a richly finished chapel in which is the broken image of a calf, and a prostrate Egyptian before it. Don't you suppose it was this custom among the Egyptians that first suggested to Aaron the idea of making a golden calf? Very likely, you say.

Well, we have now explored this tomb, let us return to the light of day and take lunch, for I am hungry. Here, we will eat in the cool shade in the mouth of the tomb—rest till the cool of the evening, and return to our boats.

• • • • •

Ghezeh! Yes, here we are at Ghezeh. We floated down here last night after returning to our boats from the Bull Tombs. Yonder are the pyramids of Cheops and Belzoni, and we are all in a fidget to be off. These are better donkeys than we had yesterday, and we will set off in a brisk gallop. The pyramids seem just out yonder, but they are six miles away. Were you ever so deceived in distance? But at this gait, it will not take long to get there. Stirrups and bridles are luxurious appendages to donkeys—are they not? Now we near the base of old Cheops. Here we pass by the great Sphynx, about which we have read, and whose picture we have so often looked at in Olney's Geography. Although it is a perfect figure hewn out of a mountain, and one of the most wonderful things in the world, we will not stop to see it now, but hasten to the pyramid, which is more wonderful still. Are you not astonished and bewildered? Do you not wilt right down before this, the greatest work ever conceived by man? I do. I feel oppressed—a sensation something akin to nightmare—and not the least inclination towards an effort to comprehend the great pile. Now, first, before we yield ourselves into the hands of these savage-looking Arabs, who wait here to carry travellers to the top of the pyramid, let us ride around and view it on all sides. Wonderful! wonderful! you exclaim; and so it is. To give our friends at home some idea of its size, I think we may say that its base covers *four times* as much ground as the public square of Huntsville!—perhaps more—certainly not less.

But here we are now, in a crowd of a hundred Arabs—great stalwart fellows. What a scuffle! Each one claims the privilege of conducting us to the top of the pyramid; and we shall be fortunate if we get out of their hands with whole bones. We are clutched by as many as can possibly get hold of us at a time, and each one seems determined to hold his grip. Fighting with donkey-boys is child's-play to this. But here comes the old sheik of the tribe to our rescue. He orders our tormentors to desist, and appoints two for each of us, who hurry us rapidly from rock to rock up the rugged steep before us. Pausing to rest when about one-fourth of the way up, we see all our party winding their way up behind us, except Smith. He is still at the base, fighting with the Arabs. Before reaching here he swore roundly that no yellow-skinned devil of an Arab should carry him up the pyramid; that he had failed yesterday to reach the top of Sakhara, and that he would to-day go up Cheops unassisted, to retrieve his character—for Smith is an ambitious man. He fights bravely, but in vain, for it is not the Arab policy to let any one go up without aid and "backsheesh." Poor Smith is exhausted, and is now borne up the rugged height in the arms of his tawny friends. He has ceased to struggle, but swears at every step that he will not pay them a cent for their labor. Now here we are at the top, higher than we ever were before, being nearly *two hundred* yards from terra firma. On top is a plateau twenty feet square perhaps, so that we can sit and rest and look about securely. People on the ground do not seem to us near so large as grasshoppers. From here we have a fine view of Cairo and the

Nile—and to the west we see away off for perhaps a hundred miles into the great Libyan desert.

We now descend, and go into the heart of this great pile of stone. This part of our day's work will not leave a favorable impression. We shall only remember it as a laborious winding and crawling through dark, hot, dusty labyrinths, where suffocation seemed almost inevitable. We find two large chambers, one called the King's, and the other the Queen's tomb. This is all.

Smith, you observe, has got over his passion, and is in excellent humor. Instead of refusing to pay the fellows who carried him up the pyramid, he has paid them more than double. They have been expatiating upon the beauty of Mrs. Smith, and have thereby struck the old gentleman in a tender place—for Smith has his weak points.

We will now lunch and rest, after which we will return to our boats, marvelling at the greatness of the works of Egypt. It will be night when we get there, and so we will sleep as we float down the river.

. . . . .

Cairo, the Grand! the Magnificent! the Beautiful! Here we are again in "Cairo the Victorious!" How delightful to get once again into a fine city, after wandering for weeks among mud huts and squalid villages! How gay the streets, and with what glee we mount the fat, round Cairo donkey, and dash through them! This pleasure almost counterbalances the regrets we experience in leaving our dear little "Minnehaha," in which we have dwelt with so much ease and delight for more than six weeks. The removal is a sad one, but the bustle and gayety in this great city of five hundred thousand people will soon dispel the sadness.

We take rooms at the "Hotel des Pyramides," and will now be off for a ride. Here we go, down the street, full speed to the park, or great square, by the "Hotel d'Orient." Hold! "Halloo, Captain! is that you? Sure enough it is! Captain Jim Williams, of Tennessee, United States Minister to the Sublime Porte. Glad to see you, Captain. Give us your hand. You are looking remarkably well. First home-face I've seen in the East. Just from Constantinople, eh? Waiting here for your family, who have gone up the Nile? Yes, we heard of them up there. Return home in eight days, do you? Thank you. We will call at the Legation, when we reach the Golden Horn. No; we have heard no news from home for many weeks, nor do we seek any. Don't tell us any, if you please. Sorry you told us of the election of Speaker of the House of Representatives. Thank you. We will call at your room this evening, and get what information you can give us about travelling in Syria, as you have recently taken a tour in that country. We leave for Jerusalem in three days. Good-day!"

We spend three or four days in Cairo, shopping and riding and walking, visiting mosques and such places of interest as we failed to see when here before.

. . . .

Now let us be off for Alexandria; for the steamer sails from there to-morrow for Joppa, and we must be on hand. We go to the dépôt and buy our tickets from a big black nigger, who cheats us out of several pennies, in making change. There are only ten of us now—two of our party, Mr. and Mrs. S., passengers of the Hiawatha, having stopped in Cairo. We give them up with much regret. The train reaches Alexandria about eleven o'clock at night, and we again domicile at the India Hotel. Smith of course quarrels with the landlord, and beats him down in his prices. Smith always argues the great difference between wholesale and retail, and generally gains his point. It would be hard for our party to get along without Smith, although I must confess that I am sometimes seriously provoked with him.

The time has now come for us to go aboard the steamer. We all settle our bills at the hotel, except Mr. Smith, who seriously disputes his, because there is an item of sixpence in it that he contends ought not to be there. He swears he will not pay it, and the landlord swears he shall. We start for the door, but Smith is stopped by the landlord, backed by all the servants about the hotel, from the head-waiter down to the bar-tender. The door is closed on him, and, by main force, they wrench the entire sum of sixpence from the enraged Smith, before permitting him to depart. I will not say that they frightened the brave Smith, but then a dozen stalwart waiters, including the cook, with a huge butcher-knife, is not just the crowd for one man to contend with, when a sixpence will settle the difficulty. The old gentleman thinks a little hard because the rest of us did not back him in the fight; but I guess he will get over it soon. We are all glad of it; for penuriousness is his besetting sin, and we wanted to see him taken down.

We have a smooth and pleasant sail of thirty-six hours, when the towers of Jaffa (ancient Joppa) loom up before us. The country before us is Palestine! We are about to tread upon holy ground. We hardly realize it, but it is so. We leave the steamer and go ashore in small boats, and here we are, actually in Joppa—a city that is said to have existed even before the flood, and to be the very place where Noah built the ark. It was at this port that Hiram, King of Tyre, landed the cedar timbers which he sent from Lebanon, for the building of Solomon's temple. Hiram and Solomon were very great friends. This, too, is the place where Jonah came, when he wanted to run away, to keep from going to Nineveh to preach. He found a ship about to sail for Tarshish, and—but you know the story about the whale. The Apostle Peter came down here once, and lodged with one Simon, a tanner, who had his tan-yard somewhere by the seaside. Part of the house of Simon you see standing here yet, and here in the court is a well, by which stands a very large stone trough, which they tell us was a vat used by Simon for tanning leather. Peter had a remarkable dream while sleeping upon the top of this house, an account of which you will find by reading the ninth chapter of Acts. During that same visit Peter performed a wonderful miracle—even the raising of Tabitha from the dead. Joppa, you see, is not a very large place, but is very beautiful to look at—from a distance. It is built upon a rock, which is in shape something like a potato-hill. The houses are all of stone, and very substantial. The streets are from four to six feet wide, and in many places we ascend them by steps, like going up stairs. We all go in a body now, and call upon Rev. Mr. Sanders, American Consul and Missionary at Joppa. We are delighted with the family, for they receive and entertain us like home-folks.

But we must not tarry in Joppa. Our dragoman has procured horses, and we must be on the road to Jerusalem. We sleep at Ramleh (ancient Arimathea) to-night, some ten or twelve miles on the way. Let us mount and be off. But wait! Smith, Brown, and myself go down and take a sea-bath first, after which we sally out at the Jerusalem gate, (which, by the way, is the only gate on the land side of Joppa,) and take our way through the finest orange-groves perhaps in the world; for Joppa, you know, is noted for oranges. The different groves or orchards are fenced with prickly-pear hedges, which grow to enormous size. We see some with trunks three feet in diameter. We soon leave the orange-groves and enter upon a most beautiful plain, everywhere blooming with flowers.

Two hours' ride brings us to Lydda, a very ancient town; the same where the Apostle Peter cured Eneas of the palsy, after he had kept his bed eight years.

About night we arrive at Ramleh, and sleep in a convent, being well received and entertained by the monks. Early in the morning we visit an old ruin, with a very high tower, just outside the town, of the history of which we know nothing. From its summit we have a fine view of the hill country towards Jerusalem; but owing to the fog in that direction, we cannot see Mount Carmel.

Leaving Ramleh, we soon strike into the mountains, where locomotion is exceedingly difficult, owing to the stony road, or, we might say, owing to the *absence* of a road. It is a sterile country, the rocks showing their teeth on every side, with scarce soil enough to afford any green thing, except in the little valleys. We pass through the valley of Ajalon, which will be for ever memorable, on account of the great battle fought there between the Israelites and Amorites, when Joshua commanded the sun to stand still upon Gideon, and the moon in the valley of Ajalon. You will find an account of the fight somewhere in the book of Joshua. We see little more of interest in the way, except the tomb of Samuel, which is covered by a mosque on the summit of the mountain.

We are getting near Jerusalem, and our impatience to see the Holy City increases. We spur our jaded horses on, and after climbing another and another mountain, the glorious sight appears! We pause and look. We see little of the city except the high walls and the domes of the highest houses. We see that mountains are truly all around about the city, and that the city and its surroundings are beautiful. We exclaim, " Beautiful for situation, the joy of the whole earth, is Mount Zion, the city of the Great King!" We enter by the Jaffa or Bethlehem gate, and wind our way through the dark, narrow streets, to the Mediterranean Hotel, which is hard by the Church of the Holy Sepulchre. We are intensely interested in every thing we see; for there is not a locality in or around the city that is not holy.

After spending a few days here, we shall go down to Jericho, the Jordan, and the Dead Sea, then to Hebron; after which we will return here, and spend a few more days before setting out to the North, towards Damascus.

Yours truly,   HAL.

LETTER XXVII.

JERUSALEM.

I HAVE now been ten days in and around Jerusalem. I have gone about Zion; have walked upon the walls and told the towers thereof. Have stood upon Calvary, and sat upon the Mount of Olives! Strolled down the valley of Hinnom, and humbled myself in the valley of Jehoshaphat. Knelt in the Garden of Gethsemane, and sung songs of rejoicing upon the Mount of Ascension. Drunk from the Pools of Solomon, and washed in the Pool of Siloam. Worshipped in the city of Bethlehem, and rested in the quiet village of Bethany. Sat in the shade of the broad-spreading oaks of Mamre, and walked through the vineyards of Eshcol. Slaked my thirst at the Fountain of Elisha, and bathed in the waters of the Jordan. Have indeed wandered for many days amid sacred scenes, and in holy places, of the which I would love to present you a faithful account, but that were impossible. The undertaking would be too great. If, however, you are disposed to make a little excursion, we will pay a hasty visit to some of the interesting localities.

We will start from St. Stephen's Gate, on the east

side of the city. It is called the Gate of St. Stephen because the martyr Stephen was led out here to be stoned to death. Here, just within this gate, is the Pool of Bethesda, the same around which the "impotent folk, of blind, halt, and withered," used to lie and wait for the troubling of the waters. Here Jesus healed a man who had been diseased thirty-eight years. The pool is three hundred and sixty feet long, one hundred and thirty broad, and thirty-five deep. It is almost dry now. Leaving this pool, we go up through the city along the Via Dolorosa, or the "mournful way," so called because it was up this street our Saviour went to Calvary bearing his cross. The first place of interest we reach is the house of Pilate, the same, or at least on the same ground, where the mock trial was had and Jesus condemned, and where he was scourged, and a crown of thorns placed upon his head. From the top of this house we look down upon the plateau on which stood the Temple of Solomon. In the midst of it, and just over the spot where the Ark of the Covenant stood, stands the Mosque of Omar, which is guarded strictly to prevent Christians entering. This is the nearest approach we can make to it, the Moslems believing that the touch of a Christian would defile their sacred edifice. The mosque is a fine octagonal building with a graceful dome, and the square around it very beautiful—a fine position for the splendid building which once occupied it.

Leaving the house of Pilate, we proceed up the

street towards Calvary and the church of the Holy Sepulchre. Our guide points out many stations along the way where incidents occurred as the Lord passed along. The places where he fainted are shown, and the place where the cross was taken from him and placed upon Simon the Cyrenean.

We enter the church of the Holy Sepulchre, and near the door see multitudes of people falling down and kissing a large marble slab. This we are told is the "stone of unction," where the body of the Lord was embalmed for the burial. Without pausing, we hasten to the interior, and after crowding, squeezing, pushing, and jamming for half an hour, in a dense crowd of the most motley people we have seen this side of Naples, we gain admittance into the room in which is the Holy Sepulchre. We stoop down and look in, and then enter the very tomb in which the great Redeemer of mankind lay for three days! It is a holy place, and we enter it with no little awe. Coming out of the sepulchre, we ascend a flight of steps in another part of the building, and stand upon Calvary, and see the very rock in which the cross was planted. We only tarry in these places for a moment, promising ourselves more time upon some future occasion. The crowd here is too dense for enjoyment, for this is the season for the pilgrims to be in Jerusalem, and they of course all flock first to the Church of the Holy Sepulchre. These pilgrims are not just the kind of people we would desire to see them. They are rough, ignorant, superstitious creatures, many of whom have journeyed from far countries to Jerusalem without once changing their garments, and are, consequently, any thing but clean. They believe that a pilgrimage to the Holy Sepulchre seals their everlasting salvation, and they make the pilgrimage at all hazards. The smell in such a crowd is not so sweet as roses, and we only stop long enough this time to see the most noted localities in this large building, such as the tombs of Melchisedek, Godfrey, and Baldwin—the place where the Saviour appeared to many after he was risen, the place where the cross was found, etc. We observe in passing that the church is exceedingly rich in gold and silver lamps and chains, and some parts decked out in such profusion of gilded ornaments as to appear ridiculous. The church is cut up into almost innumerable chapels and compartments, and when all the different sects claiming rights here are worshipping, it is a Babel, if not worse. The Greeks, Latins, Armenians, and Copts occupy different parts of the house, and each sect does its level best to make more noise than its neighbor, which is hard to do. The Greeks are in the ascendant, and outsquall the rest, but then the cracked and crazy organ of the Latins comes in for a large share of glory in the way of making a noise. These different sects hate each other like cats and dogs, and, but for the body of Turkish soldiers always on hand, would fight as such. This is a humiliating thought for Christians. My friend Smith talks like a book on this subject, and says if he had the power he would wipe the whole establishment from the face of the earth, and disperse the fanatical zealots who worship here to the four quarters of the globe. Smith is right. The scenes enacted here are disgraceful instead of honoring to Christianity.

Leaving the church of the Holy Sepulchre, we traverse the narrow, gloomy street through the Jewish quarter of the town, and enter the Synagogue of the Jews, where worship is going on. The house is crowded with men, while the women stand outside in the open court. The leader of the meeting delivers his discourse sitting, after which the whole congregation join in chanting the Law. A scroll is exhibited, and the people seem almost frantic at the sight of it, and as many as can possibly do so, rush to and kiss it or the veil which had concealed it. It is a copy of the Law—very ancient. Their worship seems to be sincere, and their reverence for the Law of Moses profound indeed. I believe these Jews worship God in spirit and in truth, and look perhaps more anxiously for the first coming of the Messiah than Christians do for his second coming.

Leaving the Synagogue, we wind through some narrow crooked lanes, which it would be vain to attempt without a guide, and reach a section of the ancient wall that surrounded the Temple of Solomon. This is the "Jews' Place of Wailing." Here the Jews have been permitted for many centuries to approach the precincts of the Temple of their fathers, and bathe its hallowed stones with their tears. It is a touching scene: Jews of both sexes, of all ages, and from every quarter of the earth, are here raising up a united cry of lamentation over a desolated sanctuary. Old men may be seen tottering up to these massive stones, kissing them with fond rapture, while tears stream down their cheeks. Well may the poor Jews repeat the words of the Psalmist, (lxxix. 1, 4, 5:) "O God, the heathen are come into thine inheritance; thy holy temple have they defiled; they have laid Jerusalem on heaps. We are become a reproach to our neighbors, a scorn and derision to them that are round about us. How long, Lord? wilt thou be angry for ever? Shall thy jealousy burn like fire?" These Jews may be seen here in this little paved area weeping and wailing every Friday.

We now leave the Place of Wailing, and emerge from the city at the Zion gate, and stand upon that portion of the hill of Zion which is now without the walls. It is a "ploughed field" now, according to the prophecy concerning it. Not far from the gate is the tomb of David. A large mosque stands over it, and it is considered by Moslems too holy a place for Christians to enter. So we cannot see the tomb of the great Shepherd King, the mosque being closely guarded. Near the tomb is the house of Caiaphas, now an Armenian convent. We enter, and are shown the little room in which Jesus was imprisoned on the same night in which he was betrayed and led away from the garden of Gethsemane to Caiaphas. We also see the rock which was rolled before the door of the sepulchre, and which the angels rolled away.

We pass on round the city wall, and at the Joppa Gate enter the Tower of Hippicus, in which Herod had his palace. David's palace was also here. It is a very strong fortress, and bears marks of great antiquity. Scattered along the different roads that lead away from this gate we see many poor lepers sitting begging. They are the most pitiable-looking objects we ever saw. I suppose they sit here now just as they did in the time of our Saviour; but there is none to heal them now. We see these miserable wretches sitting without every gate. From this Joppa gate we go down into the Valley of Hinnom, which lies between Mount Zion and the Hill of Evil Council. Passing by the upper and lower pools of Gihon, which are immense reservoirs, we enter the deeper portion of the valley, and sitting down in a quiet shady place, beneath the olive trees, where the early spring grass is green and beautiful, we sing some of the songs of Zion. Continuing down the valley, we come to the well En-Rogel, at the junction of the valleys of Hinnom and Jehoshaphat. It was at this well that Adonijah once got up a great feast, or barbecue, to which he invited all the people, and in the midst of the hilarity he caused himself to be proclaimed king, instead of his father David. Adonijah, like his brother Absalom, was an ambitious young man, but not very successful. This well is one hundred and twenty-five feet deep. The water is sweet and good.

Leaving the well, En-Rogel, we now turn up the Valley of Jehoshaphat, following the road along the margin of the brook Kidron. Two or three hundred yards bring us to the King's Gardens, a beautiful spot, highly cultivated. Hard by is the Pool of Siloam, into which we descend and drink of the pure water, which is clear as crystal. Nehemiah (iii. 15) mentions the King's Gardens as being beside the Pool of Siloah. On the opposite side of the valley from this pool is the village of Siloam, clinging to the rocky side of the Mount of Offence. It was here the tower fell and killed the eighteen men. As to the Pool of Siloam, you of course remember the story of the man who was born blind, and restored to sight by washing in this pool. We all likewise wash in it. Not far above this pool is the Fountain of the Virgin, at which, says the legend, women accused of adultery in former times were compelled to drink. If innocent, it harmed them not; but if guilty, they died immediately. When the Virgin Mary was accused, she submitted to the ordeal, and thus established her innocence. Hence its name. We now pass innumerable tombs. The slope of the hill to the right is full of them, and many are hewn out in the rocky cliffs, and now stand open and ghastly. Higher up the valley we pass the tombs of Absalom, Zechariah, and the Apostle James. They are near together, are large and finely ornamented tombs, cut in the side of the mountain. The tomb of Absalom is the finest, but the massive stone monument is defaced by the millions of pebbles that have been cast against it by the Jews, who continue to this day to throw stones at it as they pass. Absalom was a comely youth, and no doubt had a most beautiful suit of hair, but he was an undutiful, rebellious son, and the Jews have not forgotten his wicked rebellion. Hence they cast stones at his tomb.

Continuing up the valley, we reach the tomb of the Virgin Mary, a very large grotto, into which we descend by an easy flight of stone steps. It is finely decorated, and scores of gold and silver lamps are kept burning here continually, before and above the resting-place of the mother of our Saviour. The body of the Virgin's mother also lies in this grotto.

A stone's-throw from the tomb of the Virgin is the garden of Gethsemane, on what may be called the first bench of the Mount of Olives. It is enclosed with a high wall, and occupies perhaps an acre of ground. We enter by a low iron door, and find the garden well kept, being ornamented with many pretty flowers. There are a dozen or more olive trees in the garden which bear marks of very great age. At the lower side of the garden, in a little summer-house, we all assemble and join in religious service: reading the Scripture account of the sufferings and betrayal in this garden, singing, and prayer. After gathering a small bunch of flowers, we leave the garden, and ascend to the summit of the Mount of Olives. What a splendid view we have from here! We see the entire city. Every house is in view, and as nearly every one is surmounted with a dome, the scene is very pleasing. We rest here and gaze at the city and its environs for a long time. Our Saviour has sat here many times and overlooked his beloved city—ay, and wept over it too. We open the book and read the account of his weeping over it, and of his oft retiring here to pray. And now we read of his triumphal ride upon the ass from here into the city, when he entered the Temple and drove out the money-changers and them that bought and sold in his Father's house. From where we sit we see the "gate called Beautiful," through which he passed. It is walled up now, but we see the beautiful double arch in the wall. While our party rest and read, we climb an olive tree (there are hundreds of them still upon the Mount) and cut several walking-canes, which we will carry home as souvenirs. We get half a dozen, which we shall present to Rev. Mr. —— and others, if we are fortunate enough to get them home. We will come to-night and get more, as the keeper of the grounds is coming this way.

We now go across the hill and descend to the quiet village of Bethany. It is but a Sabbath-day's journey (about two and a half miles) from the city. We find the village cosily nestled in a little glen surrounded by high hills, the sides of which are covered with olive, fig, apricot, and almond trees.

Many of the houses are in ruins, but still there is a considerable population. We first sit down on the grass, in the shade, and read in the Scriptures about Martha and Mary and Lazarus, and about the great miracle wrought here. Then descend into the cave which was the tomb of Lazarus. Coming out, we go up the hill a little way to the ruins of an old stone building which is said to be the same in which that happy family lived, and where our blessed Saviour used to retire and commune with them as his dearly beloved friends. The house of Simon the leper is also shown, close by. Gathering a few flowers, we retrace our steps towards the city, and enter the gate of St. Stephen, by the sheep-market. Here we find more lepers. They are about the only beggars we find in Jerusalem. We pass through the city, and emerge from the Damascus gate at the north, and go through a large olive-grove to the Tombs of the Kings—massive excavations in the rock, where it is said the shepherd kings of Israel were entombed. A description of the deep recesses and windings of these excavations would be profitless.

Returning to the city by the Bethlehem gate, we mount the wall and make the circuit of the city, a long but interesting walk.

Descending from the wall, we take a look at the interior of the city. Half a minute's walk satisfies us that Jerusalem is a city more pleasant to look at from a distance than to walk in. The streets are from eight to twelve feet wide, and in many places arched over, which renders them quite gloomy.

They are substantially paved, but as no rubbish ever seems to be removed from them, they are not so clean as could be desired. The main streets, and especially the bazaars, are densely crowded with people. It is hard to make way through some of them. We see every variety of costume, and every cast of feature, and hear almost every language that is spoken under the sun. No danger of losing our way in Jerusalem; for the streets cross each other at right angles, and there are various landmarks to guide us. The bazaars are well supplied with almost every variety of goods, which look like they have been handled for years. Beads seem to be the principal article of merchandise in that portion of the city convenient to the Church of the Holy Sepulchre; nor are mother-of-pearl crucifixes, and other ornaments, forgotten. I think several wagons might be loaded with these things.

But we must not long linger in Jerusalem at this time. However interesting the ground on which we walk, we must leave it; for there are other places intensely interesting that must be seen. We love to sojourn in the city where the Lord of the whole earth has walked and talked and suffered and died; to walk over the ground and gaze upon scenes once familiar to David and Solomon, and the kings and priests who succeeded them; where Peter, and Paul, and James, and John, and the other apostles, have preached the gospel of Jesus Christ; to linger about the hill of Zion and Mount Moriah, where the ark of the covenant rested, and where

God himself was wont to meet face to face with his peculiar people. But we must leave these scenes for a season. Our dragoman tells us that the horses and all things are now ready for our departure for Hebron. We shall now be dwellers in tents for a few weeks. We are all glad of it; for there is a romance about tent-life really charming, especially at this season of the year, when the sky is cloudless, the air balmy, and the whole face of the earth covered with beautiful wild flowers.

Mrs. Smith is almost crazy to get under way. Smith has loaded himself down with pistols and swords, and swears he is a match for forty Bedouins; which gentry are said to infest the region through which we travel, and sometimes relieve travellers of their extra change and clothing. He has also bought him a lance, to which he has fastened the American flag, the same we had on the Nile.

The horses are brought to our hotel door. We mount and issue forth from the Bethlehem gate, and file down through the valley of Hinnom, the gallant Captain Smith leading the party. I wish I could paint you a picture of our leader, as he now appears at the head of the column. He looks venerable, for his gray beard is long and flowing. He has ignored his hat, and now wears an enormous turban and tarbouche. Is almost buried to his waist in high-top boots, with huge spurs attached to them. A red silk Damascus shawl around his waist, in which are a couple of long navy pistols, and two more hung at his saddle-bow; his long lance gracefully couched, and the stars and stripes gayly streaming from his head. And then to see how proudly the old gentleman sits upon his Arab steed—the picture is refreshing. We are all proud of Smith, feeling assured that, with him to lead, we shall have a safe passage through all the Bedouin tribes in Syria.

We take the high road to Hebron, which, in any other country but this, would not deserve the name of road at all. The first object of interest that attracts our attention along the way is——

But perhaps I had better reserve the account of our excursion for another letter, which I will write when I feel like it. I am tired now.

Yours truly,   HAL.

LETTER XXVIII.

JERUSALEM TO HEBRON—THE JORDAN, DEAD SEA, JERICHO, ETC.

My last letter left our party winding up the "Hill of Evil Counsel" from the valley of Hinnom, having just emerged from the Bethlehem gate of Jerusalem, and taken the high-road to Hebron. With your permission, we will now continue that journey. Our tents and camp-equipage have gone forward on baggage mules, and we will amble on at our leisure. Smith is riding proudly at our head, looking as much like a brigand chief as civilized man ever looked; and, to confess the truth, his followers (except the ladies) look little less suspicious than himself. The only redeeming feature in the picture is the American flag, waving gracefully from the spearhead of our gallant and venerable leader, whose horse is rearing, pitching, and curvating like a tight-rigged ship on a rough sea. We should like it if our friends could see that horse. Smith calls him "Dare-devil," and a dare-devil he is, and no mistake. A "hard"-looking animal he is, but "mettle" to the back-bone. Has a long and exceedingly gaunt body —legs ditto. A slim neck, which inclines to bow up instead of down, and the head attached to it is longer than a flour-barrel. His ears point straight up, and his tail, almost innocent of hair, points straight out behind. Baskets could be hung upon his hip-bones. But what an eye! It is one of the most villainous eyes ever stuck into a horse's head, and protrudes so far that you might knock it off with a stick, and never touch the head! We greatly admire this "Arab steed," and so does Smith, who selected him solely on account of his villainous eye. The rest of our horses were like unto Smith's in appearance, but wanting in mettle. They all have "bottom," however, and possess that quality peculiarly necessary to horses in Palestine—i. e., the ability to climb ladders, stone walls, and to walk on stilts. None but those who have travelled over the roads of this country will understand what this means.

The morning is a delicious one. The gentle spring sun is just warm enough to make us feel comfortable. The whole face of the earth seems to be covered with wild flowers of every hue and color, and we all press forward with glad hearts and buoyant hopes. The natives stare at us as we clatter over the hard stone road, in our unique costumes, but in our hilarity we heed them not.

The first object of interest that attracts our attention in the way, is a well in the middle of the road, called the "Well of the Wise Men," because there is a tradition that the wise men who came from the East to Bethlehem to worship the infant Saviour, drank and rested here after their conference with that bloody villain, Herod. One hour farther on, and we reach the tomb of Rachel, the wife of Jacob, and mother of Joseph and Benjamin. The tomb is enclosed in a little white stone building, and is alike venerated by all sects—Jews, Christians, and Moslems. The account of the death and burial of Rachel in this place is familiar to every Bible reader. It is brief and graphic, and we read it here on the spot with more than ordinary interest: "They journeyed from Bethel, and there was but a little way to come to Ephrath. . . . And Rachel died, and was buried in the way to Ephrath, which is Bethlehem. And Jacob set a pillar upon her grave; and that is the pillar of Rachel's grave unto this day." Lamps are kept continually burning before this tomb. Half an hour farther is Bethlehem, but as we have set out for Hebron, we leave Bethlehem to the left and go forward. Two hours' ride brings us to the "Pools of Solomon." These pools are so much more magnificent than we expected to find them, that we are struck with astonishment. We had not expected to see works of half the magnitude. But then we must remember that Solomon was a very rich man, and generally "bored with a big auger;" that is, did up things on a large scale. He certainly did in the way of building pools, for here they are yet to speak for themselves. They are mostly excavated in the solid rock. The largest one is two hundred yards long, two hundred feet wide, and fifty feet deep! The other two are immense, but not quite so large as the first. They are perhaps half full of water now. Here King Solomon had his country-seat—his gardens and vineyards—and here too, no doubt, he, with his many wives and concubines, used to have good times wandering through the groves and gardens, and bathing in these pools.

Leaving the pools, we continue towards Hebron, over the ancient road which was doubtless trodden centuries upon centuries ago by Abraham, Isaac, and Jacob, and many prophets, priests, and kings. The road is sadly out of repair now, and as we view the great heaps of stones over which our horses pick their way, we are tempted to doubt the possibility of war-chariots ever having passed this way. The country through which we pass is mostly barren and desolate, and nothing of peculiar interest attracts our attention until we find ourselves entering the vineyards of Eshcol. Here we find cultivation carried to perfection. Every hill-side (and there is scarcely any thing else) is terraced, and every foot of ground that can bear a vine is planted, and the stones so arranged as to prevent the earth washing. Every vineyard has its stone "tower" in the centre, and in some places we can see as many as fifty of these "towers" at one time. These vineyards were once owned and cultivated by the gigantic sons of Anak, and it was from here that the spies sent out from the Israelitish camp obtained the great clusters which so astonished their brethren. Eshcol would be a good place to pass through in the grape season.

We now approach Hebron. Its frowning stone walls and towers loom up before us. We do not enter the city now, but proceed to our tents, which are pitched in a pretty green common just before the town, hard by the pool over which King David hung the assassins of Ishbosheth, as related in 2 Samuel iv. 12. This is our first entree into camp, and we are hugely pleased with the prospect. All things look neat and in order, and we dismount and look about us. Here are four tents. The first and largest is given up to Mr. and Mrs. Smith, Miss Kissiah, and Miss Jemima; the second to Davis, Green, and Pipkins; the third to Jones, Brown, and myself, and the fourth is for the dining-saloon and servants. We glance at our furniture, and are astonished at the great display made by the few packages brought on the mules. The table is already spread, and is groaning (tables always "groan," you know) beneath the weight of a smoking dinner which has been got up with astonishing rapidity by Demetri, our new cook. The table is large enough for ten persons to sit around comfortably, and yet it can be rolled up into a bundle so small that you can almost carry it under your arm. Ten chairs surround it, which can be reduced in like proportion. As to our bedsteads, or cots, they can be rolled up in bundles little larger than so many umbrellas. Those two comparatively small boxes carry all our table and kitchen furniture. One mule carries both, besides the "kitchen," (simply a sheet-iron trough with holes punched in the bottom, and folding legs,) and a bag of charcoal to cook with, firewood being a luxury rarely enjoyed in Palestine. In short, our household and kitchen furniture is complete, and we are utterly astonished to see with what facility it can be packed (including tents and all) and transported from place to place.

Now, although we are somewhat elated with our new mode of life—the luxury and novelty of living in tents—still there is a slight sense of uneasiness in the camp this evening. We are surrounded with a horde of the natives, whose savage frowns are any thing but pleasant. These Hebronites are a savage, fierce people, and hate "Christian dogs," as they call us, with a perfect hatred; and we are therefore on our best behavior. Smith bustles about, and tries to appear unconcerned, but he frankly acknowledges the corn to me that they are not just the kind of people with whom he would like a muss. Were they Egyptians, or ordinary Arabs, Smith's "koorbash" would have played havoc among them in short order; but they are not Egyptians nor ordinary Arabs, so he lets them alone, and wisely, too. It would be a great relief to all of us if they would leave, but we dare not tell them so, for fear of a shower of stones.

Hebron is perhaps the oldest inhabited city in the world. We don't know its age, but in Numbers xiii. 22, we read that it was built "seven years before Zoan in Egypt." When Zoan was built we do not know, except that it was built seven years after Hebron. That must have been a long time ago, for

Zoan has been a heap of ruins for centuries. We care little, however, about the age of Hebron. We know that Abraham used to live here, and that his bones are still here, resting quietly in the cave of Machpelah. This "faithful" man and "friend of God" was buried here more than thirty-seven hundred years ago, and during all that time his descendants have reverenced the spot, and Christians and Moslems do the same. The remains of Isaac and Jacob, Sarah, Rebecca, and Leah, are also buried in this cave. With the exception of Jerusalem, no place on earth is more hallowed by high and sacred associations than this venerable old city of Hebron. Here the old patriarchs communed with God, and received the promises of the covenant. David once lived here—was anointed king, and made this his capital for some seven or eight years. It was here in Hebron that Joab assassinated Abner. His tomb is within a stone's-throw of our encampment. The rebellious Absalom, whose tomb we saw in the valley of Jehoshaphat, made this his headquarters during the time of his rebellion against his good old father David.

Hebron is a much more imposing city than we expected to find it. The houses are all built of large hewn stone, and look like they might stand for ever, for they stand upon a rock. It contains ten or twelve thousand inhabitants, all fierce Mohammedans, except a few miserable Jews, who only exist by sufferance. There are no Christians. Indeed, it is hardly safe for Christians to *visit* here, as we are now doing, much less reside among these bigoted, fanatical Moslems. Visitors are fortunate indeed if they get away from here without being insulted, if not stoned from the heights above the camping-ground.

Our fancy does not lead us to wander through the streets of Hebron to any considerable extent. It is not pleasant to be followed up and hooted at by crowds of yellow-skinned devils; we therefore content ourselves with a visit to the mosque which stands over the Cave of Machpelah, and make as near an approach to the bones of the old patriarchs and their wives as possible—no Christian being allowed under any pretence to enter the cave. We also visit the tomb of Abner, and the ancient pool before alluded to.

Having seen all of Hebron that we desire to see, we start back towards Jerusalem over the same road we came, making a little detour just after leaving the city, to see the last surviving oak in the vale of Mamre. It was here that old Father Abraham first pitched his tent, and dug a well, which still affords an ample supply of excellent water. We drink of it, and rest beneath the shade of this broad-spreading oak, and read in our Bibles about the visit of the angels to the old patriarch, when he dwelt perhaps just here where we sit. The scene around us is one of the most beautiful in Palestine, the rugged hills standing out in bold relief, each possessing a distinct feature of its own, unlike the hills of any other country, while the rich olive-groves and vineyards remind us the while that we are not in the land of the West. We feel that we are upon holy ground. Every view the eye rests upon was seen as we now see it by Abraham, Isaac, and Jacob, by Samuel, David, and Solomon. The cities they built or dwelt in are now heaps of ruins, but the features of nature remain unchanged—the mountains, the valleys, the fountains, the rocks are all here. Many a time and oft have these good men of old walked up and down this lovely vale of Mamre, communing with the great God himself, and covenanting to serve him faithfully. They, too, like other men, have wept before the Cave of Machpelah.

But beautiful as is the scene, and pleasant as is the shadow of this brave old oak, we must not linger here. No, the Vale of Mamre, the well and oak where Abraham and righteous Lot have oft communed together, the very ground where angels have stood, and the vineyards of Eshcol, must all be left behind, for we must rest in Bethlehem to-day. We cut a few slips from the grape-vines to carry home with us, and then take the highway towards the city of David. At the Pools of Solomon we rest, and partake of our noonday repast. We here leave the Jerusalem road, and strike off to the right, down a beautiful valley, filled with clusters of olive, fig, almond, and apricot trees. Two hours' ride brings us to Bethlehem, whose streets we traverse, feeling that every footfall is upon holy ground. Our party enter the gates of the city chanting that good old song,

"The star, the star of Bethlehem."

We go first, of course, to the "Church of the Nativity," whose sacred walls we enter with awe and reverence. The story of the Child of Bethlehem is known to the world. We enter the grotto, and stand before the very place where the Saviour was born. Near by is the manger in which he was laid. We open our Bibles and read the interesting story, which seems now more interesting than ever before. We read about the wise men coming in and worshipping the child, and presenting their costly gifts; and also about the shepherds coming in from the field, after the light had shone about them, and the angel, with a multitude of the heavenly host, had appeared unto them, praising God and saying, "Glory to God in the highest, and on earth peace, good-will toward men." These shepherds knew that a Prince and Saviour was born into the world, and "they returned glorifying and praising God for all things that they had heard and seen." This place was a stable then, and a gloomy place, no doubt; but Joseph and Mary were thrust here "because there was no room for them in the inn." This grotto with its costly trappings, and the other sacred places about this great old church, have been so often described that we deem it unnecessary to do more than to look on and try to realize the fact that we are actually in the very place where Jesus was born.

Bethlehem, although an imposing little city, as seen from a distance, is not a place in which one desires to tarry long. When we have seen the

"Church of the Nativity," and its appendages, we depart toward Jericho, the Jordan, and the Dead Sea, not forgetting to take with us a guard of Bedouins—thieves whom we hire to protect us from other thieves; for there is nothing more certain than that, if a man undertakes to go down to Jericho without an escort, he will fall among thieves, and be left wounded and naked on the way. The country through which we pass is indescribable. The hills are utterly barren, and look as though a scathing fire had just passed over them, consuming every green or combustible thing. Smith says these hills seem to have been dropped down at random, and then stirred up. If they looked in old times as now, I wonder much that Moses did not turn away with disgust when he viewed them from Mount Pisgah. To be gathered to his fathers just at that time, should have been matter of congratulation, rather than regret, with the great leader of Israel. But they possibly may have been fruitful then, or he may have had a spiritual view of the goodly country beyond these hills.

But we must hasten on, or this letter will be too long, if it is not already verging that way. It is hardly worth the time and space to record the confusion, not to say consternation, into which our party is thrown by our foremost escort, who comes galloping back at full speed, with the startling information that a large force of robbers is in a ravine just ahead, waiting for us. It is now that our gallant Smith shows his "grit." He takes command in earnest, forms us into compact order, and takes his position at the head. Examines his pistols, couches his lance, and, looking as fierce as a thunder-cloud, puts "Dare-devil" into a gallop, and cries, "Come on, boys!" We follow, each man ready with his revolver, keeping a sharp lookout. We gallop on, and on, and on, and finally reach the margin of the Dead Sea, without meeting with the enemy, or even seeing his track. We now know that the alarm was a mere trick of our guard, to see if we were spunky. Had we shown the "white feather," they would have robbed us themselves. All honor to Smith for his gallant bearing on the trying occasion.

We arrive at the shores of the Dead Sea. Like everybody else who comes here, we pull off our clothes and "pitch in," and, like everybody else, we of course find the water intensely salt and tremendously buoyant. We lie on the surface, and float without an effort. Come out, and by the time we get our clothes on, are encrusted with a thin layer of salt. Fill our bottles with water, pick up a few handsome pebbles, mount our horses, and make tracks for the Jordan, to wash the salt off our bodies, which begins to sting and prickle rather uncomfortably.

An hour's ride across the plain brings us to the banks of the Jordan, whose rushing waters come down like a mill-race. Before us, beyond the river, the mountains of Moab loom up, dark and frowning. We see the peaks of Pisgah, and also Mount

Gilead. These mountains and this river we have read of from our youth up, and we now look upon them with gladness. We are soon stripped and in the cooling waters, splashing and diving in the most hilarious manner; for it is a great relief to get the salt washed off. After bathing to our hearts' content, we come out and sing that good old song,

"On Jordan's stormy banks I stand," etc.,

which certainly are not "stormy" now. Eat our lunch, and, under the shade of the trees upon the bank, we read in our Bibles about "those days" when John came preaching and baptizing, perhaps in this very place. It was here that the great multitudes flocked to hear the preaching of John; and it was here, or hereabouts, that the Saviour himself was baptized, when the Spirit of God descended upon and proclaimed him the Son of the Almighty. And it was in this immediate neighborhood that Joshua led the conquering hosts of Israel over into the promised land.

But evening approaches, and we must needs sleep at Jericho to-night, and that is two hours away; a very pleasant ride, however, across the level plain. Our ride is enlivened, too, by a tilting match between Smith and Brown, who seize this first opportunity (it is the first level ground we have passed over) to test the real mettle and speed of their charges. They perform their parts to admiration, both horses and riders, until toward the close of the fun, when Smith is thrown at least twenty feet into the midst of a patch of thorn-bushes; from which we extricate the old gentleman with no little difficulty. He is wounded and bleeding, and will bear the marks of the thorns longer than his sojourn in Palestine. His spear-head is broken off, but our dragoman repairs the damage soon after we get into camp.

Jericho we find a miserable village, filled with the poorest kind of Arabs. Even the traces of the old walls which fell down at the blowing of the rams' horns are gone. The glory of Jericho has long since departed, and its palaces are heaps of ruins, outside the village. Our tents are pitched in a beautiful situation on the banks of the brook Cherith, which flows from the fountain of Elisha— the same fountain whose waters were once bitter, but were healed and made sweet by that prophet. He healed them by putting in a cruse of salt, and they remain healed unto this day. There are remains of an old house here, which tradition says is the house of Zaccheus, where our Saviour stopped when in Jericho. The tree that Zaccheus climbed is not to be seen. Jesus was in Jericho when word was brought him that his friend Lazarus was sick at Bethany. We leave our encampment here, and follow the same road which our Saviour travelled, when going up to Bethany to raise Lazarus from the dead. About half-way to Jerusalem we pass by the ruins of a large stone building, said to have been once an inn, possibly the same in which the

Samaritan lodged the poor fellow who fell among thieves. The road all the way to Bethany is despicable, and the country most of the way utterly barren, and encumbered with large rocks. Our horses know their business, however, and take us safely through. Smith says he don't believe there is a more truthful passage in Scripture than that which says,

"Jordan is a hard road to travel;"

and we all agree with Smith; for a worse road is not to be found.

We pass through Bethany—over a shoulder of the Mount of Olives—through the valley of Jehoshaphat, and again enter the walls of Jerusalem, where we shall remain a few days, and then proceed on our tour in the North of Palestine and Syria. Adieu. HAL.

LETTER XXIX.

JERUSALEM TO TIBERIAS.

INASMUCH as you accompanied our party on a tour from Jerusalem to Hebron, the Dead Sea, the Jordan, Jericho, and back to Jerusalem, it is but right and proper that you continue with us during the rest of our wanderings in the Holy Land. Therefore, if you will consent to go, you shall see what you shall see.

Great preparations have been made for our departure to the North. Smith has been the main spirit in fitting out the expedition, and has thereby brought the rest of us under renewed obligations to him. I do not know how we should get along without Smith, for he is certainly an "institution," and the most active one I ever knew. He attends to every thing—dragoman, servants, and horses— and when things don't go to suit him, he swears like a trooper, in Arabic—for he has picked up at least twenty words of the language, which he uses upon all occasions—especially when in a passion, and that is more than half the time. (Smith says it is wonderful how soon a man picks up the language of a country.) Through his influence we have almost doubled the number of our arms, for there are frightful rumors afloat about the ferociousness of the Bedouin Arabs in the mountains; and it is said that the plains of Sharon and Esdraelon swarm with banditti. But our party is large, and we stand in but little fear of the savage descendants of Ishmael. With our bold captain to lead, we feel as if we could ride through a troop of them.

But we must be under way. Pleasant as it is to linger about Jerusalem, we can stay no longer. The jingle of the bells of the baggage mules reminds us that our tents will be pitched at Bethel to-night, and to reach them we must be stirring. While our horses are being got ready, we watch those patient mules filing away under their heavy burdens, and pity them. There are Mrs. Smith's two great heavy trunks strapped across the back of one little animal, so small that it could be put inside of either one of them, and have ample stable-room. It is astonishing to see the amount of baggage carried by a fashionable woman. One-tenth part of the contents of these trunks would be sufficient for the tour of Palestine, and yet the fastidious Mrs. S. insists upon carrying it all. I fear it will be a tempting invitation to the Bedouins to fall upon us. Miss Kissiah Jones is the most sensible woman I have seen travelling in the East. She is content to carry a small valise, in which she carries but one extra dress. She has worn that old brown travelling-dress in which she now appears, until it seems to be a part and parcel of herself.

It is woefully faded under the influence of the pelting African sun, and is becoming beautifully fringed about the bottom of the skirt; but still, Kissiah, with her beaming face, looks well even in it. She wears her other dress only on Sundays. (It is a black silk.) She says she is determined to stick to the "old brown" until the end of the journey—and she is right.

But here are our horses. Let us mount and be off. Smith is first in the saddle, and of course leads the way. Look at him as he rides off; and see with what pride and dignity old "Dare-devil" walks away, with head and tail up, evidently proud of his master. A prouder horse and rider have never sallied forth from the Damascus gate since the days of Saul of Tarsus, who emerged from the same portal about eighteen hundred years ago, breathing out curses upon Christians, while Smith goes forth breathing out Arabic curses upon the head of our dragoman, who is reeling under the influence of a quart of mean brandy; for be it known, that Ibraheem, our Syrian dragoman, is no Mohammedan, but a Christian, and is therefore privileged to indulge in villainous drinks. The order of Good Templars has not yet penetrated Jerusalem. Achmet, our dragoman on the Nile, never drinks, for he is a strict Moslem.

We are now fairly out on the Damascus road, pacing along in single file, for the road is too narrow for two to ride abreast. It is only a camel road, for there are no wheeled carriages in this country—

not even a wheelbarrow. The only thing I have seen on wheels is a cannon on the Tower of Hippicus in Jerusalem. Our road, although narrow and very rough, is a great thoroughfare, as we can see by the long trains of camels we meet. They are mostly laden with goods from Damascus.

Here we leave the Tomb of Helena on the right, cross the upper end of the Kidron, and ascend the hill of Scopus. And here we take our farewell glance at Jerusalem—its domes, and minarets, and gray walls, and the mountains that compass it around, with Olivet at their head. We take a long lingering look back at the sacred spot, and only turn away when the picture grows dim and indistinct through the quivering tear-drop. Jerusalem is enshrined in our affections, and was even before we saw it. We can almost adopt the plaintive, passionate language of the captive Israelite by the waters of Babylon: "If I forget thee, O Jerusalem, let my right hand forget her cunning. If I do not remember thee, let my tongue cleave to the roof of my mouth."

Here on our right, on the top of the hill, is where stood the ancient city of Nob, and just over there is the site of Gibeah. In this little valley between is where the interview between Jonathan and David took place. That large rock we see peering above ground may have been the rock "Ezel," behind which David lay concealed. We sit down here and read 1 Sam. xx., xxi., and xxii., and learn therefrom that tragical events have occurred here and hereabouts. We now go over to Gibeah, on the opposite hill. From the summit we have an intensely interesting view. We see away down into the valley of the Jordan, and the purple-tinted mountains of Moab beyond. On the south we get a peep at some of the buildings on Mount Zion. On the west we see the tomb of the prophet Samuel, over which stands a mosque. On the north is a picturesque village — Ramah, of Benjamin. The sites of Anathoth, Geba, and Michmash, are visible from this point.

On this ground where we now stand once stood the city of Gibeah. Saul, the first King of Israel, lived here; and here occurred that awful tragedy which well-nigh annihilated the tribe of Benjamin. We remember the horrible story of the Levite and his concubine; and here, on the spot, we read the nineteenth, twentieth, and twenty-first chapters of the book of Judges. Here, too, we read, in 2 Sam. xxi., of the hanging of the seven descendants of Saul, and of the maternal tenderness of the bereaved mother, Rizpah.

A little farther on we pass the village of Ramah, of Benjamin, and notice nothing else of interest until reaching Bethel. Here we read the story of Jacob's slumber and dream, etc. Here the country begins to grow better, and olive-groves, vineyards, and fig-orchards now begin to take the place of that bleak, barren sterility through which we have been coming ever since leaving Jerusalem. Wild flowers cover the ground, and we pass in sight of some pretty villages perched upon the tall hills. We have now left the territory of Benjamin, and entered that of Ephraim, and the fertility around us reminds us that he was blessed with "the precious fruits brought forth by the sun, . . . and the precious things of the lasting hills."

Now we approach a dark and narrow defile between two high mountains. It has a startling name, and is the dread of faint-hearted travellers. It is called the "Robbers' Glen." Scarcely a season passes that murderous deeds are not committed here. Before entering it we look well to our pistols and ride as close together as possible. Smith unfurls his flag and takes the lead with as much pride as Don Quixote ever rode forward to attack an audacious windmill. "Dare-devil" seems to snuff the battle afar off, and enters the gorge with as little trepidation as his bold rider. See the old gentleman as he rises in his stirrups and presses forward! Bold indeed will be the brigand who hurls a lance at that figure. A whole troop may well pause and consider before attacking our brave captain, for his arms are numerous and in good order—and Smith is a man who will not hesitate to use them. Besides his long, keen lance, he carries two of Colt's repeaters at his saddle-bow, two "volcanic repeaters" in his belt, and a double-barrel gun strapped to his back. So you see he is capable of firing thirty shots, besides doing immense execution with his shining spear. And then, too, the appearance of the man will do much towards gaining us a victory. His tall figure, flowing gray beard, huge turban, red shirt, brilliant sash, high red-top boots, and ponderous spurs—these things are enough to strike terror into the ranks of the most daring banditti. We all glory in Smith, and well we may, for he is a jewel.

But we pass the "Robbers' Glen," and see "nary" robber. The country still improves, and our ride is most charming. The terraced hills are so quaint, the winding valleys so picturesque, the wild flowers so brilliant and so plentiful, the sombre foliage of the olive, the deep green of the fig, and bright green of the growing wheat on the terraces, all give such exquisite hues to the landscape! Add to this the gray ruins perched upon the hilltops, and the peasants in their gay dresses, red and green and white, and the strings of mules and donkeys and camels, defiling along the narrow paths, their bells awaking the echoes; and the Arab with his long spear, or old brass-bound, flint-lock musket; and the shepherd leading his goats along the mountain-side, or grouped with them around a fountain; and then—the oddest figure of them all—the traveller from the far-west, with his red face and nondescript trappings! These are the scenes and pictures around us.

But we hasten on to Shiloh—a most interesting spot. We stop under the shade of this huge oak, (the only tree to be seen,) and read some portions of Scripture relating to Shiloh. We find that here the Tabernacle of the Lord was first permanently set up in Canaan; and here the Israelites assembled to receive each his portion of the promised land. It was to this place Samuel, when a child, was brought and dedicated to the Lord. There was a great annual feast held in Shiloh in honor of the ark, at which the village maidens were wont to dance; they probably did up their dancing in this little valley just below us. It was on one of these festive occasions that the remnant of the Benjaminites concealed themselves in the vineyards near by, and suddenly rushing upon the unconscious damsels, carried off two hundred of them. It is to be hoped they got the old maids. The glory of Shiloh departed with the capture of the ark, and it is now but a heap of ruins. We see a few swarthy, thievish-looking rascals prowling around while we read, but either the size of our party, or the formidable appearance of Smith, keeps them at a distance. They would no doubt like to finger our cash.

Leaving Shiloh, we soon enter a rich and most beautiful valley. The country has been improving ever since we entered the domains of Ephraim, and there now seems but little room for further improvement. Such fertile districts are unknown in Judah or Benjamin. Every step we advance proves to us that Ephraim was indeed blessed with the "chief things of the ancient mountains." The first high hill we ascend after leaving this valley reveals a most glorious view. Away over yonder we see on a very high point a little white building of some kind. That is the landmark of Mount Gerizim, and marks the spot where the Samaritan Temple once stood.

Beyond it we see the point of Mount Ebal. Between the two lies the valley and city of Shechem, or Sychar. And far, far away on the northern horizon we discern a peaked cone tipped with snow; that is Hermon!

Two or three hours' riding brings us to Jacob's Well, just at the entrance of the valley of Shechem, and near the base of Gerizim. Here the Saviour rested at noonday, wearied no doubt with the long walk up the hot plain, having come, like ourselves, from Jerusalem. There is but little to be seen at this well, for it is almost filled up, but we stop and read the story of that strange interview between our Lord and the Samaritan woman. The little white enclosure we see near by is Joseph's tomb. His body was brought up from Egypt, and buried in this place. Half an hour's ride up the valley brings us to Shechem, situated among the finest scenery in Palestine, and one of the most beautiful sites for a city from Dan to Beersheba. It is in a narrow valley, with the steep mountains of Ebal and Gerizim towering up on either side. Shechem has a population of about eight or ten thousand, the most villainous set of people we have seen since leaving Hebron. They take pride in hating Christians, and we must be particular not to offend them, or we may get up an unpleasant affair. We go into the synagogue of the Samaritans, (there are still a few here,) and are shown a manuscript copy of the law, which the high-priest tells us is three thousand five hundred years old.

It was in Shechem that Abraham first pitched his tent in Canaan; Jacob also settled here, and perhaps lived near where he dug his well. He bought that "parcel of a field" where his well is from Hamor, Shechem's father, and there was buried his favorite son Joseph. After removing from Shechem down to Hebron, Jacob still retained his plantation here, and it was to his fields here that he sent Joseph in quest of his brethren, to see if "it was well with them and well with their flocks." They had removed to Dothan, twelve miles farther. The little fellow in his "coat of many colors" followed them up with the message of his good old father, and they sold him to the Ishmaelites.

As this was the place where the patriarchs first settled in Canaan, so it was, many hundred years later, the place where their descendants gathered after coming up out of Egypt, and here, on Mount Gerizim and Mount Ebal, the blessing and cursing took place that we read about in Deuteronomy, xxvii. and xxviii. In different parts of the Scriptures we find that many highly interesting and important events occurred here in old times, but we will read them at our leisure, when we have more time. Those villainous Shechemites who eye us so closely would perhaps rather see us move on.

The next place of importance at which we halt is Samaria, once a great and royal city, but now only a village. Within the walls of an old ruined church is said to be the tomb of John the Baptist. From the commanding position, and the numerous evidences of fine architecture, Samaria must have been a most beautiful city. None of the ancient buildings are standing, but the great hewn stones and the multitude of columns show that it was superior, in beauty at least, to any thing we have before seen in Palestine. There are hundreds of columns still standing, and hundreds more lying prostrate, scattered over a vast extent of ground. In one place, on a beautiful terrace along the hill-side, stands a row of columns near three-quarters of a mile in length. There was once a double row of them fifty feet apart, but nearly all of one of the rows have been thrown down, and have rolled down the hill. In many other places columns are standing in rows and squares. Vineyards and olive-groves now cover the grounds, and magnificent specimens of carved stones lie scattered about among them, from the top of the hill even down into the valley. The origin of this city is told with simplicity and clearness, in 1 Kings xvi. 23, 24. Its destruction was foretold by Micah; and, as we stand on the hill and look on these columns shooting up from clustering vines and green wheat, and the great heaps among the olive trees in the valley below, we read with thrilling interest the striking and fearful prediction of that prophet, "I will make Samaria as an heap of the field, and as plantings of a vineyard; and I will pour down the stones thereof into the valley, and I will discover the foundations thereof." This prophecy is fulfilled to the very letter. The cause of this destruction we learn from Hosea

11

xiii. 16: "Samaria shall become desolate, for she hath rebelled against her God."

Leaving Samaria, we traverse a most picturesque and highly cultivated section of country. A ride of six miles brings us to one of the richest and most beautiful little plains we have seen. It is Dothan. Here is where Joseph found his brethren with their flocks the day they sold him. Elisha the prophet once lived here.

A few hours' ride, and our hearts are rejoiced as we enter that celebrated and extensive plain of Esdraelon. It is extensive, rich, and beautiful, and is drained by the river Kishon. This has been the great battle-field of Palestine. The names of the mountains which surround this plain are familiar to every one who reads the Bible—and the towns are also known. Upon entering the plain, we pass through Jezreel, once the royal city where Ahab built his palace. We stop and open our Bibles, and in the twenty-first chapter of First Kings read the story of poor Naboth and his vineyard, and the cruelty of the crafty Jezebel. We are now at the base of Mount Gilboa, where Saul and Jonathan fell. Tabor and Little Hermon are in plain view. We pass through the towns of Shunem, Nain, and Endor. In fact, every village, hill, and valley we see in this section, possesses scriptural interest. There have been innumerable battles fought and rivers of blood shed just where we now are. Here the Israelites have fought with the Midianites, the Amalekites, the Philistines, the Syrians, and all the

Canaanitish tribes, time and again. Here, too, many of the prophets lived. We pause in Nain, and read the touching story of the raising from the dead of the widow's son by our Lord. In Endor we read of Saul's interview with the witch, when she called up the Prophet Samuel.

In the distance, away to the left, we see the blue summit of Mount Carmel, and straight ahead, away across the plain, rises Tabor, a tall single cone standing all alone. We press forward to the latter, for we must camp there to-night. As we cross the rich plain, we are amazed to see what a small proportion of it is cultivated. But then we must remember that there is no encouragement here for industry. This is the home of the thievish Bedouin, who scours the smooth surface of the plain on his fleet mare in search of plunder. This region has always been insecure, both for farmer and traveller, since history began. The Bedouins make frequent incursions from beyond the Jordan, destroy whole crops, and drive off as many cattle as they desire. This knowledge is very annoying to my friend Smith, and he now openly declares himself in favor of fillibusterism. He wants to go home and raise a company of fillibusters, and bring them over here to exterminate the thieving Arabs. He thinks a few hundreds of Uncle Sam's boys would either civilize or exterminate them; but rather favors the latter. Smith generally has very correct notions of things.

We now approach Mount Tabor, certainly the most beautiful mountain we have seen, for it is thickly dotted with small oak trees, a sight we have not before met with in Palestine. A hard climb of fourteen hundred feet brings us to the summit. The view from here is lovely beyond description. We take in the whole plain of Esdraelon at a glance, from the foot of the hill below us to the base of Carmel and Gilboa, one unbroken sea of verdure. Little Hermon is before us, and the villages of Nain and Endor clinging to its side. To the east we see a long stretch of the Jordan valley, and the mountains of Gilead beyond it. To the north-east we see a small portion of the Sea of Galilee, and away, very far away beyond we see the towering cone of snowy Hermon, and a portion of the Lebanon range. On the summit of Tabor we find massive ruins of an ancient city. We know nothing of these ruins. It was evidently a fortified city of immense strength. Many suppose Tabor to be the Mount of Transfiguration. It was in the plain near the base of this mountain that the bloody battle between the French, under Napoleon I., and the Turks, occurred. This would have been a glorious point from which to view the battle.

We now leave Tabor, and proceed to Tiberias, about five hours' ride, where we shall spend the Sabbath—and a fitting place it is to spend the day of rest. Tiberias is a walled town, containing about two or three thousand inhabitants, just on the margin of the Sea of Galilee. It is noted for filth and fleas, the latter of which are without number, and of marvellous size. It is said that the flea congress assembles here, and if so, we can readily believe that they hold night sessions, and present "bills" incessantly. We can here sing with *feeling* that beautiful parody which runs thus:

> "Oft in the stilly night,
>   Ere slumber's chains have bound me,
> I feel the cursed bite
>   Of something crawling round me."

Smith carries the bass beautifully, and Miss Kissiah screams out the treble enchantingly.

Almost every spot around this little sea is holy ground, for here is where our Saviour lived, after he was rejected by the people of Nazareth. He taught the multitudes on these shores, and chose some of his apostles from the fishing-boats on its waters. But these shores at that day were not so silent and desolate as now; they were teeming with life. Several cities lay at intervals along its margin —such as Capernaum, Chorazin, the two Bethsaidas, Gamala, Hippas, Scythopolis, Gadara, Tiberias, etc., etc. Vast multitudes lived here, and they followed the Lord daily to hear his preaching. Sometimes he was so thronged that he would enter into a boat and thrust out from the shore. Just over yonder we see the place where he once fed five thousand people with a few loaves and fishes; and just here, on this little hill, he fed another company of seven thousand in a like miraculous manner. We read our Bible here with intense interest, because the scenes to which they relate were here. Just opposite to where we now stand is the place where

Gadara stood, and where the Gadarenes were so alarmed at the teachings and power of the Lord.

We take a boat and sail partly round the sea, (it is but a little sea,) and visit the ruins of many of the ancient cities, such as Capernaum, Chorazin, etc., all of which possess wonderful interest. We spend most of Saturday and the whole of Sunday in wandering, and reading the Scriptures—not forgetting to bathe in the sacred waters. The only inhabited city on this sea now is Tiberias, and it seems going to destruction.

Our sail upon the sea is very pleasant, for there is just breeze enough to waft our little ship merrily along. As we sail we read the story of the great storm that once occurred here, and the great calm which followed, when our Saviour rebuked the winds. We read, too, of his walking upon the water, and of Peter's daring attempt to do the same.

We leave Tiberias to-morrow for Nazareth, having changed the plan of our route. The danger of robbers along the road, and some of our party being pressed for time, we shall not go to Damascus, but proceed to Beyrout, by way of Tyre, Sidon, etc.—a more interesting route, I think, than the one by Damascus, for it will take us by Cana and Nazareth and Carmel, and many other places I desire to see. Farewell till I write again. HAL.

LETTER XXX.

TIBERIAS TO BEYROUT.

There is a commotion in our camp this morning —a running to and fro of our party, and an expression of alarm on every countenance. Brown is missing! Yes, the daring Brown, whose long hair and immense beard and moustache have rendered him the admiration of the ladies of our party—especially Mrs. Smith—is gone, and nobody knows where, though all believe that he is kidnapped by the Bedouins. Search has been made for him upon the hills and all along the sea-shore, and whoops and yells have been echoed from crag to crag in vain. Brown answers not. He went quietly to bed in his tent last night, and has not been seen since. He must be in the hands of the banditti, for breakfast has now been ready and waiting for half an hour, and still he comes not—a circumstance never before known since the commencement of our travels—for Brown is not a man to slight the table comforts. Perhaps he has gone up on the Mount of Beatitudes, (which is hard by,) to meditate, perhaps to pray. But no. Brown is not addicted to such practices, that we are aware of. Besides, we have fish—fresh fish from the waters of Galilee—for breakfast, and Brown is astonishingly fond of fish. But we must not stop supinely here. Captain Smith has given the word of command, and we must be in the saddle and away. The country must be scoured, and Smith swears he will kill the first Arab we meet if he give not information of our lost friend—and Smith's oaths are fearful. Arming ourselves is but the work of a moment, and we gallop away from our encampment vowing to eat not until our comrade is found—for it will never do to give Mr. Brown up so! "Dare-devil" and his rider are of course in the lead, and the flag is again unfurled to the morning breeze. We take our course along the margin of the sea of Galilee towards the outlet of the Jordan, for in that region, it is said, the robbers most do congregate.

A brisk ride of a mile brings us within a few hundred yards of the hot springs, which issue from the base of the mountain and flow off into the sea, when—lo, and behold! we see the comely form of the lost Brown issuing from the old building which covers the springs, and innocently taking his course towards us—evidently as much surprised to see us in battle array as we are delighted to see him. He has only been taking a hot bath for his rheumatism, having got up and left the camp before the rest of us were astir. Smith gives him a round cursing (Smith will be profane, notwithstanding the sacredness of the scenes around us) for his imprudence, and we wind our way back to the encampment, feeling a little foolish, where we find the ladies in mortal terror, having seen a couple of armed Arabs prowling near them during our short absence. The delight of again seeing Brown return unharmed, soon recovers them, and Mrs. Smith kindly pats his ruddy cheek, and smilingly tells him he must not do so any more. Mrs. S. seems to have a growing fondness for Brown's moustache.

We sit down to a cold breakfast, and by the time we are through, the tents are struck, the baggage packed, and the jingle of the little bells on the baggage mules is soon heard as they wind their way up the steep mountain side. We mount our horses, take a last look at the beautiful little sea of Galilee, bid farewell to Tiberias and its swarms of fleas, and take the road towards Nazareth—for we must sleep there to-night.

The country through which we travel is very pretty and picturesque—rich, but poorly cultivated. We pass by some very pretty towns—only pretty, however, at a distance — surrounded with rich groves of olive trees. In the distance we see snowy Hermon, and peaks of the Lebanon range. The first town we arrive at possessing scriptural interest is Cana, which, for a wonder, is a neat village, prettily situated on a hill-side, and surrounded by olive and other fruit trees. Cana of Galilee is memorable as the place where our Lord performed his first miracle of changing water into wine at a marriage-feast. Nothing else is recorded of it that I know of. There is a large spring of water just outside the town, from which no doubt the water was taken at the time of our Lord's visit, as it is the only spring near. We see a number of the village damsels around it with their water-pots. In an old Greek church here some water-pots are shown, said to be the same which contained the miraculous wine. We believe as much of the story as we choose. There are remains of an old house here, said to be that of Nathanael.

We now hasten on to Nazareth—one of the most sacred spots on the face of the earth. We find it a picturesque little city, built upon a hill, but surrounded by mountains overtopping it. It contains a population of over four thousand, two-thirds of whom are Christian, and decidedly the cleanest, best-looking, best-mannered people we have found in Palestine. It is the cleanest and best built town we have seen—the houses all built of light-colored stone, with flat roofs.

Nazareth is as a household word throughout Christendom, for it was the home of the Saviour's boyhood, the scene of his early labors, his prayers, and his whole private life. How often must he have run in boyhood about these streets! How often must he have accompanied his mother to this very fountain here, hard by our camp! How often must he have sat with his parents in the quiet evenings on the housetop, as is still the custom! How often must he have wandered over these rocky hill-tops, meditating on his divine mission, and holding sweet communion with his Father! But we have no memorials of this period of the Saviour's life. It is enough for us to know that the Lord dwelt here; that for thirty years he trod this spot of earth, and that his eyes were familiar with the objects spread around. In his public life we know of only two incidents recorded in connection with "the city in which he was brought up." In one instance the Nazarenes were so offended and exasperated when he preached that "they thrust him out of the city, and led him unto the brow of a hill on which their city was built, that they might cast him down headlong." Upon glancing round we can see more than one "brow" which might have answered their wicked designs. From that moment Nazareth ceased to be his home, for " he came and dwelt in Capernaum." When he visited "his own" people again they sneered at him, and said, "Is not this the carpenter, the son of Mary, the brother of James, and Joses, and of Judas, and Simon? And are not his sisters here with us? And they were offended at him."

While in Nazareth we go round of course to see the holy places which the monks are always ready to point out—for money—such as the place of Annunciation, Mary's house, Joseph's carpenter-shop, etc., etc.; but we care for none of these things. It is sufficient for us to know that Jesus and Mary and Joseph lived here. These localities are but guessed at by the monks.

This fountain here just by our camp is called "Mary's Fountain;" and it is said that she was there drawing water when the first salutation of the angel came to her.

From Nazareth we proceed towards Acre, passing near the base of the beautiful Mount Carmel. We do not climb the steep acclivity, but from the plain we see the place where the event occurred which gives to Carmel its chief interest—the place of Elijah's sacrifice. We open our Bibles and read the story as recorded in 1 Kings xviii. 17-46. It was just up there the great multitude of people were assembled to witness the conflict between the one prophet of God and the eight hundred and fifty prophets of Baal. The people no doubt looked on with intense interest, while from morning till noon, and from noon till the time of the evening sacrifice, the priests of Baal cried in vain. When the sun was sinking behind the mountain, Elijah's sacrifice was accepted. The last act of the tragedy was performed on this plain—possibly near where we now stand—when Elijah brought the eight hundred and fifty defeated prophets down to this little river Kishon, and slew them here. Now, reader, get your Bible and read the eloquent portion of Scripture relating this tragedy. Carmel is truly beautiful, its slopes being covered, like those of Tabor, with small trees.

We pass through a lovely region to-day. The plain of Acre is one of the richest in Palestine—producing alike luxuriant crops, and the rankest weeds in the country. The city of Acre is not mentioned in Scripture, so far as I know, but it is certainly one of the most important towns in the country. It is a very strongly fortified place, and contains about five thousand inhabitants, including a garrison of Turkish soldiers. Napoleon called it the key to Palestine. Acre is also called Ptolemais. Many battles have been fought here, and the blood of thousands of brave men has drenched these plains. It was a place of much importance during the time of the crusades. But we must not stop to recount the scenes that have occurred here.

From Acre we take the road to Tyre, which is most of the way along the seashore, and over exceedingly rough spurs of the Lebanon mountains, that jut out into the sea occasionally. In crossing these spurs our horses are called upon to exercise that peculiar talent known only to the horses of this country—to-wit, "getting up stairs" and climbing ladders. We have left Palestine, and are now in Phœnicia, and to-night we sleep at Tyre, the ancient "mistress of the seas." These snowy mountain peaks to our right are the mountains of Lebanon. Just before arriving at Tyre we pass some remarkable fountains and reservoirs of immense size, and which are as old as history itself. The water is brought down in aqueducts from Lebanon, and served in ancient times to supply the great city of Tyre with excellent water. The water is ample to turn any amount of machinery, but it is only used now to turn one solitary mill. Near the fountains we see some beautiful gazelles feeding, but they flee at our approach.

We now approach Tyre, where we rest to-night. We find its walls broken down, and every thing about it having an old and dingy appearance; but still it is not the desolate place we expected to find it. It has a population of three or four thousand, and upon entering the gate we find the streets comparatively clean, and the people looking decidedly respectable for Asiatics. This was once the greatest of the Phœnician cities, even greater than its mother Sidon; and the great number of old columns and sculptured stones we see lying about convince us that a superb style of architecture prevailed here in olden times. These stones and columns are almost innumerable, built up in the modern walls, and piles of them lying in the water, and all along the beach. We are reminded at every step, and by every glance, of the prophecies uttered against this city: "And they shall make a spoil of thy riches, and make a prey of thy merchandise, and they shall break down thy walls, and destroy thy pleasant houses. . . . They shall lament over thee, saying, 'What city is like Tyrus, like the destroyed in the midst of the sea!'" and again, "They shall break down the towers of Tyrus, and make her like the top of a rock. It shall be a place for the spreading of nets in the midst of the sea." Here we see scores of fishermen's nets spread upon the old broken walls, to dry. We sit down here on this exquisitely wrought capital, which once no doubt adorned a graceful column in some magnificent building, and read with intense interest the 27th chapter of Ezekiel, which, for graphic power of description and prophetic accuracy, is probably unequalled in the whole compass of literature. We recommend a perusal of it to our friends.

We are also interested in this city of Tyre because it was once the city of King Hiram—and a very clever man he was, too, no doubt, for he was a particular friend of King David, and furnished that monarch with both materials and workmen to build his palace. There also existed a good understanding between Hiram and Solomon—as always should be the case between high-minded gentlemen—and the former furnished the latter with an immense amount of cedar-wood, etc., for the building of the Temple at Jerusalem. I told the story of Hiram's benevolence to my friend Smith this morning, but he was not disposed to do justice to the Tyrian king. He thought that Hiram knew "which side of his bread was buttered," and only furnished materials to the kings of Israel because he feared them. We think differently.

We make a little excursion to the tomb of King Hiram, which is some distance outside the town. We find it rather a remarkable monument, standing alone, apart alike from human habitation and ancient ruin—a solitary venerable relic of remote antiquity. It is an immense sarcophagus of limestone, hewn out of a single block, twelve feet long, and eight wide, (according to the measure of my walking-cane,) and six high, covered with a lid five feet thick, and resting on a massive pedestal ten feet high. The monument is perfect, though weather-beaten. And here was deposited the remains of Solomon's friend and ally!

Leaving Tyre, we take the road to Sidon, which is through the plain of Phœnicia, where a mournful, solitary silence prevails. The plain between the mountain and the sea is little more than a mile wide, and very rich, but, sad to say, most of it lies waste. The mountain sides and wild glens above are clustering with villages; while every available spot is cultivated in terraces; but the plain is desolate. The only signs of life we see as we ride along are a few Arab tents, and an occasional horseman, armed to the teeth, and oftener a little troop of gazelles. Security for life and property is unknown here save beneath the walls of cities, or amid the mountain-fastnesses. Hence the plains lie waste, while the steep mountain-sides and crevices are cultivated. We find some ancient ruins along the way, but know nothing of them. The only place of scriptural interest we pass is the village of Sarepta, the place where the Prophet Elijah came during the great famine, and met the poor widow woman gathering sticks to prepare her meal. We remember the interview between them, and the sequel: how the widow's meal and oil were miraculously multiplied, and how her dying son was subsequently restored to health by the prophet. These miracles impressed Divine truth upon that poor woman, and she confessed—"Now by this I know that thou art a man of God, and that the word of the Lord in thy mouth is truth." We open our Bibles here and read the touching story in the 17th chapter of 1 Kings. It is said that here is where the Syrophenician woman met the Saviour during his visit to the "coasts of Tyre and Sidon." We read the little story in the 15th chapter of Matthew, and also in the 7th chapter of Mark.

We here get our first view of Sidon, away in the distance, embowered in luxuriant gardens and orchards. The view is most lovely, though three hours' ride distant. Upon entering the city we find the streets after the usual Eastern type, with the usual amount of filth, and running in no particular direction, but winding about promiscuously. Some of the houses, however, approach elegance, especially those along the wall overlooking the orchards. It contains a population of about five thousand. Just outside the town on the seashore we find our tents pitched, and, as usual, surrounded by a swarm of the natives, who are always curious to see strangers. Among the rest we are met by a venerable old gentleman and all his family, consisting of his wife, a son, and four grown daughters. They are Protestant Christians, and meet us as brethren. We are glad to see them, and shake them heartily by the hand. The daughters speak English, having been taught at the Beyrout Mission. They are all dressed in the true Eastern style—the flowing trowsers and long white veils. They carry on a school here, and tell us that they occasionally gain additions to their little Church. A Protestant

Christian is a rare sight in this seemingly God-forsaken country. We do not remember the name of this family—and who could remember a regular Arab name?

We see very few remains of antiquity about Sidon, although it is one of the oldest cities in the world, as we find it mentioned in the tenth chapter of Genesis, along with Gaza and Sodom and Gomorrah. It is said to have been founded by the great-grandson of Noah—and that, you know, was long, long ago. We find many allusions made to this city in various parts of Scripture. Paul touched here when on his voyage to Athens. Sidon was once the mistress of the seas, but afterwards Tyre took the wind out of her sails, and became the great city of the East.

We leave Sidon, and take the road along the seashore to Beyrout, one of the most bleak, barren, desolate roads we ever travelled. We plunge through deep sand, and climb rugged spurs of the mountain from morning till night, with a most withering Syrian sun pouring down upon us without mercy. We shall remember this day's ride as the most—in fact, the *only* disagreeable day of our journey.

But we rejoice not a little as we approach Beyrout. It is like entering Paradise. Before entering the city we pass through a forest of oranges, lemons, figs, almonds, apricots, peaches, pears, olives, pines, and mulberries, all growing luxuriantly, forming a forest of beautifully tinted foliage.

Going into Beyrout is like getting into the "white settlements" after wandering long among savages, for here we see white men, and many buildings that really look European in style. It is a city containing about fifty thousand inhabitants, a good many of whom are Protestant Christians, for the American missionaries have done wonders here.

Here ends our tent-life in Palestine and Syria. Here we bid farewell to mules and horses, for our next ride will be upon the troubled waters of the restless ocean. It is affecting to see the parting between Smith and "Dare-devil;" for truly if man ever loved horse, Smith is the man, and "Daredevil" the horse. Smith has clipped a whisp of hair from the horse's mane, (he has none on his tail,) which he intends to carry as a souvenir. I think a few tears were shed at the parting. We also take leave of Ibraheem, our dragoman, and he, from absolute sorrow, immediately gets on a spree. The same may be said of Halleel, his assistant, and poor Demetri, the cook—for they all claim to be Christians, and are therefore privileged to indulge in villainous drinks. Our tents are furled up, our camp equipage stowed away, and we betake ourselves to the good cheer of the Hotel Bellevue, where we find some other Americans, one of whom, a Mr. Boots, seems to know something about every thing in the world, and takes much delight in telling all he knows. I may tell you something about him at some future time. He is to accompany us to Constantinople, at which we are all of course wonderfully pleased—for Mr. Boots is a man not to be lightly regarded, being a man of huge preponderosity, and marvellous ability. We have already set him down as a trump card.

We remain in Beyrout two or three days to rest, and during the time wander about the city and through the groves and gardens to our hearts' content. We visit the American Mission School and Publishing House, where we are courteously received by Rev. Dr. Van Dyck, Dr. Thomson, and others connected with the Mission. We are all invited to Dr. Thomson's to tea, where we spend one of the most agreeable evenings we have passed since leaving home. We meet many missionaries, and other Americans, among them Rev. Dr. Hatty, from Damascus, Rev. Mr. Porter, from Sidon, and Rev. Mr. Jessup, from Aleppo. Dr. Thomson is a veteran in the missionary cause, having labored here for eighteen years. He is the author of the "Land and the Book," a most excellent work on Palestine.

This country is greatly disturbed now. An old feud between the Maronite Christians and the Druses is being revived, and much bloody work is anticipated. A great many murders have been committed within the last few days in the mountains of Lebanon, between here and Damascus. An open war of extermination between these two sects is anticipated. It matters little which exterminates the other, for they are villains all.

We are now preparing to leave Beyrout. Our

HAL'S TRAVELS.   341

steamer sails for Constantinople to-morrow. I may write you another letter one of these days. Till I do, good-bye.   Yours,   HAL.

P. S.—I must not forget to tell you that I have bought some splendid Arab horses, which, if I succeed in getting them home, will create quite a sensation, I think. In spirit they are of the "Daredevil" breed. The Arab horses, you know, have long been celebrated throughout the world for their fleetness and bottom. It is said that they can run all day. They are also horses of great beauty. They are mainly noted, however, for long wind.

CEDAR OF LEBANON.

LETTER XXXI.

BEYROUT TO PARIS.

From the rumbling noise that comes floating across the great waters, I am convinced that the political caldron at home is boiling over, and perhaps scalding folks. The grandiloquent farce recently enacted in Charleston has, I see, burst the Democratic party wide open, and that some of the actors in that funny scene now threaten, for mere spite, to tear the Union into several separate and distinct pieces. The Black Republicans, I observe, sneer and slyly laugh in their sleeves at the farce; but they too—many of them—are willing to assist in the threatened destruction; and, between the two destructive factions, the danger seems imminent, judging from the sputtering noise they make. But while these things are going on, I calmly smoke my pipe, and trust that the fool-killer may come along in time to save our country from the claws of those ranting cock-sparrows who bestride the editorial tripod or mount the stump, to preach destruction to gaping multitudes. With this comfortable hope I shall smoke on, and leave politics alone, and tell you something more about my travels in the East.

Now, if you would accompany me, it is absolutely necessary for you to again draw on your seven-league boots, and nerve yourself for the longest course you ever ran; for this letter must take us all the way from the coasts of Asia Minor to the shores of sunny France—from Beyrout to Paris. Nor shall we go direct, for we must needs go by Smyrna, Constantinople, and Athens, taking a bird's-eye view of these cities, and several other interesting points along the route.

My last letter left us, I think, on the point of sailing from the city of Beyrout, which we shall now proceed to do. We expect a row with the custom-house officers, and are not disappointed in our expectations. They deem us proper subjects for plunder, and consequently proceed to plunder us. They examine our baggage most rigidly, and unblushingly declare that most of the little trinkets we have picked up in the Holy Land are forbidden by law to be taken out of the country. We bluster a good deal, and my friend Smith even goes so far as to get out one of his "six-shooters." But it's no use: they are too many for us. Finally, rather than lose our little souvenirs, we pay a liberal "backsheesh," which is wonderfully efficacious in making an official blind to the law. We shake the dust from our feet, and go aboard the steamer that awaits us in the harbor.

All aboard, and the whistle has sounded for the last time. We all stand on deck, and, as the noble vessel steams out of the bay, we take a last look at one of the most lovely scenes man ever looked upon. Beyrout, with its white houses embowered in green groves of olive, pine, mulberry, fig, and orange, backed by the picturesque mountains of Lebanon, and the still taller peaks of Anti-lebanon, tipped with eternal snow, and all these gilded by the setting sun, make a scene which no painter ever has or ever can portray.

Now let us see who are our companions du voyage. A glance tells us that it is a motley company, composed of representatives from almost every nation under the sun—Greeks, Arabians, Turks, Persians, and Europeans. Here we have an old English Consul, who has recently "gone and got himself married," and has been taking a little bridal tour; a Turkish Pasha, who sits like a fat, lazy beast, as he is, and smokes continually; several of the German nobility—quite respectable-looking people; (we should like Countess Jaw-breaker better, however, if she did not sit upon deck with the gentlemen and smoke cigars;) also a number of Greeks of the better sort, and a goodly number of Americans. And here is our new friend Mr. Boots, the knowing man. We are glad to have him along; for he has travelled the route before, and knows it all by heart, and can tell it too. Besides, he has read Virgil and Homer and Ovid, and all them Greek and Latin fellows, and can tell us all about the classic ground over which we travel. How fortunate we are, to fall in with Mr. Boots! He speaks French, German, and Arabic!

But we are in a great hurry to finish up our Eastern tour, and have no time to dwell upon the varied accomplishments of Mr. Boots. We must push ahead, and only note the points of most interest along the way; for we are heartily tired of the Asiatics, and long to get among more civilized people. Our first stop is at the city of Marino, Island of Cyprus, where we go ashore and ramble through the town for a few hours, visiting two or three churches, and a Greek school, said to be somewhat celebrated. We see some ancient ruins, but don't know what they are. The most enjoyable portion of our visit is an hour spent with Mr. Barclay, United States Consul, whose Cyprus wine we all pronounce excellent. In a distant part of the island Mr. Boots points out Mount Olympus, and discourses learnedly about the Titans, etc.; but we don't exactly get the hang of his remarks. The Apostle Paul landed here, I think, when on his way to Greece. Our next stopping-place is the Island and city of Rhodes, where the great Colossus used to stand, with its feet straddled across the mouth of the harbor, for ships to sail in between its legs. The Colossus is gone now, and the glory of Rhodes has long since departed. It is the most strongly-fortified town we have seen; but a ramble of an hour or two through its streets satisfies us that it is a most miserable place. Boots tells us that in ancient times Rhodes was one of the most magnificent cities of the world, and gives us a thrilling account of how, in more modern times, it became famous as the stronghold of the Knights of St. John of Jerusalem, and was the scene of the most heroic defences on record. But the valorous Knights were finally beaten by the barbarous Turks. Their city was taken from them, and they escaped to Malta. No Christian is now suffered to dwell within the walls of this city. Rhodes is the most eastern island of the Ægean Sea. The apostle also touched here in his journey to the West. We pass many other of the Ægean Islands, but have not time to note the classic harangues delivered upon each by our learned friend Boots. We note the island of Coos, because it was one of Paul's stopping-places, and Patmos, because it will ever be memorable as the island to which John the Evangelist was banished, and where he wrote the book of Revelation.

We now approach the beautiful city of Smyrna, a large city situated at the head of a long bay and good harbor. It is beautiful to look at from the sea, but an entrance into it convinces us that it is not what it promised to be. Smyrna is the great fig market of the world. Most of the figs we have in the United States are brought from here. A great many American ships are loaded here annually. In wandering about the town, we are surprised to see the great number of lambs that are being slaughtered, and conclude that the Smyrnians are certainly the greatest sheep-eating people in the world. At the door of almost every house the bloody work is going on. Our surprise, however, somewhat abates when we are told that it is the eve of the Passover, and that it is the paschal lamb that is being slain. These people all seem to join in the great feast. We find the bazaars of Smyrna extensive and rich, almost equal to those of Grand Cairo. It is a much better built city than Cairo. One of the seven Churches of Asia, mentioned in Revelation, was located in this city. We visit the remains of an old amphitheatre, on the heights just above the city, where it is said that Polycarp, an early Christian martyr, fell a victim to the fury of the people and the wild beasts. His tomb is hard by. The massive ruins on these heights attest the greatness of this city in ancient times.

Leaving Smyrna, we soon pass by the Island of Mytelene, and Tenedos, and the Plains of Troy—and here our friend Boots waxes eloquent indeed. Talks about the Greeks and the Persians, the Macedonians and the Trojans, the Phœnicians and the Romans; about Xerxes, and Ajax, and Achilles, and ever so many other ancient worthies—all of whom he speaks of as familiarly as if he knew them personally. He then enters into a lengthy dissertation upon the gods and goddesses of old, and talks so learnedly, that we all gape and wonder with an admiration equal to that manifested by the rustics when the village schoolmaster spoke, as told by one Goldsmith. He told us of one Cœlus, first King of Heaven, who gave his crown to his son Titan, who afterwards abdicated in favor of his brother Saturn, on condition that he (Saturn) should raise no male children. Saturn's wife, Ops, soon after had twins, whom the father had baked into a pie for the dinner of himself and wife. Saturn did this barbarous thing without his wife's knowledge, and treated it as a good joke; but she fainted outright, as most women would have done, as soon as she knew that she had helped to devour her own children. Ops, like a dutiful wife, however, soon presented her husband with another child, whom she called Jupiter. This Jupiter would no doubt have followed the other children into a pie, had not Ops deceived her cannibal husband by giving him a stone to eat, telling him it was the child. She was vastly pleased at the success of her stratagem, but she was forced to keep the child hid in a cave on Mount Ida, (now in sight,) out of the way of Saturn, where he was fed on milk and honey, and grew up. Old Titan made war upon Saturn as soon as he found that he had a grown-up male child—a violation of the condition upon which he obtained his throne. Jupiter proved himself a real Jack the Giant-killer, in assisting his father against the monster Titans. After subduing the Titans, Jupiter drove his papa from the kingdom, and assumed the reins himself. After firmly establishing himself upon the throne of the kingdom of Heaven, he divided the empire of the world with his two brothers, who had grown up in secret as he had. To Neptune he gave the sea, and to Pluto the infernal regions. All these things Mr. Boots tells us as we quietly steam along among the Grecian Isles, where the occurrences are supposed to have taken place. He tells us of a war waged against

Jupiter by the giants who wished to revenge the death of their relations, the Titans. These giants were earth-born monsters of great power, and used rocks, oaks, and burning woods for their weapons, and heaped Mount Ossa upon Pelion to scale the walls of heaven. The gods fled from before them; went into Egypt, and assumed the shape of animals, to screen themselves. Jupiter, however, soon rallied, and, with his son Hercules, put the giants to flight. After this war, Jupiter gave himself up to pleasure, and as there was no law against bigamy or polygamy, he married him several wives, and among the rest his sister Juno. These wives could not agree, and many black eyes and bloody noses were the consequence. Jupiter and Juno were in the habit of indulging in regular "set-to's," the Madam generally coming out second best; but she paid Jupiter with interest, by pitching into his son Hercules, and giving him particular thunder. For this injustice she was suspended from heaven, with an anvil tied to her feet. Her son Vulcan, a deformed blacksmith, undertook to release her, seeing which, Jupiter raised his foot and kicked him clear over the battlements of heaven, when he fell to earth, performing the journey in nine days. He alighted on the island of Lemnos, (past which we are now sailing,) where he set up a blacksmith-shop, and employed his time in forging thunderbolts for Jupiter. But it would be tedious to recount all the wonderful stories told us by Mr. Boots. He left Juno still suspended from heaven with the anvil tied to her feet. Suppose she is still there. What a comfort it is to have such a learned man in our company! He knows some story connected with the gods, about every island we pass.

We now enter the Strait of the Dardanelles or Hellespont, which divides Europe from Asia. The strait is narrow, and fortresses frown upon us from every height. We pass but one town that seems to be important—Gallipoli. Boots tells us a story about this town, but we don't remember it. He points out to us the very place where Lord Byron swam across the Hellespont. We now leave the strait and enter the sea of Marmora, through which we ride in a storm that threatens to break things— but don't. We get through safe. The storm dies away, and we glide smoothly into the still waters of the Bosphorus, when—O ye powers! What a scene bursts upon us! The Queen of the East! The city of the Sultan—Constantinople—so beautiful that we are bewildered. It looks like a city made without hands. Had all the gods and demigods known to heathen mythology put their heads together and wrought for centuries, their united labors could never have fashioned any thing more beautiful. At the sight of this queenly city our steamer seems to dash forward with increased speed, and the white buildings and minarets rapidly grow more and more distinct, until we distinguish the celebrated mosque of St. Sophia and the Sultan's palace. The steamer now turns a jutting point of land called Seraglio Point, and glides at half speed into the Golden Horn, the splendid harbor of Constantinople. At this moment the gorgeous panorama that opens to our view is one of the most extraordinary that it is possible to conceive—and an attempt to describe it would be a dead failure. A bay surrounded by an amphitheatre of hills, rising one above another, covered with buildings, domes, minarets, and fairy palaces, down to the water's edge, intermingled with foliage of cypress groves. The harbor is filled with ships, steamers, and caiques, (pleasure-boats,) skimming about in all directions. The scene is not surpassed in the world. We stand upon the deck of our steamer and take a protracted view, drinking in the beauty around us. Get into a caique and are rowed to the shore, and find ourselves actually in the city of Stamboul. It is well that we took a lingering look at the city before landing, for the poetry vanishes immediately, as we start up the steep, narrow, muddy street, in search of a hotel. The contrast is even greater than being transported from the Fifth Avenue to the most filthy alley in Five Points.

But as we design only to take a bird's-eye view of the cities we visit, we must hurry through Constantinople in high-pressure style. We first call upon our clever American Minister, Mr. Williams, who kindly receives us, and gives us a clue to the "ropes" of the city. There are nearly three hundred mosques here, but we only visit a few of the most noted, going first, of course, to the Mosque of St. Sophia, the largest and most noted, having once been a Christian church, built by Emperor Constantine. Christians are only admitted into this mosque by special firman from the Grand Vizier, which we obtain through much tribulation and large "backsheesh." After the mosques and the tombs of the Sultans, we visit the celebrated palace and gardens of the Seraglio, a faithful description of which might possibly interest you; but you must seek it elsewhere. We next take a caique and make an excursion of many miles up the Golden Horn, amid scenes that can be properly called nothing but fairy-like. Then we charter a diminutive steamer and steam up the Bosphorus, and take a look at the stormy waters of the Black Sea. The scenery along the way is as grand as it is beautiful. A great many graceful palaces dot the shores of the Bosphorus. The rest of our time we spend in wandering promiscuously about the city, through streets that are as filthy as they are narrow, and as crooked as they know how to be. There are many open spaces and squares, however, to relieve the monotony, and fountains are innumerable. The bazaars are rich and gorgeous beyond description, and are as numerous as they are rich; for all the business of Constantinople is transacted in these bazaars. It is said that an honest trader has never yet been found in one of them; and our experience has not been such as to make us discredit the assertion. Villains all, we believe them to be, but still we love to linger among them; for in these bazaars we see much to amuse us. Every trade has its particular quarter.

In one street nothing is seen but arms and weapons of different descriptions; another is filled with jewels, diamonds, and precious stones; some are lined with the costly goods of India, while numbers of streets are occupied by shoemakers, cooks, confectioners, etc., each being confined to a distinct district. The different trades are appropriated to different nations, and each dresses in the costume of his country: the Armenians, with their huge black caps; the Turks, with their immense turbans; the Persians, with their high conical sheepskin caps; the Greeks, with their long red tarbouches hanging gracefully on one shoulder; then the passengers in every costume—Turks, Albanians, Egyptians, Circassians, Greeks, merchants, sheiks, dervishes, slaves, water-sellers, and occasionally a European or American, in a trim black coat and a two-story stove-pipe hat, looking altogether out of place—all these give a motley yet picturesque appearance to the bazaars. And not the least attraction here is the great number of Turkish women, pushing along through the crowd, and peeping roguishly at us from under their thin veils. Beware of them; for, in their intense curiosity, they may pick your pockets.

But a few days' rambling must satisfy us with Constantinople. We are anxious to hasten on to a country where there is less thieving and more civilization. We go aboard the fine French steamer "Carmel," and take a last look at the fairest city upon earth, (but very like a whited sepulchre,) and set sail for Athens, leaving, with much regret, our knowing friend Boots. In due course of time, and the usual amount of sea-sickness—for the weather is rough—we arrive at Piræus, the port of Athens. Landing from the steamer, we take carriages and drive up one of the most lovely vales we ever looked upon, surrounded by classic mountains, so grouped as to form a landscape surpassed by none. We whirl rapidly up the broad road five miles, and in little more than one hour we are standing upon the Acropolis, amid the ruins of the great Parthenon. A more lovely day never dawned, and the scene around us is perfectly enchanting. We know not which to admire most—the landscape around, or the massive yet graceful ruins amid which we stand. We glance alternately at one and the other, and then look down upon the neat, clean-looking modern city at our feet. The lovely plain of Attica lies before us, dotted with vineyards and olive-groves, and surrounded with the picturesque and the beautifully tinted mounts of Parnes, Pentelicus, Hymettus, Ægaloos. The south is open to the sea—the Gulf of Salamis. It is hard indeed to take our gaze from the delightful prospect, seemingly more harmonious and pleasant to look upon than any we have before seen. After gazing long, however, we turn to the ruins, and grope amid scenes of fallen splendor till we are weary with walking. You have no doubt often read descriptions of the great Athenian temples, and it would be but a waste of time for me to attempt it. We find the Parthenon and the Erectheum in a more ruinous state than we expected; but the Temple of Theseus we find almost perfect, and one of the most graceful buildings we ever saw. It is filled with broken statues and works of art, found by the modern Athenians in their excavations. Of the Temple of Jupiter Olympus nothing now remains but some twenty or thirty columns, very massive, and adorned with highly-wrought capitals. We visit the Amphitheatre of Herodes, the Prison and Tomb of Socrates, and many other places of interest to the reader of Athenian history.

One place we visit with feelings of more than ordinary interest. It is Mars Hill, on the top of which the great Apostle of the Gentiles once stood and delivered a stump speech that will be read and remembered as long as time shall last. We sit down upon the very spot and read a report of that speech, which we find in the seventeenth chapter of Acts. This little hill stands just between the temples of the Parthenon and Theseus, and is an admirable place from which to address a large audience—and methinks the speaker had a large audience that day—"for all the Athenians and strangers which were there spent their time in nothing else but either to tell or hear some new thing." We can imagine that we almost see those philosophers of Epicureans and Stoics, as they came forward and sneeringly asked, "What will this babbler say?" Then Paul proudly arose and stood "in the midst of Mars Hill," and told the proud Athenians of their ignorance and superstition; and pointing up to the gorgeous temple of the Acropolis, we can almost still hear his words ringing in the quiet air as he said, "God that made the world, and all things therein, seeing that he is Lord of heaven and earth, dwelleth not in *temples made with hands!*" But, as might have been expected, some of those philosophers mocked when they heard the sermon. Some of the same sort live at the present day, and would no doubt mock if Paul were to return to earth and preach as he then preached.

But we must leave Athens. This document is already getting lengthy, but we are bound to make it carry us to Paris. We go through the modern city of Athens, and are much pleased with the beauty and cleanliness of the new part, but the older part is horrible. The palace of King Otho is a tasteful but not a gorgeous building. We go through the King's gardens and gather a bouquet of flowers, but as neither King Otho nor Queen Otho are at home, we do not call at the palace. Rev. Dr. King, the high-standing and popular American missionary and teacher, is our guide through the city, to whom we return many thanks. Athens contains a population of about fifty thousand.

We are off again on the bounding billows, and, after doubling Cape Matapan, see no more land until we strike the coast of Italy, and enter the Strait of Messina, when we "fetch a compass and sail to Rhegium," and thence to the city of Messina, which we find in a terrible state of confusion, the place being in a state of revolt, and the soldiers having possession of the city. It is with much difficulty we get permission to land, the government being terribly alarmed on account of a rumor that Garibaldi is coming down upon them with fillibusters. Our Consul finally gets permission, however, and we go ashore, to see nothing but closed houses, gaping cannon in the streets, and myriads of soldiers swaggering about, ready to cut down any defenceless citizen who may chance to look like a revolutionist.

A short visit satisfies us with Messina, pretty as it is, and we return to our steamer, and, steering clear of both Scylla and Charybdis, leave the Strait, and gain the open sea, and are off for Marseilles, which we reach in little more than two days, without incident, except two or three little storms, which can be got up at any time on the Mediterranean with five minutes' notice. Soon after leaving Messina we pass the mountain and volcano of Stromboli, whose glowing furnace looks most brilliant at night. We leave the coasts of Sicily, expecting and hoping soon to hear a good report from it, for the Sicilians have taken a notion to free themselves from the galling yoke of tyranny that has so long pressed them; and if Garibaldi should effect a landing with his daring fillibusters, the work will be done—and woe to the house of Bourbon! woe to the upstart King of Naples! Could we meet with Garibaldi's expedition, we should be half inclined to join it and help him in the glorious work of freeing a downtrodden people. If the revolutionists in Sicily succeed, Naples will follow—and then the powers at Rome may tremble!

But we have no time to speculate. We approach Marseilles. The verdant shores of France are before us. Glorious sight! We have longed to quit the troubled sea, and to reach a land where order prevails. And here we are at last. How beautiful the city! Not like the cities of the East, only beautiful from the sea, but its elegant houses, broad, clean streets are refreshing. Marseilles, for elegance and beauty, is only second to Paris. But we tarry not here. Paris is before us, and two days' travel will land us there, if we go straight through by rail. But we must halt a little on the way. We must see the extensive and magnificent remains of Roman works, especially the old Amphitheatre at Arles. It is next in size perhaps to the great Coliseum at Rome. And it will not do to pass through the ancient and important city of Lyons without stopping. Perhaps we may see some of the descendants of the "Lady of Lyons" and "Melnotte." Who knows? But if we do not, a look into some of the great silk manufactories will pay us for stopping. There are more than seven thousand such establishments in Lyons! These things, in connection with the beautiful city, so well situated at the junction of the Soane and Rhone rivers, make it well worth while to tarry a day.

And Fontainbleau must be seen. We give a day to it, driving through its extensive forest and garden, and walking through the palace. One day is not satisfactory, but we are in haste.

Paris at last! and snugly housed in the Hotel de Luxembourg, with my old friend John G. to keep me company. How glad I am to find him once more!—and now for a good long rest.

Smith is here, Jones is here, and Miss Kissiah is here. Brown and the rest are dispersed—some in Italy, and some gone home. So our party is now clean "busted up." We shall remain here some time, for it will not do to leave Paris in May.

When I feel sufficiently rested, I shall perambulate Paris with my good and faithful friend Smith, after which I may write you again.

       Yours, etc., HAL.

LETTER XXXII.

PARIS.

I HAD intended to write you a letter this morning, but upon reflection have concluded to write only an apology. In piping times like these, commonplace letters from plodding correspondents are of no interest whatever to the reading public of our country, the taste of which has been wound up to a blood-and-thunder pitch by politicians, bully members of Congress, and "fancy" gentlemen of the "ring." It is, therefore, unnecessary for me to shed ink with the vain hope of interesting the worthy people who have so many public interests to look after, and who have so much to talk about. The world is in a ferment, and things are happening and are likely to happen everywhere—especially in our own country, where the tug of war is setting in on a larger scale and more fiercely than that of Garibaldi with the Neapolitan Government. I am awfully afraid that that horrid monster, so long looked for, and so often predicted, is about stalking in at last to frighten our people into spasms with his gaunt, spectral visage, and gory locks. I mean *the crisis!* The signs of his coming are vivid, and if he come, woe be to the faint-hearted!

But, as I said above, I write this note merely as an apology, instead of a letter, and to reveal to you the important fact that I am on the point of leaving the capital of His Imperial Highness for that of Her Royal Majesty. In other words, I have accepted an invitation to eat roast-beef and drink 'alf-and-'alf with my English cousins, and herrings with my Scotch friends, not forgetting to call by and indulge in a mess of "praties" with the honest Hibernians. In short, I am going to "do" Great Britain. My friend John accompanies me.

I have been trying to get my good friend Smith to go, but can't. He is willing enough to go himself, and anxious, but the Madam says she is not through with Paris yet. Smith groans in spirit, and submits, but says he cannot hold out much longer. Mrs. S. goes shopping "at all hours of the day and in all kinds of weather," and has bought more goods than poor Flora McFlimsey ever dreamed of. Smith says the expenditures of his wife are intolerable. But still he submits. A day or two ago the Madam announced her readiness to leave, whereat the old gentleman was in ecstasies, and came and informed me of the decision with a beaming face. But an hour after, the decision was revoked. She has now determined to stay till after the funeral which she feels confident will come off in a few days. Prince Jerome is very ill, and is expected every day to die. She wants to witness the grand funeral pomp, which she thinks will be one of the most imposing ceremonies ever got up in Paris. She has a passion for grand spectacles. (My private opinion is that it is more of a passion for the company of Major Fitzdoodle than any thing else that keeps Mrs. S. in Paris; but Smith must not know this.)

I regret leaving my good and faithful old friend; and I verily believe he is sorry to part with me; but the parting must come. We have roamed the streets of Paris both by day and night for several weeks together—in fact, we have been together daily for months past: what wonder, then, that we should part in sorrow?

Latterly the old gentleman goes to the circus almost every night, while the Madam goes to the opera with Major Fitzdoodle. She will not go to the circus because she considers it "low," but is willing, and even anxious, for her "kind and obliging" husband to go there. Smith says he don't care a "cuss" for the circus, but he feels certain that the fellow who performs upon the slackrope will break his neck some night, and he is anxious "to be in at the death."

Paris is very gay at this time, and is a hard place to leave. But this is "the season" in London also. We go by the Isle of Wight, where Her Majesty is sojourning at this time.

The Emperor reviewed his troops in the Bois de Boulogne a few days ago, assisted in the arduous duty by the Empress and the little Prince. It was a brilliant spectacle. In returning from the review, Mr. Smith and myself had the honor of riding near the Emperor for a mile or more, and, as we rode in a slow walk, had an excellent opportunity of entering into a conversation with His Grace—but we did n't. We took off our hats to him, and he took off his hat to us; but, like a modest man that he is, he said nothing.

But I must close and pack up my duds, for I leave for Havre, etc., at 12 o'clock. Good-bye.

HAL.

P. S.—My friend Smith has just been in to unbosom himself to me. He informs me with a very long face that Mrs. Smith has gone and bought a monkey, and has dressed it up in a suit of clothes just like his. He is terribly distressed, and swears roundly that he will not stay in Paris three days longer. He was somewhat put out when his wife bought the poodle dog, but the monkey has almost filled the cup of his patience. H.

LETTER XXXIII.

PARIS TO LONDON.

I sent you a brief apology from Paris last week instead of a letter. You may think you are going to get off again as easily. But don't flatter yourself. I feel rather desperate to-day, and shall bore you just as long as I please. This is a real London day—dark, chilly, damp, and smoky—and as I cannot go out to see the sights of the great metropolis, I must let off steam by inflicting upon you a most burdensome document.

On the same day I wrote you last, I bade farewell to Paris and my friends there—especially the Smiths—and John and myself made tracks, on the rail, for Havre, tarrying long enough by the way to take a bird's-eye view of the ancient and classic city of Rouen, where relics of antiquity meet the eye at every turn, and where stands a statue of Joan of Arc. Arriving at the great commercial city of Havre—" the Liverpool of France"—we, for the last time, before embarking for a land of freedom, went through the nonsensical ceremony of having our passports overhauled and *viséd*. Then, after partaking of an enormous beefsteak, and a quantity of claret, we sallied out and took a look at the quaintly built and eminently French-looking city; after which we deposited ourselves at midnight on a couple of shelves (called berths by courtesy) on board the little wheezing steamer that plies between Havre and Southampton. These shelves are said to have been made to sleep on. That may be, but the individual must have a copper-lined stomach who can sleep on such a sea as we passed over that night. The little steamer heaved and set all night long—and the great load of passengers did likewise, until we arrived in the quiet waters of Southampton bay at nine o'clock the following morning. I never saw people "cast up accounts" (that's quoted from Smith) with more earnestness than did that squad of passengers. Tartar-emetic is a mere circumstance to a troubled sea. So, landlubbers, take warning.

Having arrived at Southampton, we made all haste to get away from it, for it is not a place for one to hanker after, particularly in bad weather; besides, we were greeted on every hand with that vulgar vernacular, the English language. Everybody spoke English, and we found our French, which we had acquired with so much labor, utterly useless. It was downright shocking, and strange as it was shocking, to hear great round oaths rolled out in English, after having been deprived of such a luxury for nearly a year. You have little idea how strange it seems to hear everybody speak

English, after the ear has been so long accustomed to different sounds.

Leaving Southampton, we whizzed through a portion of, perhaps, the best-improved and best-cultivated country on earth, and about two o'clock found ourselves enveloped in a dark mist, and almost suffocated with coal-smoke. And this, if nothing else, would have told us that we were entering London. Its horrible smell, dark smoked houses, and crowded streets, were the same that we had left them months and months before.

And so, here we have been now for six days—and if I were to tell you that we had good weather for one-sixth of the time, you might well doubt the story. It has rained twice since I commenced this letter, (and I am not a slow writer,) and at the present moment it looks like we are going to have a storm. It would be but little exaggeration to say that this is the character of the weather we have had all the time. If it be thus in June, what must it be in winter?

Such being the character of the weather, I can't say that we have enjoyed London to an enormous extent, although we have been pretty constantly on the pad. Between showers we frequently employ the time in looking at London and its masses of humanity from the top of an omnibus. One day we found it dry enough to visit the Royal Zoölogical Gardens, which paid very well, for we there saw animals, birds, reptiles, and fishes from all lands and all waters. Another day, when it was raining, we had ourselves shown through the Bank of England, the greatest institution of the kind in the world. It covers four acres of ground, and employs a thousand clerks, etc. Between two and three million dollars in notes are cancelled there daily. We were politely shown through all the departments, and the stories told us about the amount of business transacted in each were so enormous that I have not been able to retain them in my head. I remember one thing, however: In the printing department we were told that six hundred reams of paper were used per month to print bank-notes upon! In one room a gentleman placed in my hand a bundle of notes which he said contained two millions and a half. The bundle was not large nor heavy, but the same amount in gold would have loaded several wagons. (The threatened storm is upon us!)

Thursday morning last was dark and lowering as usual, but John and myself determined to get the soot and cobwebs from our throats and lungs by breathing a little pure air. The Ascot races were going on some twenty-five miles from the city, and Thursday being the big day, there we determined to go and witness the sports of an English turf. These races are patronized by the Queen, and Thursday is called the "Queen's Day." We went, (it is but little more than an hour's ride by railway,) and, although it was a showery day, everybody and all their families seemed to be present. Hundreds of temporary booths were reared on every hand for the sale of refreshments—principally beef, beer, and cakes—and John Bull did his whole duty in the way of eating and drinking. The racing was spirited, and so was the betting. The finest horses of the kingdom, and the noble patrons of the turf, were all there. Upon the whole, it was a very gay scene. A little after twelve o'clock the Queen and all the royal family, accompanied by many noble foreigners, arrived on the ground, in a procession of fourteen fine carriages and a numerous host of outriders in the most brilliant uniform. Their Royal Highnesses were received with shouts of welcome, loud and long—for these English people love their good little Queen very much. She acknowledged the welcome with graceful bows and waves of her hand, after which she took her place in the royal stand, where we could all see and admire her as much as we pleased. She is a dumpy little body, but, according to my taste, has a remarkably sweet, pleasant face—more rounded and fleshy than I expected to see—decidedly blooming and healthy—which is a great blessing to her people, for if she were a pale, delicate-looking woman, the English ladies would ruin their health trying to look like her. She was dressed like any other lady, in plain black, with a white bonnet, not gorgeously trimmed. Prince Albert is a fine-looking man, but begins to show age a little. I thought the Prince of Wales looked rather verdant for a young man of his advantages. The little ones of the Royal Family all had clean faces, and looked as neat as if they had just popped out of the bandbox.

Up to the time of the Queen's arrival, the racing had been of minor importance; but then the celebrated horses were brought out, and the great races of the day commenced. Five, seven, eight, nine, and, in one race, fourteen horses were started. The people became frantic, and for a time seemed unable to hold themselves upon the ground. Even royalty itself stood on tiptoe, until the result of the latter race was announced, and then the air was rent with yells that would have aroused the envy of any savage; and if throats were not rent, it was not for want of an effort Don't understand me to say that everybody yelled. Far from it: some were sad enough; for some were hundreds, and some thousands of pounds poorer than when they arrived on the race-course.

The great race being over, the royal family retired, and so did we, and reached London in time to take our six o'clock dinner of roast-beef and brown-stout.

Horse-racing is a national institution in England. So is foot-racing, jumping, lifting, wrestling, etc. Consequently there are more fine horses, and more stout, healthy-looking men, than I have found in any other country, except it be some parts of Germany, where manly sports are a pastime. The French are not near so stout or fine-looking as the English, and the Italians are pigmies in comparison. The Arabs, with few exceptions, are contemptible specimens of humanity, and the Turks are little if any better. Americans, in appearance, occupy a medium place between the English and French, approaching perhaps nearer the latter than the former standard. Perhaps it may be, in part, owing to the immense amount of beer that is swilled by the Germans and English, that gives them their superior portly appearance.

Since the races, we have been circulating at random in the parks, on Regent street, Piccadilly, in the Strand, and steaming it up and down the Thames. Nights we spend variously: one night to the opera, another to the Haymarket Theatre, another to the Adelphi, to see the performance of a first-rate play, called, "Our Female American Cousin," which is done up to admiration by Miss Daly; then we go to the Royal Prince's Theatre, to see Richelieu and Pauline, and again to see the Christy Minstrels, who are doing a smashing business in a very poor way. They sing the oldest songs, play the oldest tricks, and get off the most stale and contemptible jokes and conundrums that you can imagine. But the people laugh and applaud, and that is sufficient. A joke or conundrum that would be hissed in Huntsville, will "bring down the house" here. After seeing the Christys once, I must say that negro-shows are degenerating. Their plantation melodies and dances, as sung and danced in London, are about as true to nature as the Democratic party is to its pledges.

Yesterday (Sunday) we went to Exeter Hall, to hear the big gun, Spurgeon; but the big gun had "gone off," and we didn't hear him. We heard a good sermon, nevertheless. A Mr. Northrup, from the United States, (I don't know what part,) did what he could towards filling the pulpit of the big gun. I expected a "flash," but was agreeably disappointed. He preached an excellent sermon; one that, had it been from Spurgeon, would have been considered one of his best. But it was not Spurgeon, and therefore many excellent people were sadly disappointed. It was a good, old-fashioned, plain sermon; and I liked it, because it reminded me of some that I had heard from board pulpits in the woods, long, long ago, when people used to come together and pitch their tents in the cool shady groves, and worship God beside some silent stream or bubbling fountain. Mr. Northrup is a good preacher, be he whom or what he may, or where from. He is drawing great crowds here, and is, I doubt not, doing good. Success to him, and all who preach simple truth!

To-day we shall call upon our Minister, Mr. Dallas, to get tickets, and to-morrow shall visit the two Houses of Parliament. The day after, we go to Sydenham, to visit the Crystal Palace. Then we must go to Hampton Court, and many other places of interest in and about London. Then ho! for other parts! Isle of Wight, Stratford-on-Avon, Kenilworth, etc., etc., etc., etc. And some time, when we get tired of seeing, we shall call and see you all—perhaps.

I was thinking, a day or two ago, that I ought to have written you a letter or two from Paris, giving an account of what I saw and enjoyed in that city. But then perhaps it was more merciful in me to spare you; for I could have written you nothing but a batch of such stuff as this. I saw nothing particularly new. Spent my time in the most useless way—dodging in here and out there, popping up here and down there; bobbing around generally, as much pleased with every thing I saw as a child at a Punch and Judy show. Lounged in the Garden of the Tuileries, watching the gay and giddy throngs of men, women, and happy children; strolled through the galleries, and admired the pictures of the old masters, as well as the sculpture. And then I walked the most gay and beautiful of all thoroughfares—Champs Elysees, admiring the fine equipages, the beautiful women, and the fine store-goods they carried on their graceful persons; also the Rue de Rivoli, and the Boulevards; staring in at the brilliant shop-windows, the like of which is to be seen nowhere but in Paris. Then, often the afternoon would find me in the Bois de Boulogne, (the finest park I ever saw,) where everybody goes to enjoy themselves—to see each other—to show their fine horses, fine carriages, and fine clothes. There too the Emperor and Empress are to be seen almost every pleasant evening, his Imperial Highness often driving his own horses—a span of splendid blacks—one gentleman sitting beside him, and two on the back seat. He dresses as other gentlemen, and has no guard. The Empress seldom rides with the Emperor, but in her own carriage, with one or two ladies of the Court. She is always accompanied by a guard of honor. So is the little Prince Imperial, who also has his own carriage. I have seen the Emperor on horseback, and little Prince on a little white pony beside him. He is a remarkable little fellow, to be little over four years old. He rides his pony in a lope.

When looking at Napoleon III., like my sensible friend Smith, I thought it *something* even to *see* a man who is destined to fill as many pages of history as any man who has preceded him—a man who is emphatically *making* history. I am persuaded that he is the greatest man living, if not the greatest man who ever lived. When he speaks a word, it is repeated oftener, goes farther, and more importance is attached to it than the word of any other man. And I doubt if the man ever lived whose word influenced the world as does that of the Emperor of the French. He says little, but he does a great deal. Like a truly great man, he is even great in little things. While managing his own great empire, and at the same time looking over the affairs of the other nations of Europe, he neglects not the smaller matters. He has works of public improvement going on in every part of France—canals, railroads, turnpikes, and public buildings; he encourages agriculture, horticulture, and mechanics; has an eye to the public schools, and patronizes the fine arts, nor does he neglect science; gets up fairs in every section of the country for the exhibition of every species of industry, and awards munificent prizes. He knows the healthful influence of public promenades, places of resort, fêtes, and amusements for the people, and provides them. Under his guidance the police regulations approach very nearly perfection, and you will as vainly look for riot and disorder in a French city, as for sobriety and decency at a New York election. Order, cleanliness, and industry are visible everywhere in France. In short, Emperor Napoleon seems to have an eye to and to promote every thing calculated to advance his people, be it small or great. His great mind seems to comprehend all, for while he conducts minor matters, he commands his armies and his navy, and has but to shake his finger to make proud nations tremble before him! Who but Louis Napoleon could have taken the mass of vagabonds and fierce red republicans, such as the French people were a few years ago, and made such a people and such a government! I doubt if the man lives who could have done so much. Happy indeed is it for the French people, and for the world, that a man with such a mind and such vast power is disposed to do right.

But where am I running to? I did not intend to say so much about the French Emperor, much as I admire him. Hope you will excuse it.

When I left Paris I expected (or at least hoped) to have been joined before this time by my friends Mr. and Mrs. Smith. They have not come, nor do I now expect them to arrive during my stay in London. I have just received a letter from Mr. S. informing me of their change of plan. It is in real business style — short, and to the point. It runs as follows:

Friend Hal:—You needn't expect me in London. Can't come. Sorry to disappoint you, but can't help it. Mrs. S. has changed her mind. Prince Jerome didn't die, as was expected, consequently my dear wife will not be gratified with the sight of a royal funeral-procession. She thinks it very provoking. She has now taken a notion to go down to Fontainbleau instead of London. The Emperor and all his folks have moved down there. We go to-morrow. Major Fitzdoodle goes with us. (And, privately, my friend, between you and me, I say d—n Major Fitzdoodle.) He is an upstart. And yet I don't know how to get rid of him, unless I pull his nose. And that would not do, as it would wound the feelings of my dear wife, for she thinks the Major a very nice man. And, true, he has been very kind to her.

The Snob family leave to-day for London. You will no doubt see them, as they intend stopping at the same old place in Piccadilly. I did hope that that young flirt, Julia, would take the Major with her. But not so.

I am glad to say that Mrs. S. is growing tired of her monkey. Think she will give it up soon. She has now bought a big green parrot, and a most infernal noisy thing it is.

Hope you will have a good time with the Britishers. Sorry I cannot be with you.

That cussed fool of a rope-jumper at the circus came very near breaking his neck last night.

Respectfully yours,   SMITH.

So, in all probability, I shall see my good friend no more. I shall therefore hurry through my travels in the British Isles, and make a break for a country where I can get corn-bread.

Wish Smith a pleasant sojourn at Fontainbleau, and hope that something may turn up to give him a chance to pull Fitzdoodle's nose.

The sun has now come out, and I will close and go out to enjoy its pleasant smiles.

Yours, etc.,   HAL.

P. S.—The steamer "Great Eastern" will sail for New York next Saturday. I would take passage on her but for a few reasons. First, I have not seen enough of this country. Second, John is afraid to risk his life on the first voyage of the monster, and I can't leave him. Third, I understand the places are all taken, and I could not get a berth even if I wanted it. Fourth, and lastly, the great ship will cause an immense sensation when she reaches America, and my own arrival, I fear, would be comparatively unnoticed by the great public; and that would be mortifying, you know. The New Yorkers, I guess, will find it difficult to contain themselves when they see the Great Eastern in their waters. Wonder if they have got their City Hall rebuilt, so they can get up another bonfire, as in the case of the telegraphic cable?

I guess you read the papers, and know what Garibaldi is doing; that he has flogged the Royal Neapolitan troops, and captured Palermo, the capital of Sicily. He has sworn that the King of Naples shall no longer rule the Sicilians, and has made a glorious beginning towards carrying out his oath. If he does not take the Bourbon yoke from the whole Neapolitan kingdom, I shall be mightily deceived. I once thought seriously of going to Sicily, but when I thought of the intensely hot climate, and the heating nature of the work likely to be encountered, I thought it more prudent to keep at a distance. I might, if seriously and urgently requested to do so, consent to die for my own country. But then, to die for the priest-worshipping, macaroni-eating Italians, is another thing altogether.

But still, I swing my cap in the air, and cry, "*Vive le General Garibaldi!*"

It is now preparing to rain again, and I am tempted to write several more pages, to kill time. But I'll spare you.   H.

LETTER XXXIV.

LONDON TO ISLE OF WIGHT, STRATFORD-ON-AVON, ETC.

I AM on the wing now, and cannot take time to burden you with much of a letter. I must, however, bring myself up "to the scratch" long enough to pen you a running account—very brief—of the incidents, adventures, and experiences, picked up along the way since my last letter.

Before leaving London, John and myself spent one day in the Crystal Palace; but to undertake to give an account of so huge an establishment in one little letter, would be downright presumption, not to say foolishness. In fact, what I saw there is so promiscuously jumbled and tangled in my mind, that I doubt if I could write intelligibly about it. I only have a confused idea of an immense building, stored with some of almost every thing under the sun. I have a dim remembrance of a thousand little shops, and a thousand pretty girls behind a thousand little counters, selling thousands and thousands of little trinkets and gimcracks to the visitors; also have a faint impression that there was an immense amount of machinery, agricultural implements, statuary, paintings, gardens, fountains, beasts, birds, fishes, and reptiles; wax-works, and specimens of every style of architecture, ancient and modern; restaurants, beer-saloons, and music in various parts of the establishment. Also have an idea that the building is made entirely of iron and glass, and think that something was said by somebody about its covering nineteen acres of ground—perhaps three stories high. I remember that I did a most excellent day's work in the way of walking through the different departments of the palace. Blistered feet impress this fact vividly. Was decidedly pleased with my visit, and am resolved to stay a week next time I go.

Another day we spent at Windsor Castle—the grand and magnificent old pile—founded by William the Conqueror, and which has been the seat of royalty ever since his day. Palace very fine, but not so rich as some in France. Park very extensive, stocked with deer and buffalo, and in it an equestrian statue of George III., in bronze—the largest I ever saw. Was shown "Herne's Oak," immortalized by Shakspeare. The stock of "Merry Wives" is not entirely extinct, judging by the gay and flaunting dresses we saw flitting about the lawns of Windsor. The celebrated Eton College is at Windsor.

Went to Exeter Hall one night in London, to hear John B. Gough deliver himself of one of his thrilling temperance lectures. He spread himself for two hours, and poured out more eloquence than I ever heard before—presenting figures gaunt and ghastly, such as made the hair stand on end, the blood run cold, and the very marrow chill in the bones. And all the while he spoke he paced his long stage from end to end like a chained bear, looking more like a maniac than a rational being. Should not be surprised if the man does go totally deranged, for he really seems verging that way. Towards the conclusion of his lecture, when he seemed to have finished the work of annihilating the monster intemperance, and just at the point where he ought to have stopped, he travelled considerably out of his way to lug in his abolitionism, and denounced slavery, (stealing the words of that Congress fellow,) as "the sum total of all villainy." And this of course "brought down the house," as might be expected of an English audience. He wound up by announcing his determination to go home and preach a crusade against slavery during the Presidential canvass. I predict that John B. Gough will be in the Lunatic Asylum before very long.

Three or four days ago, having "done" London as well as circumstances permitted, we packed up our duds, and with perfectly dry eyes bade farewell to our sorrowing landlady. At London Bridge station we took the train, and a last look at the eternally-befogged and besmoked old city. Two hours express time, through a country of rare richness and beauty, brought us to Brighton, on the seacoast—a city remarkable as a place of fashionable resort for London sea-bathers—and more remarkable as a resort for London Sabbath-breakers, as you may judge when I tell you that excursion trains run between London and Brighton every Sunday, carrying passengers at less than one-fourth the regular fare. Consequently, many thousands who desire to get on a "bust," escape from the vigilance of the city police, and go to Brighton—provided they can raise two-and-a-sixpence to pay their fare.

Without tarrying at Brighton, we hastened on to Portsmouth—two hours farther—where we desired very much to get a peep into the great Government Dock-yard, where war-ships, cannon, and all sorts of destructive materials are turned out. In this we failed, for none but Her Majesty's faithful subjects are permitted to see the savage preparations there going on. We tried very hard to look like regular beef-eating Britons, and in addressing the gate-keeper I even adopted the cockney lingo, telling the faithful guardian that we were "hanxious" to see the "hoperation" of making the "'orrid himplements" of war. But the man at the gate, with a knowing look, gave us to understand that he was "up to snuff," and that we could not come it over him with our "haitches." Intimated that he knew a Yankee as far as he could see him. So, not being able to see the Dock-yard, we had to content ourselves with the other lions of the town, the which we were kindly shown by Mr. B., a gentleman connected with the public works, and to whom I had a letter of introduction. We saw the fine old man-of-war "Victory," the same on which Lord Nelson fell in an engagement with the French fleet.

Late in the evening we quitted Portsmouth, and on a little cockle-shell of a steamer were brought safely to Cowes, and here we have been luxuriating ever since in the beauties of one of the most lovely isles of the ocean—the gem of all islands—the crowning jewel of Great Britain. The Garden of Eden could have been little fairer than the Isle of Wight.

Yesterday we spent the entire day in riding about from place to place in a carriage, visiting Carisbrooke Castle, some old ivy-covered churches, and other interesting spots. To-day we have made almost the complete circuit of the island on the top of a stage-coach.

Yes, the stage-coach! Who does not love to travel by coach? Ay, but it is glorious! The four large prancing horses—the hugely proportioned coach—the short pursy driver in high-topped boots, with fair round belly, fat red face, and two peering little eyes, twinkling on each side of a big purple nose, on which the delicate gin-blossoms are just beginning to bloom! And then the proud flourish and cracking of the long whip—the "winding of the mellow horn"—the start, and brisk clatter through the village streets, to the mortal terror of old women and little children, who scramble out of the way, and look enviously at us as we pass! How like the olden time before the innovation of the railway! It is a good thing to travel by stage-coach over these firm, smooth English roads! I was honored with a seat on the box by the side of our dumpy little driver, whom I soon found to be a very knowing man, and not at all disposed to hide his light under a bushel. He had imbibed a sufficient number of "horns" to make him "mellow," and was therefore in a capital humor for imparting just such information as I desired. He knew the island perfectly, and could tell the history of every old church, castle, and ruin upon it. He told me he had been driving the coach here for just twenty-one years; but to hear him talk, one might think he had been driving for centuries, and had known the island intimately since the days of its Norman conquerors. He knew the very spot on which the fugitive Charles I. landed, the room in which he was imprisoned in Carisbrooke Castle, and pointed out the very window from which the unfortunate King made several unsuccessful attempts to escape. Knew Osburn House perfectly, and seemed intimately acquainted with the private chambers occupied by Her Majesty during her visits to the island. Had heard of Legh Richmond, and the Dairyman's Daughter, and had even gathered flowers from little Jane's grave on one occasion for one of his lady passengers. His knowledge, however, was confined entirely to the island, as I discovered when I took out my pipe for a smoke. He asked me where I had got such a "'orrid houtlandish pipe?" Told him it was a pipe I had got an artist to carve for me in Jerusalem, from a knot of olive-wood. He repeated the word "Jerusalem" several times, and said he thought he had heard of the place before. Asked if it was in the United States.

You must know that the Isle of Wight seems almost like holy ground to me. Many years ago I read some little books which gave me a strong desire to see the island; and now that I am upon it, it seems that I am treading upon sacred soil. The little books I allude to are those written by Rev. Legh Richmond, the foremost and best of which is, I think, "The Dairyman's Daughter," a little book that no one can read attentively without profit; and I heartily recommend it to all my young friends—ay, and older ones too. Also, the "Young Cottager," and "Cottage Conversation." Also, some little books of perhaps no less value, by Rev. W. Adams: "The Shadow of the Cross," "The Distant Hills," "The Old Man's Home," and "The King's Messengers." The reading of these little simple stories gave a charm and a beauty to the whole island that I could not have otherwise seen. I trust they may all continue to be read as long as time lasts. A visit to some of the old churches and churchyards has been exceedingly interesting, and even edifying. Brading Church, where the good Richmond used to preach the pure and simple gospel truth, is a pleasant place to visit. And just beside the church is the grave of "Little Jane," the pure "Young Cottager," whose simple story has been so extensively and profitably read by multitudes of people. I have copied the lines inscribed on her tomb:

> "Ye who the power of God delight to trace,
> And mark with joy each monument of grace,
> Tread lightly o'er this grave, as ye explore
> The short and simple annals of the poor.
> A child reposes underneath this sod—
> A child to memory dear, and dear to God.
> Rejoice, yet shed the sympathizing tear,
> Jane, the 'Young Cottager,' lies buried here!"

In Arreton churchyard is the grave of the good and lamented Mr. Adams. It is a simple, unpretending tomb, and above it is suspended a metal cross, so that whenever the sun shines, its shadow is cast upon the white marble slab which covers the tomb. This was done in honor of the little book he wrote, entitled, "The Shadow of the Cross." I thought the monument quite appropriate.

In the same churchyard is the tomb of Elizabeth Wallbridge, "The Dairyman's Daughter." There are three grassy hillocks side by side. One of these has a tombstone to the memory of Elizabeth; another has a stone in memory of her sister; the other, which has no stone at all, is over the father and mother. I also copied the lines from this tomb, rather long, but at the risk of being tedious I shall insert them here, for I know they will be gladly read by all who have read the touching story of "The Dairyman's Daughter:"

> "Stranger! if e'er, by chance or feeling led,
> Upon this hallowed turf thy footsteps tread,

> Turn from the contemplation of the sod,
> And think on her whose spirit rests with God.
> Lowly her lot on earth; but He who bore
> Tidings of grace and blessings to the poor,
> Gave her, his truth and faithfulness to prove,
> The choicest treasures of his boundless love:
> Faith that dispelled affliction's darkest gloom;
> Hope, that could cheer the passage to the tomb;
> Peace, that not hell's dark legions could destroy:
> And Love, that filled the soul with heavenly joy.
> Death of its sting disarmed, she knew no fear,
> But tasted heaven e'en while she lingered here.
> O happy saint! may we, like thee, be blest—
> In life be faithful, and in death find rest!"

We also found it pleasant to visit the cottages once occupied by the "Dairyman's Daughter," and "Little Jane." A description of these cottages and churches, and the surrounding scenery, will be found vividly and beautifully depicted in the little books I have mentioned.

I have written more than I intended, but I hope you will read it with good nature. I shall close now, and take a little sleep. To-morrow we go north, to visit Oxford, Warwick, Stratford-on-Avon, Kenilworth Castle, etc. Will finish this letter, and mail it, after I have seen those places. For the present, adieu.

. . . .

STRATFORD-ON-AVON, June 21, 1860.

The thoughts and emotions in my heart this morning are almost too big for utterance. To be silent would therefore be more seemly. I *must* tell you, however, that I am here—here in Stratford-on-

Avon—the place where Shakspeare was born, and lived, and died—and where his bones are buried. I have seen the room in which he was born—where he was nursed, "mewling and puking in his nurse's arms"—the great broad fireplace by which he was taught his A B C, and where he was no doubt often spanked and sent to bed for his waywardness. I have sat in the chair in which he sat, and seen the table on which he wrote. His tomb is in the great old church which stands on the margin of the sweet flowing Avon, and his family repose beside him.

And besides the emotions caused by the knowledge that I am where Shakspeare lived, and look upon scenes that he looked upon, I am even domiciled at the "Red Horse Tavern," in the same room, and writing upon the same table on which the immortal Geoffrey Crayon wrote his sketches. His picture hangs upon the wall, and the identical sceptre he held in his hand, when "monarch of all he surveyed," is reposing by the fireplace, in the shape of a huge iron poker. The words "Geoffrey Crayon's sceptre" are engraved upon it, and shown by mine host with much gusto. Washington Irving is almost as well known here as Shakspeare.

I have just returned from a pleasant walk of a mile across the fields to the cottage of "Sweet Anne Hathaway." Travelled the same road, no doubt, that wild Will used to travel, when paying stolen visits to his Anne, when she was less reputable, perhaps, than in later years. It is a neat thatch-roofed cottage, with a venerable look, and is said to be still occupied by descendants of the Hathaways. They show some ancient furniture, said to have belonged to Anne.

I have been to Warwick, visited Warwick Castle and Guy's Cliff, and seen many things there, old, quaint, and curious. Have also visited Kenilworth Castle, a venerable old ruin. Saw the tower in which the lovely but unfortunate Amy Robsart was confined, and was shown the grotto in which she was discovered by Queen Elizabeth, on her visit to Kenilworth. But all these things are too much to put in this letter.

We now leave for the ancient city of Chester, and from there we go to Bangor, in Wales, to see the great tubular and suspension bridges across the Menai Straits, and the immense slate quarry near that town, where four thousand eight hundred men are engaged in quarrying slate. Then, ho! for a visit to the "cannie Scots" and the "wild Irishmen." So, till you hear from me again, good-bye.

HAL.

P. S.—I will not bore you with the political news from this side the water; but really the Eastern world seems to be in a ferment. Sicily, under the influence of Garibaldi, is boiling like a pot—Naples seems on the eve of being wiped out—the Vatican is thundering ominously, and Ireland is in a stew, sending off recruits for the army of his Holiness—Sardinia is trembling between the menaces of Rome and Austria—Turkey is cowering beneath the outstretched claw of Russia; and even John Bull is turning pale before the fancied hostile intentions of the French Emperor. So you see Europe is in a perfect hubbub. And even in Asia Minor the work of blood is going on. I have just received a letter from the American Consul in Beyrout, which closes as follows:

"Syria is now in a blaze of civil war. More than sixty villages have been burned. Hundreds of Christians have been killed, and the work of blood is still progressing. The Druses, aided by the Turks, obtain the victory everywhere. We are only saved from a Moslem insurrection in Beyrout by the presence of a Russian frigate."

This war was brewing when I was in Beyrout.

H.

CONCLUSION.

Now, good friends, we will cease our wanderings. We have had a long tour, which I trust you have found pleasant, and not altogether unprofitable. We have seen much to condemn, and much to approve; much to laugh at, and much to sorrow over. We have pressed through swarms of gaunt beggars, and jostled against gilded nobility—the oppressed and oppressors crowding along the same streets. The latter we looked upon with indignation, while we enjoy the consoling thought that our coppers have often appeased the gnawing hunger of the former. We have been often vexed by police and custom-house officers, and cheated times almost without number. But these are petty annoyances that all must submit to who go out to see the world as it is, and they should be borne with patience.

At some future time I may ask you to accompany me further through the kingdom of Great Britain, when we will visit the manufacturing cities and rural districts of England, the mountainous regions of Wales, the cities and highlands of Scotland, when we will climb the Bens and sail upon the Lochs of that classic country; and then through Ireland, where "praties" abound, and many queer things are to be seen.

For the present, farewell; and may the remainder of your journey through life be as pleasant as our late travels have been to me! So mote it be.

THE END.

www.ingramcontent.com/pod-product-compliance
Lightning Source LLC
Chambersburg PA
CBHW032021220426
43664CB00006B/328